WARREN ZEVON

Tempo
A Rowman & Littlefield Music Series on Rock, Pop, and Culture

Series Editor: Scott Calhoun

Tempo: A Rowman & Littlefield Music Series on Rock, Pop, and Culture offers titles that explore rock and popular music through the lens of social and cultural history, revealing the dynamic relationship between musicians, music, and their milieu. Like other major art forms, rock and pop music comment on their cultural, political, and even economic situation, reflecting the technological advances, psychological concerns, religious feelings, and artistic trends of their times. Contributions to the **Tempo** series are the ideal introduction to major pop and rock artists and genres.

Bob Dylan: American Troubadour, by Donald Brown
Bon Jovi: America's Ultimate Band, by Margaret Olson
British Invasion: The Crosscurrents of Musical Influence, by Simon Philo
Bruce Springsteen: American Poet and Prophet, by Donald L. Deardorff II
The Clash: The Only Band That Mattered, by Sean Egan
Kris Kristofferson: Country Highwayman, by Mary G. Hurd
Patti Smith: America's Punk Rock Rhapsodist, by Eric Wendell
Paul Simon: An American Tune, by Cornel Bonca
Ska: The Rhythm of Liberation, by Heather Augustyn
Warren Zevon: Desperado of Los Angeles, by George Plasketes

WARREN ZEVON

Desperado of Los Angeles

George Plasketes

ROWMAN & LITTLEFIELD
Lanham • Boulder • New York • London

Published by Rowman & Littlefield
A wholly owned subsidiary of The Rowman & Littlefield Publishing Group,
Inc.
4501 Forbes Boulevard, Suite 200, Lanham, Maryland 20706
www.rowman.com

Unit A, Whitacre Mews, 26-34 Stannary Street, London SE11 4AB

British Library Cataloguing in Publication Information Available

Library of Congress Cataloging-in-Publication Data

Names: Plasketes, George.
Title: Warren Zevon : desperado of Los Angeles / George Plasketes.
Description: Lanham, Maryland : Published by Rowman & Littlefield, 2016. | Series: Tempo : A
    Rowman & Littlefield music series on rock, pop, and culture | Includes bibliographical refer-
    ences and index.
Identifiers: LCCN 2015041682 (print) | LCCN 2015043652 (ebook) | ISBN 9781442234567
    (cloth : alk. paper) | ISBN 9781442234574 (electronic)
Subjects: LCSH: Zevon, Warren. | Rock musicians–United States–Biography.
Classification: LCC ML420.Z475 P53 2016 (print) | LCC ML420.Z475 (ebook) | DDC
    782.42166092–dc23 LC record available at http://lccn.loc.gov/2015041682

Always, for Julie
"...we will float."

CONTENTS

SERIES EDITOR'S FOREWORD

Out in Los Angeles in the 1970s, sat Warren Zevon at his piano, precariously perched on the edge of America's dream factory. He was at home on the edge. At the start of his adolescence, in 1960, Zevon's parents moved from Chicago into the Southern California sun. Since then, Zevon had spent most of his years not so much basking in that sun, its culture, and its music, but rather dehydrating the L.A. romance of living forever as a media (and mediated) creation. By 1976, when Zevon was 29—at the trailing edge of what everyone would call youth—he released his first major-label debut album, titled *Warren Zevon*. The buoyant sounds and parched sentiments eponymously announced a new artist headed in a new direction: here was one bound to enjoy the ride through canyons overheated from an interminable sun, singing intimations of mortality.

Zevon's wit, wordplay, and wonderment at life's shortcomings, all wrapped in smartly arranged pop-rock songs, played against the sun-kissed California singer-songwriters of the 1970s much like a tonic is to an Orange Julius. George Plasketes tells this story with a scholar's assessment of Zevon's career and cultural influence, and a fan's appreciation for his artistry. Plasketes's writing complements Zevon's lexical dexterity, and each chapter is itself a delightful direction toward pinning down a renegade's craft. Zevon expended some effort to cultivate his outlaw persona, but not much. Being drawn to the edges by temperament, Zevon drew from real life to compose fictions to say what he saw underneath all the glamour. A consummate reader, making him one of rock's most literate songwriters, he knew the power of a story of a character in crisis, and seemed to court peril as his muse. Zevon greedily stepped over borders when he could, to blur the edges and combine forces. He brought a classical musician's training to the rock culture milieu; he used more, and more challenging, words than rock and roll had typically thought necessary to say life was short and then you die, so savor it; he drank his human tenderness to the brink of destruction, then, after having enjoyed a long stretch of regained health, had cancer take him all the way.

For his intelligence, poetics, musicianship, and cultural criticism, Zevon earned the respect of his contemporaries—the likes of Jackson Browne, Neil Young, Bruce Springsteen, and Bob Dylan—and many more in the 1 percent of the showbiz industry. His signing to David Geffen's Asylum Records in the 1970s would prove monumental for Zevon and Geffen, not to mention all the artists on the label, and by the end of his life in 2003, he was much revered and beloved as a result of having lent his hand to many musical projects. Postmortem celebrations and affections for Zevon continue to this day, perhaps ironically, as Plasketes charts throughout this book. For as much as he has been a central figure since the 1970s in the history of American singer-songwriters, Zevon has never had the popular appeal of a Neil Young or a Springsteen. He continues to cling to the edges, but rewards all who come out to find him.

Scott Calhoun

TIMELINE

Cultural Events	Warren Zevon's Life and Career
	January 24, 1947: Warren William Zevon born in Chicago, to parents Beverly Simmons and William "Stumpy" Zevon (Zivotofsky), a boxer and gambler
January 1949: RCA introduces the 45 rpm record	
June 1950: The United States enters the Korean War	
September 1956: Elvis Presley on *The Ed Sullivan Show*	Christmas 1956: First piano is a Chickering that Zevon's father won playing poker on Christmas Eve
February 3, 1959: Buddy Holly dies in plane crash	
November 1960: John F. Kennedy elected president	1960: Family moves to California; Zevon begins to study classical music, inspired by several meetings with composer Robert Craft and Russian maestro Igor Stravinsky

August 1963: Martin Luther King Jr.'s "I have a dream" speech

1963: Parents divorce; Zevon drops out of high school junior year, travels cross-country to New York to follow his Bob Dylan folksinger dream

November 22, 1963: JFK assassinated in Dallas, Texas

February 9, 1964: The Beatles' first appearance on *The Ed Sullivan Show* helps launch the British Invasion

1964: As "stephen lyme," forms folk-pop duo, lyme and cybelle, with high school classmate Violet Santangelo. The duo signs a recording contract with the White Whale label and cuts a few singles, though never records an album

August 1964: The Beatles film *A Hard Day's Night*

May 1966: The Beach Boys' *Pet Sounds* released

April 1966: "Follow Me" reaches number 64 on *Billboard* charts; duo performs on the teen dance show, *The Lloyd Thaxton Show*

June 1967: The Beatles' *Sgt. Pepper's Lonely Hearts Club Band*, "Summer of Love," and psychedelia

1967: Labelmates the Turtles record the "Follow Me" B-side, "Like the Seasons," as the B-side to their number-one hit "Happy Together." They also record Zevon's "Outside Chance"

November 1967: Debut of *Rolling Stone* magazine

June 1968: Robert Kennedy assassinated

1969: Zevon records first solo album, *Wanted: Dead or Alive*, on Imperial label, produced by L.A. cult figure Kim Fowley. "She Quit Me" (as "He Quit Me") is included in the *Midnight Cowboy* film soundtrack.

August 15–17, 1969: 500,000 gather for "three days of peace and music" at Woodstock Festival at dairy farm in Bethel, New York

August 7, 1969: Son Jordan is born to Marilyn "Tule" Livingston

April 1970: Paul McCartney announces the breakup of the Beatles

Early 1970s: Bandleader for the Everly Brothers. After Everlys break up, moves to Berkeley briefly, playing the nightly club circuit

September 18, 1970: Guitar legend Jimi Hendrix dies

August 9, 1974: Richard Nixon resigns as president

1974: Marries Crystal Brelsford

April 1975: End of Vietnam War

Summer 1975: Discouraged with music industry and with funds dwindling, Zevon moves to Spain, lives and plays music at Dubliner Bar in Stiges near Barcelona, owned by former mercenary David "Lindy" Lindell, who becomes songwriting collaborator

October 11, 1975: Lorne Michaels' late-night satire *Saturday Night Live* premiers "Live from New York . . ." on NBC, with George Carlin as guest host

September 1975: Returns to L.A. after receiving encouragement from Jackson Browne, who negotiates a major label recording contract for Zevon

May 18, 1976: Self-titled major-label debut album produced by Browne on David Geffen's Asylum Records, receives rave reviews in the rock and popular press. Linda Ronstadt records four songs from the album

July 1976: Celebration of U.S. bicentennial

August 4, 1976: Daughter Ariel born

November 1976: Opens for Browne on nine-country European tour

August 16, 1977: Elvis Presley (allegedly) dies in Memphis

November 1977: *Saturday Night Fever* soundtrack, a double album of disco and Bee Gees, stays at number 1 for 24 weeks, remaining on the charts for 120 weeks until March 1980

January 18, 1978: Second Asylum album, *Excitable Boy*, reaches number 8 with the single "Werewolves of London" reaching number 21. Struggles with alcohol escalate, leading to numerous episodes, interventions, and revolving rehabilitations

May 22, 1978: Profiled in mainstream magazine *People*

February 15, 1980: release of *Bad Luck Streak in Dancing School* which includes excerpts from Zevon's unfinished symphony

August 1980: United States boycotts the Summer Olympics in Moscow

May 11, 1980: Appears on the King Biscuit Flower Hour with Willie Nile

December 1980: John Lennon murdered in New York City

December 26, 1980: Series of performances from the Roxy in West Hollywood released as live album *Stand in the Fire*

August 1, 1981: MTV debuts

March 19, 1981: Appears on cover of Rolling Stone as subject of Paul Nelson's transcendent "crack up and resurrection" feature on Zevon's struggles with alcoholism Separated off and on since 1979, Warren and Crystal Zevon officially divorce; begins relationship with actress Kim Lankford

July 16, 1982: *The Envoy* released

November 1982: Michael Jackson's *Thriller* released

1982: First of many appearances on David Letterman's *Late Night/ Late Show*, including substituting for Paul Shaffer as bandleader

March 1983: Compact discs introduced in the United States

1983 Relocates to East Coast, briefly engaged to Philadelphia DJ Anita Gevinson

May 1983: Asylum drops Zevon, leaving him without a record label for nearly five years

May 1984: Soviet Union boycotts Olympic games in Los Angeles

1984: Checks into rehab clinic in Minnesota

March 1985: USA for Africa Charity single, "We Are the World"

January 1986: Space Shuttle *Challenger* disaster

March 1986: Begins sustained period of sobriety that lasts for 17 years.
New manager Andrew Slater connects Zevon with members of popular college/alternative band, R.E.M. Together, as hindu love gods, release a 7-inch single, "Gonna Have a Good Time

Tonight/Narrator" on R.E.M.'s IRS label

October 24, 1986: First of three "Best of" collections during career, *A Quiet Normal Life*, completes the Asylum catalog;
Martin Scorsese uses "Werewolves of London" on the soundtrack to *The Color of Money*

August 28, 1987: Strong "comeback" album, *Sentimental Hygiene*, after being one of the first artists signed to newly launched label Virgin Records

November 1989: Fall of the Berlin Wall marks end of Cold War

October 1989: Dropped by Virgin following the conceptual, science fiction-influenced *Transverse City*

August 1990: Operation Desert Storm

1990: Signs with Irving Azoff's new label Giant Records; hindu love gods' album of mostly blues covers released; version of Prince's "Raspberry Beret" charts at number 28. Scores *Drug Wars: The Camarena Story* NBC mini-series; increasingly involved in music for television and film throughout the decade

1991: "Casey Jones," with David Lindley, on Grateful Dead tribute, *Deadicated*, marks only guest spot on any record

December 1991: Dissolution of the Soviet Union

October 15, 1991: *Mr. Bad Example* released

May 21 1992: MTV's *The Real World* launches reality TV era,

1992: Writes music for episode of HBO's *Tales from the Crypt*

accelerating the decline of
civilization as we know it

January 1993: Inauguration of Bill
Clinton, first Democrat president
in 12 years

1993: Oversees music for the NBC
remake of *Route 66*

April 13, 1993: "Unplugged"
album *Learning to Flinch* released

September 1993: Appears in scene
on HBO comedy, *The Larry
Sanders Show*

April 5, 1994: Grunge icon Kurt
Cobain dies

1994: Music for William Shatner's
USA/SciFi network series, *TekWar*

1995: Self-produces album
*Mutinee*r, with two songs
cowritten with novelist Carl
Hiaasen

August 1995: Grateful Dead head
Jerry Garcia dies

September 1995: Cameo on HBO
comedy, *Dream On*

1996: Rhino Records releases two-
disc, 44-song *I'll Sleep When I'm
Dead* anthology

1998: Writes liner notes for
Stranger Than Fiction, a charity
compilation by the band of bards,
the Wrockers. Also performs on
several songs with reconfigured
Rock Bottom Remainders, who
formed in 1992

January 16, 1999: Performs at
inauguration ball of Minnesota
governor-elect Jesse Ventura of
the Reform Party

March, May 1999: Appears on
NBC sitcom *Suddenly Susan* as
himself with Rick Springfield

2000: Cast as Billy Bob Thornton's silent sidekick, "Mr. Babcock," in Dwight Yoakam's existential Western, *South of Heaven, West of Hell*

January 25, 2000: Following another five-year label hiatus, returns on Artemis Records with one his strongest records of his career, *Life'll Kill Ya*

September 11, 2001: World Trade Center and Pentagon terrorist attacks

November 29 2001: Beatle George Harrison dies

May 7, 2002: *My Ride's Here* includes multiple songwriting collaborations with writers, and hit hockey single, "Hit Somebody!"

August 2002: Diagnosed with mesothelioma, an inoperable cancer, and given a three-month prognosis

September 2002: Begins writing as many songs as he can with longtime friend Jorge Calderón. VH1 begins filming *(Inside)Out* documentary

October 2002: Release of *Genius*, third "Best of" collection, with 22 songs. On October 30, David Letterman devotes entire *Late Show* to Zevon, who performs three songs in his final live performance

November–December 2002: Zevon's music contemporaries gather in L.A. to contribute to final recording, with VH1 documenting the sessions

March–May 2003: United States leads invasion of Iraq, one of seven countries named as "axis of evil"

March 18, 2003: Release of *The First Sessions* compilation of early recordings and demos, including lyme and cybelle

April–May 2003: Records final two songs for farewell album; Virgin albums reissued

June 2003: Twin grandsons Maximus Patrick and Augustus Warren born June 11; movement underway via Internet petitions for induction into Rock and Roll Hall of Fame

August 2003: 24 VH1 *(Inside)Out: Warren Zevon* documentary premieres without commercial interruption on Sunday evening, August 24; two days later, *The Wind*, benefitting from "terminal exposure" sells 48,000 copies its first week, opening at number 46 on the charts, the highest position for a Zevon album since 1980; and certified gold (100,000 copies) in December and receives five Grammy nominations

September 7, 2003: Zevon dies at his home in Los Angeles, age 56

November 2003: String quartet tribute, *Dad Get Me Out of This*, released

February 8, 2004: Posthumously wins two Grammys; ceremony features live choral performance of "Keep Me in Your Heart" as tribute to artists who died in 2003. VH1(*Inside*): *Out* documentary on DVD two days later

March 3, 2004: Marilyn "Tule" Livingston Dillow, Jordan's mother, dies at age 57

October 12, 2004: Jordan Zevon and Wallflowers perform "Lawyers, Guns and Money" on *Late Night* preceding release of multi-artist *Enjoy Every Sandwich* tribute record on Artemis

August 2005: Hurricane Katrina ravages Gulf Coast region

July 2005: Indie tribute, *Hurry Home Early*, released

December 2006: Saddam Hussein executed

January 31, 2006: Jordan launches recording career with five-song EP *Reconsider Me: The Love Songs*; Irish poet Paul Muldoon publishes "Sillyhow Stride," a three-part elegy to Zevon

March 27, 2007: Rhino reissues Asylum catalog, including long-out-of-print *Stand in the Fire*

May 2007: Crystal Zevon publishes 452-page oral history, *I'll Sleep When I'm Dead: The Dirty Life and Times of Warren Zevon*; release of *Preludes: Rare and Unreleased Recordings* two-CD set

2007–2014: Central presence in soundtrack, lead character Hank

Moody, and vibe of Showtime series *Californication*

November 2008: Barack Obama elected first African American President

2008: *Warren Zevon* reissued/ remastered in a double-disc edition

September 24, 2013: Stephen King dedicates *The Shining* sequel, *Doctor Sleep*, to Zevon

December 2013: Animated Zevon figure and "Carmelita" reference in Killers' "Christmas in L.A." video

December 2014: Masha's sultry version of "Werewolves of London" used in Three Olives Vodka video/ad campaign

April/May 2015: Jason Isbell and Amanda Shires, and Dawes perform Zevon songs on *Late Show* during David Letterman's final month

ACKNOWLEDGMENTS

Writing about the Late Great Warren Zevon and chronicling and curating his remarkable songbook has been a dream writing project for me; a haunting and consuming labor of love. I am profoundly grateful to Tempo Series Editor Scott Calhoun, and Senior Editor Bennett Graff at Rowman & Littlefield for the opportunity to contribute to this series. Since Tempo's inception, I have admired the vision, design, and scope of the series, and am honored to be a part of its impressive roster of authors and musical artists. As the adult supervision—Scott and Bennett, along with fellow Rowmans Monica Savaglia, Natalie Mandziuk, publicist Jacqline Barnes, cover designer Devin Watson, and Lara Graham, who, with her merry band of proofreaders and production staff steadfastly provided the finishing touches on the pages—have displayed qualities commonly associated with saints and scout troops. They have provided guidance, wisdom, and encouragement, while allowing creative freedom, and patiently accepting most, if not all of my writing whims, quirks, and compulsions, without heavy handedness or hovering. Thank you, again, again, and again, for the privilege and the pleasure.

I want to express my appreciation to the Zevon family, specifically Crystal, Jordan, and Ariel, with hopes that reverence rings in my Warren narrative without intrusion or misrepresentation. Also a note of indebtedness to the critics, writers, musicians, and artists who have written about and commented on Warren Zevon, his music and life, with such insight and style. Those perspectives informed and enriched my critical view along the way.

My "Thanks always to Jackson" list of continuous gratitude extends to Gary Edgerton, Gary Burns, Bill Kolar, Ron Shapiro, Jim Dees, John Lang, George Lewis, Remy Miller, and John Fortenberry. Always above and beyond, the ever-resourceful and considerate Greg Metcalf sent me his way-cool Zevon *Nkisi* sculpture to empower my writing, along with his usual steady stream of references. And a nostalgic nod to George Stuart, for inaugurating *Warren Zevon* on a turntable in our Mississippi dorm in 1976.

I'm fortunate to have a sustaining strand in the School of Communication and Journalism at Auburn: Director Jennifer Adams; my Media Studies colleagues—Susan Brinson, Hollie Lavenstein, Ric Smith, Kevin Smith, Ed Youngblood, Josh Hillyer, Andrea Kelley, and cinematic Associate Provost Emmett Winn; also Rob Agne, Mary Helen Brown, Mitchell Kilpatrick, and Kathy Klick, and Shannon Solomon for her continual kindness and solutions to pretty much everything. I appreciate the generous grant from the Bronzcek Fund, which came in handy. Thanks always to our Siri, Library Resourceress, Barb Bishop, for waving her magic wand to locate elusive citations.

To the branches of my family tree—the Plasketes, Piekarski, and Williams—especially Joan and Rodger, and the spirit of my parents, Charles and Rita: thank you for the roots, nurturing, and shade.

Lastly and everlastingly . . . in memory of our sweet and lovable Lulu, at my side, at my feet, 'til the very last chapter; a Constant Companion, Muse, One of a Kind for 16 ½ years (115 in dog years)—"And I will be right next to you." And faithful sidekick Pancho. For our daughter Anaïs, our son Rivers, and my wife, artist, and best friend, Julie, I have yet to find enough words, or the right words, to express the vastness of my love, gratitude, and admiration for them. From their bicoastal locales in Los Angeles and New York, to the studio space, rooms, and gardens of our home, they color my heart and soul with abundance, and inspire and grace my every thought and word. Thanks to Julie, for her empathy and appreciation of my Occupy Zevon; for graciously hosting his extended stay while enduring my painstaking pace; for looking the other way with the "disorder in the house" from the Zevonian debris in the vicinity of my writing space and beyond; for tolerating my ragged gray writing t-shirts; and for knowing when I should seek solitude in

The Woods—"I'm lucky to be here with someone I like, who maketh my spirit to shine."

INTRODUCTION

The Grim and Grin Reaper in the Songwriter's Neighborhood

There was simply nobody else writing like Warren Zevon at that time. He was one of the most interesting writers of the era, and certainly ahead of his time.

—author Gore Vidal (C. Zevon)

Warren Zevon traveled down his own road, and it's unpaved.

—musician/songwriter Jorge Calderón (C. Zevon)

A PREMORTEM PRELUDE: "DON'T LET US GET SICK"

On October 30, 2002, David Letterman devoted his entire *Late Show* on CBS to singer-songwriter Warren Zevon. The exclusive solo scheduling for any guest, let alone a musical performer, was unprecedented in the late-night television talk show landscape. The tone of the occasion, from Letterman's lengthy interview underscored with an "enjoy every sandwich" maxim, through Zevon's intimate three-song set, was sentimental and solemnly celebratory. Zevon, whose songwriting regularly referenced and confronted death, was two-thirds into a three-month prognosis following an August 28 diagnosis of mesothelioma, a rare form of inoperable cancer.

The late-night visit with Letterman was a momentous mark in what became Zevon's compelling and prolonged desperado "Deteriorata," a parting procession that blended elements of New Orleans jazz funeral, Irish wake, and rock and roll reality television series. Two years earlier, Zevon's presciently eerie recordings provided a grimly intuitive foreshadowing of his fateful finding. *Life'll Kill Ya* (2000), beyond its unequivocal title track, included the gently imploring "Don't Let Us Get Sick," a doctor's doomed diagnosis bluntly titled "My Shit's Fucked Up;" the graceful ride "Ourselves to Know;" a song that views Elvis's demise through a "Porcelain Monkey;" and a CD booklet reinforcing the music's mortality motif with images of skeletons and a shadowy shroud of Zevon. This was followed by *My Ride's Here* (2001); the "ride" was an allusion to a hearse, with its cover image of Zevon peering out its back-seat window. Late in 2002, Jackson Browne, Jorge Calderón, David Lindley, Ry Cooder, Bruce Springsteen, Tom Petty, and members of the Eagles were among an all-star cast of music contemporaries that assembled with Zevon for a requiem recording session, out of which emerged the climactic centerpiece of his farewell trilogy, the Grammy-winning *The Wind* (2003), and a companion two-hour documentary, *VH1 (Inside) Out: Warren Zevon: Keep Me in Your Heart* (2004).

On September 7, 2003, nearly 30 years after Zevon emblazoned the defiant "I'll Sleep When I'm Dead" on his debut album, his piano-pounding pledge became prophecy fulfilled as Zevon died at the age of 56 in Los Angeles.

"THE CRAZY BAG OF LABELS"

There's no way the mainstream could be hip enough to appreciate Warren Zevon. He was our everything, from Lord Buckley to Charles Bukowski to Henry Miller. Warren made someone like Randy Newman even seem normal.

— singer-songwriter Bonnie Raitt (C. Zevon)

During a career that spanned 40 years and 20 records that accumulated with critical acclaim and intermittent ascriptions of "genius," Warren Zevon was one of the most original, intelligent, darkly droll, and quotable voices to emerge from the flourishing 1970s Los Angeles singer-songwriter sphere. Zevon was an insurgent who "traveled down his own road," marauding on the peripheries of music's mainstream with abandoned amusement, always in the fray, throwing lyrical punches and punch lines, drawing blood from bodies and broken hearts in verses he lived and wrote along his unpaved way.

Zevon's self-titled, major label debut in 1976 on nascent media mogul David Geffen's touchstone record label, Asylum Records, is a distinguishing, if not definitive, work for Zevon as a songwriter. The album also stands as one of the unsung yet integral recordings of the substantial Los Angeles and canyon country/folk/rock catalog that was *the* American sound for most of the 1970s. Though overshadowed by the Eagles' bewitching classic, *Hotel California* (same label, same year— Asylum 1976), *Warren Zevon* is a lurking, literate album that endures as one of the most delightfully dark visions of Southern California culture, demystifying the Hollywood scene, its desperation and decadence.

The distinctive debut established the fringe dweller pattern for Zevon's career. With the exception of his Top Ten platinum follow-up, *Excitable Boy* (1978), Zevon's music never transcended critical and cult status, nor had the broad appeal to consistently sustain in the mainstream. Most mentions or discussions of Zevon are commonly prone to abrupt referencing of his most familiar and successful song—the cavorting, howling Top 40 hit in 1978, "Werewolves of London." The song is a bane and badge of instant and distant recognition: "Warren Zevon . . . the guy who did 'Werewolves of London,'" rather than contextualizing him as the guy who wrote "Desperados Under the Eaves," "Mohammed's Radio," "Splendid Isolation," "Play It All Night Long," "Mutineer," or any other number of brilliant songs. Despite being what Zevon referred to as a "dumb song for smart people," and "that piece of shit" when arguing with Asylum on why the song should *not* be *Excitable Boy's* single, the lineage of "Werewolves of London" became strangely and surprisingly profuse. From the 15 minutes that it took to write on the way to reaching number 21 on the *Billboard* charts, the song's chronicle extends from a 1935 horror film to a sample in a Kid Rock song in 2008, with soundtracks, covers, Halloween hit compilations, contests, artifacts, a team and its mascot, a vodka ad campaign, and running jokes delivered by Zevon himself in cameos on television comedies, in between.

Simultaneously synonymous and stigmatizing, "Werewolves of London" is an undeniable Zevon emblem, though not by any means his complete signature. His sardonic and substantial songbook is strikingly cinematic and literary, brimming with noir narratives, lurid and lovesick lyrics, complex characters, and cultural references. Among what actor Billy Bob Thornton calls "the crazy bag of labels" attached to Zevon and his body of work is an alliterative litany of descriptions that includes idiosyncratic, iconoclastic, ironic, and imaginative.

Zevon's prodigious, albeit tormented, talents uniformly enthralled critics, as well as his contemporaries within and outside music. By most accounts, virtually everyone whom Zevon encountered—producers, songwriters, musicians, writers, actors—instantly recognized his intellectual and musical proficiencies, as well as his compulsive behavior and reckless excesses. When singer Linda Ronstadt first met Zevon, she thought he was a "psychopath" (Hoskyns 2009, 245). Nonetheless, with the encouragement of producer Peter Asher, she managed to overlook that first (un)impression to uncover and record into hits one-third of the songs from *Warren Zevon*—"Mohammed's Radio," "Poor Poor Pitiful Me," "Carmelita," and "Hasten Down the Wind," which was further appropriated as the title for Ronstadt's 1976 platinum album, also on the Asylum label.

The Zevon inauguration attracted an unusual and abundant array of literary, film, art, and music correlations that continued over the course of his career and posthumously, associations that attempted to comprehend his berserk brilliance, singular songwriting, and tempestuous presence. Bonnie Raitt invoking Lord Buckley, Charles Bukowski, Henry Miller, and Randy Newman may be the most comprehensive composite, while other entries in the lengthy index of Zevon similes include: "a Laurel Canyon version of Elvis Costello," a "Dada-ist Bruce Springsteen," "Jackson Browne's bad conscience," "The Dangerous Dean Martin," "Warren Warhol," "F. Scott Fitzzevon," "Jimmy Buffet's Evil Twin," and "a cross between Baudelaire and Johnny Rotten." Zevon was also compared to acerbic satirist Dorothy Parker and novelist/screenwriter Nathanael West, who wrote *The Day of the Locust*; and was referred to as a rock and roll version of maverick film directors John Huston and Sam Peckinpah, the latter known for his wild lifestyle and violent artistic vision, particularly in his Westerns. Even Zevon contributed to the inventive inventory. When Jackson Browne introduced him at a concert as the "Ernest Hemingway of the 12-string guitar," Zevon amended the accolade to "Charles Bronson," the actor frequently cast as a gunfighter and perhaps best known for the *Death Wish* series of films (between 1974 and 1994) in which he plays a crime-fighting vigilante.

DEAD ON ARRIVAL

Zevon established himself as rock's death-defying desperado. Demise, depravation, and desperation were occupational preoccupations and central attributes of Zevon's sneering songwriting signature. He pronounced himself "dead on arrival" as early as 1969. His independent release, *Wanted: Dead or Alive*, included songs such as "A Bullet for Ramona," which foreshadowed the tone his twisted tunes would take during the four decades to follow.

Zevon expended endless energy composing a reckless rough draft for his epitaph in lyric and lifestyle. A requisite reference and a touchstone tune in his crypt-keeper catalog, "I'll Sleep When I'm Dead" in 1976, appeared to be his short-term career objective, a self-fulfilling prophecy in progress. His life on layaway, as if composing a sequel to Ingmar Bergman's *The Seventh Seal*, Zevon spent much of his career a tortured, soul-searching, self-saboteur, wavering between praise, paradise, and self-induced paralysis, vandalizing his musical gifts and vision via a vodka vortex, accented with a fascination with loaded firearms. "He is among the wildest people I've ever met. For him it was all about trials by fire," said Zevon's longtime friend, mentor, and advocate, singer-songwriter Jackson Browne, who negotiated Zevon's major label deal with Geffen, and produced his first two Asylum albums (Boucher, F1). By his own admission and with ample supporting evidence, Zevon "chose a certain path and lived like Jim Morrison" and "was the most fucked up rock star on the block" (Gunderson, 12D). His notorious excesses are well documented, notably in renowned rock journalist Paul Nelson's stunning account of Zevon's early descent and resurrection in a *Rolling Stone* cover story (March 19, 1981), and in *I'll Sleep When I'm Dead: The Dirty Life and Times of Warren Zevon* (2007), a 452-page, posthumous oral history compiled at Zevon's request by his ex-wife Crystal.

The death motif was a lifelong haunt for Zevon, dating to his child-hood:

> My ideal as a child was a dead man—with my name, looks and career intentions. A dead warrior who'd been waylaid by his heroism. . . . I grew up with a painting of an uncle, Warren, who looked just like me. He was a military man, a golden boy, an artist. He'd been killed in action. Uncle Warren was sort of the dead figurehead of the family, and I was brought up to follow in his footsteps. I guess that kind of background gave me the idea that destroying myself was the only way to live up to expectations. (Nelson 1981, 33)

And:

> It didn't take a lot of therapy to realize I'd been ingrained with the idea that dying was going to fulfill your parents' ideas of what's good. (Alfonso, 25)

Which may, in part, explain "Old Velvet Nose," the smirking, cigarette smoking, sometimes bespectacled, skull image that grins from the covers, corners, and liner notes of Zevon's albums, like a skeletal Nike swoosh sibling logo of Edward Munch's famous lithograph, *The Scream*, from the late 1800s. The "trademark" was at once a Zevon birthmark, self-portrait, mirror image, x-ray, mask, and alter ego. Perhaps a haunting homage to the waylaid warrior, Uncle Warren.

SONG NOIR: "A CIRCUS IN REVOLT"

> *There was always this little something going on behind those eyes. He [Zevon] was always one joke away—always looking for an opening to get in a little wit, or a little slice of this, or a little sardonic this or ironic that.*
> —best-selling author Mitch Albom (C. Zevon)

Zevon's fatalistic vision and scathing, sophisticated songwriting style prompted Browne to anoint Zevon the first and foremost proponent of "song noir." The designation was often modified to "comic noir" to accommodate Zevon's mordant humor. Zevon comprehended the cinematic, hard-boiled Hollywood compliment, though he was politely indifferent, if not dismissive.

Popular music has its share of humorists beyond the Weird Al Yankovic, Spinal Tap, *Mighty Wind* parodists. Along songwriting's comic continuum, Randy Newman stands out as one of the smartest satirists. The Johns—Prine and Hiatt—routinely offer amusing takes on family and the human condition, whereas the Brit blokes, Graham Parker and Elvis Costello, can be cutting. James McMurtry's wit is West Texas dry; Loudon Wainwright III strums folksy social observations; the Roche sisters and Jill Sobule are clever lyricists who sometimes skew toward the silly end of the spectrum; and among a newer wave, Courtney Barnett delivers droll lyrical rambling.

And then there is Zevon, "always one joke away;" a unique coalition of composer, comic, and coroner, a title he actually held in Pitkin, Colorado. The honorary appointment was unofficially bestowed late one night in Aspen's Hotel Jerome bar. His noir sensibility and literate wit forge a "witerary" aesthetic in distinctly dense, darker shades, with frequent scornful strands, colored with culture and romantic tones. Not coincidentally, "up all night" and "the rest of the night" are phrases frequently found in Zevon's songwriting. Predictably, his "all night long" is a more shadowy nocturne than Lionel Richie's colorfully festive use of the phrase.

Zevon's fellow songwriters were drawn to his unique vision, among them David Crosby, who stated, "Very few people have an ability to write songs that are mocking, wry, and loving all at the same time. He saw things with a jaundiced eye that still got at the humanity of things"(C. Zevon, 427). Browne, who along with Zevon's close friend and collaborator Calderón provided some of the most astute readings of Zevon as an artist and person, expounded: "He sang and joked about things that no one had joked about before, like 'Excitable Boy.' But he could say in a few words something with great depth. His songs were like cartoons" (Fricke 2003, 49). And:

> He is the standard bearer; he's very adventurous and there's confidence and power . . . a literacy, not just of words but also an emotional literacy . . . that realm is honesty and vulnerability. But then, you know, there's a berserk quality to the whole thing when it's done. (Boucher, F1)

Zevon's ominous outlook was certainly twisted, but not over the top. His wit, savage and smart, was deftly described by Jim Dees, host and humorist of Oxford, Mississippi's live literary and music show, *Thacker Mountain Radio Hour*, as "a circus in revolt." Adroit arrangements and jaunty, merry melodies incongruously lure listeners into lyrical lair, frequently in a "Whistle While You Work" way. The gleefully grim "Excitable Boy" may be among the best examples of Zevon's slyly enticing sing-along style. Further heightening the presentation, whether live or recorded, Zevon's intermittent exclamatory bursts, "Hah!" and "Huh!"—emphatic echoes of Springsteen's holler on "She's the One"— are well-placed vocal stomps that punctuate verses or launch into a bridge or chorus.

A WROCKER: NO STRANGER TO FICTION

> *Warren was pretty enthusiastic about writers, and I think writing was what interested him, in a way, more than anything he did.*
> —novelist Thomas McGuane (C. Zevon)

> *I wondered why popular music was so square. Because I had been reading Norman Mailer from the time I was 12 years old. I don't think it occurred to me that I was trying to make some kind of breakthrough in the popular song. It seemed to me then, and it seems to me now that, for the most part, there were some kind of restrictions on the subject matter of songs. And it was quite the opposite in every other art form.*
> —Warren Zevon (Roeser)

Reveling and rollicking in the ghastly and gruesome is one of Zevon's indisputable dominant artistic traits. Yet the delightfully dark recurring themes eclipse numerous complementary facets that illuminate Zevon's distinctive noir vision, presence, and gifts as a songwriter and musician. Literature, film, popular culture, romance, and humor infuse Zevon's writing, which, in part, is why Zevon and his work are as often compared to writers and filmmakers as they are to songwriters. "I wrote like what I'd always read and what was in the movies . . . I'm sure popular music is supposed to be like this," said Zevon (Bowman, n.p.). The influences are also evident in Zevon's record dedications, which include director Martin Scorsese (*Stand in the Fire*); crime novelist Kenneth Millar (a.k.a. Ross Macdonald) (*Bad Luck Streak in Dancing School*), who was a saving grace during one of Zevon's alcohol interventions in 1979; and gonzo journalist Hunter S. Thompson (*Mutineer*).

Literature, philosophy, and poetry inform, litter, and loiter in Zevon's writing, from Fitzgerald and Hemingway to T. S. Eliot, Robert Lowell, Graham Greene, and Martin Amis, from Schopenhauer and Rilke to Mickey Spillane and countless others. "I was more interested in contemporary writing than in pop music. I wasn't a great rock and roll fan," said Zevon. "What Norman Mailer or John Updike had to say seemed a lot more interesting than what was going on in pop music in the early 1960s" (VH1.com). And, later: "Certainly you had Paul Simon and Bob Dylan. But nobody was trying to be the John Updike of rock songwriting" (Fricke 2007, 4).

Zevon's ideals included Mailer, Raymond Chandler, and Ross Macdonald, author of the Lew Archer detective mysteries set in Southern California, "a nice balance between blood and guts and humanitarianism, with just the right acceptable amount of formal poetry" (Nolan, 375). Part of Zevon's hard-boiled, novelist nature was that he identified with fictional characters, particularly the kidnaped kid in Macdonald's *The Zebra-Striped Hearse* (1962), and the rock star protagonist haunted by the delusion that his father was Jesse James in Thomas McGuane's *Panama* (1978).

McGuane was among the numerous literary alliances Zevon established, several of which resulted in songwriting collaborations, McGuane among them. Zevon also partnered with best- selling authors Carl Hiaasen and Mitch Albom, Pulitzer Prize–winning poet Paul Muldoon, and gonzo journalist Hunter S. Thompson, to write songs which were recorded for his albums. Zevon occasionally performed in the band of bards, The Rock Bottom Remainders, featuring Albom, Stephen King, Amy Tan, and Dave Barry, among many others. He also wrote the liner notes for *Stranger Than Fiction* (1998), a two-CD charity collection by the Remainders reconfigured as the Wrockers (the name a hybrid of "writers + rockers," not a reference to the "wizard rock" of Harry Potter–themed bands).

According to Crystal Zevon, Warren "took pride and pleasure in being quoted by authors." It astonished and delighted him to think that best-selling authors appreciated his songs as much as he loved their books. His library was extensive, and filled with the complete works of all the writers he admired, especially those he ended up befriending. Bookstores were always a main stop for Zevon while touring, and he was known to use character names from Norman Mailer novels as aliases on the road. Zevon routinely attended book signings of writers he liked, standing in line for an autograph and talking with fellow fans (282–83). Zevon (dis)qualified the literary pursuits with, "We buy books because we believe we're buying the time to read them" (Read, VH1).

"A MAD MAGICAL POET," AND THE LANGUAGE THAT HE USED

> *Warren rarely communicated in conventional language.*
> —Danny Goldberg, CEO Artemis Records

> *He [Zevon] really couldn't write in that more traditional way. He was always looking to do something more original and ultimately meaningful. Many of Warren's songs gave language new meaning.*
> —guitarist David Landau (C. Zevon)

> *I'm no linguist but I believe Warren Zevon may be the only man in the history of human communication to use the word "brucellosis" in a song.*
> —*Late Show* host David Letterman

Zevon's wonderful way with words outweighed his wayward ways. He is indisputably one of rock's most striking visual and literate lyricists; a "mad magical poet," as described by Billy Bob Thornton. In producer Jon Landau's view, Zevon's "intellect and sophistication were so much higher than the typical musician's," and his writing gifts unique in their multiple mastery of the psychological, description, and construction (C. Zevon, 109).

Writing was painful to Zevon. He considered himself "lazy"; saying that his ambition was "getting the third line to the second verse right." He agonized over lyrics, and was too meticulous to be prolific. Zevon's writing approach was that "there are only as many songs as there are"; there were not any more songs in a vault or in a notebook. In a 1992 interview with *Los Angeles Times* writer Richard Cromelin, he explained,

> The weird phenomenon in my songwriting is that there are never any more songs than I record. The whole Neil (Young) and Bruce (Springsteen) deal is inconceivable to me: "I wrote 100 songs and I didn't like 'em so I wrote 10 more and we cut those." I can't imagine. For some reason when I get an idea I'll always carry it through. It'll eventually get finished and recorded. (n.p.)

Guitarist David Landau, Jon's brother, thought Zevon's "thing to make up phrases and make them mean something" was a "much more ambitious thing to do." Lines and phrases in Zevon songs come from everywhere and from nowhere, often with stunning peculiarity, elegant vulnerability, and perverse pleasure: "I'd like to meet his tailor"; "how was I to know she was with the Russians too?"; "your face looked like something Death brought with him in his suitcase"; "even the Lhasa Apso was ashamed." His songs originated from sources that were mundane, strange, and sometimes unknown and unexplainable, even to Zevon. He told Salon.com's David Bowman of his songwriting that sometimes it "just sort of happened," and that he wrote "songs about things that I'm simultaneously trying to not think about."

Photographer Richard Edlund observed Zevon in the pre-Asylum era, saying "I know Warren as always pushing himself intellectually . . . psychologically, in order to extrude another song from his brain. Warren was like Poe in his writing, and occasionally there would be some mixed metaphor that would come out of conversation, and then four days later he would have some song" (C. Zevon, 32).

Zevon's songs translate into a variety of literary forms, from highbrow to low—short stories, vivid three- to four-minute screenplays, sonnets, sordid sagas, allegories, tragicomic B-flicks, detective mysteries, novellas, pulp fiction, and cartoons. His noir narratives feature recurring themes of gun-barrel justice; desperation, betrayal, bravado, and honor involving hustlers; hostages, bandits, burnouts, bottom feeders, backstabbers, and Machiavellian men of action; all across an atlas of lively and lonely locations. Zevon's sense of place is a geographical span stretching from international hot spots to local dives, famous drives such as the winding Mulholland, Hollywood hotels and haunts, 7-11s, Legion Halls and factories, to metaphorical and fictional settings such as the inspection booth, Kingdom of Fear, Dew Drop Inn, Last Breath Farm, Rehab Mountain, Say-one-thing-and-mean-another-ville, and Pleasant Station. Zevon tells jokes and ghost stories, composes dirges, crafts tender, graceful ballads, and concocts macabre, often masochistic meditations that feature unusual subjects—clowns, monkeys, karma, diseased cattle, a Rottweiler, hockey goon, root canal, gorillas in therapy, an ashamed Lhasa Apso.

As a casting director and lyrical landlord, Zevon assembles a roster of unusual suspects into bizarre bios that are at times beyond berserk, with occasional caricature qualities: "the Village Idiot/his face all aglow"; the "Excitable Boy" who, among other bad behavior, rubbed the pot roast all over his Sunday best, bit the usherette's leg in the dark, and built a cage with his prom date's bones. There's "Mr. Bad Example," "very well acquainted with the seven deadly sins" since his altar boy days, and the "Model Citizen," with a Craftsman lathe down in the basement to "show to the children when they misbehave." Brother Billy with "both guns drawn, ain't been right since Viet Nam." The "Worrier King," "hiding from the mailman"; an "Angel Dressed in Black," a "Poisonous Lookalike," and a "Basket Case"; "a bipolar mama in leather and lace."

Such consistently creepy and quirky character sketches from album to album naturally fostered misconceptions which Zevon spurned: "There's the notion some people have that I'd probably write a song about [serial killer] Jeffrey Dahmer. I don't know where they get the idea. Reaching that conclusion about me is like thinking that Clint Eastwood is actually a cop" (Lim, n.p.). Though many of his characters and narratives, particularly those delivered in first person, were conveniently presumed to be autobiographical, Zevon frequently deflected direct associations. He preferred the more ambiguous term "self-referential," reminding those making such connections that "in the songwriting field there isn't a section for 'fiction' and a section for 'non-fiction,' it's all mixed together."

Zevon's lyrics flourish with literary conceit. His vocabulary is vast, his phrasing striking and poetry peculiar, accented with Dylanesque and Dr. Seussical rhythms and rhymes. While Letterman acknowledged "brucellosis" as one of the highlights of Zevon's garish glossary, his word wellspring runs deep: an invalid haircut, nickname expires, naugahyde divan, sky looks kinda chewed-on like, trees look like crucified thieves, rhododendron days and fuchsia nights, regal sobriquet, regicidal friends, sentimental hygiene, dancing quanta, polyvinyl chloride, double helix, harvest of contusions, Ivy League voodoo, reptile wisdom, green horned chicken hoppers.

Zevon's lively language was not limited to his lyrics. During interviews, whether conducted in person or in print, Zevon was articulate and epigrammatic, similarly forthright and funny, offbeat and self-effacing. He oddly referred to his fans as "customers," and in an interview with Jody Denberg in 2000, characterized them as an "audience that accidentally stepped on a Mr. Toad's ride on the way to the funhouse." The *I'll Sleep When I'm Dead* compilation reveals Zevon journal entries with quirky phrases such as "orangutan wedding," and descriptions— "displaced earthquake people and pets . . . who look like they belong at a Bulgarian bridal shower." Others are caustically comic, referring to managers as "shit handlers," his dry cleaners as "floor shitters," and an interviewer as a "dreary bedwetter." When one of his songs was a last-minute cut from a movie scene, costing him considerable royalty revenue, Zevon's entry read: "$35,000 disappears in seconds like a colored hankie in a shitbird magician's fist" (C. Zevon, 362). In the VH1 *(Inside)Out* documentary, Zevon remarks that photos of him resemble "a baboon from Newcastle trying to get a job in a toothpaste commercial," further evidence of his acute monkey fixation.

CLASSICAL COMPOSER AND CULTURAL CURATOR

Zevon frequently displays his erudite, worldly ways beyond literature and film, culture and geography. Foreign languages—Spanish, French, Russian, Latin, and Hawaiian among them— layer and accent his lyrics, in phrases, choruses, and entire songs, such as "Laissez-Moi Tranquille." Musically, Zevon lists his influences as classical, folk, blues, and rock, in that order, as specified during an interview on the BBC music series, *Later . . . with Jools Holland*, on May 13, 2000, though he has on other occasions simplified his status to "folk singer."

Zevon's classical training and proficiencies are exhibited in his accomplished piano playing, impressive arrangements, and excerpts of his unfinished Symphony No. 1 that are placed as interludes throughout his album, *Bad Luck Streak in Dancing School* (1980). The miniatures were inspired by one of his idols, celebrated Canadian pianist and Bach interpreter, Glenn Gould, and more notably, Zevon's encounters at age 13 with composer/conductor Robert Craft and Russian maestro Igor Stravinsky, who had taken up residence in Los Angeles around Hollywood. Despite his classical background, Zevon avoided piano solos on his records because he didn't like them and wasn't interested in what he called "rock and roll piano," which he found "a little grating" (Roeser, n.p.). Zevon said in an interview with Jody Denberg that he "hated to admit" that he "never had as much fun playing the piano as he did the guitar."

Composing music may have been an easier process for Zevon than writing lyrics, though the method seemed somewhat mysterious. Zevon said he didn't really hear music but rather saw it, often in dreams, written out in formula like a mathematical equation. He would then write the little piece down, then compose and expand it on his computer or portable Steinberger (C. Zevon, 235).

Zevon was also a keen cultural consumer and observer, well informed beyond literary works and highbrow. Ronstadt oddly recalls in her memoirs that Zevon was the only person she knew who had a subscription to *Jane's Defence Weekly*, a publication devoted to global military intelligence activity and weapon technology. Referencing familiar and obscure people and places was a complementary component of his songwriting approach. Zevon's array of pop portraits, citations, and allusions in song are analogous with pop artist Andy Warhol's attraction to fame and the celebrity images in his silkscreen prints, figures which included Jacqueline Kennedy, Elvis, Marilyn Monroe; and those depicted in his "Myth Series" in 1981—Howdy Doody, Mickey Mouse, Dracula, Santa Claus, Mammy, Superman, the Shadow, the Wicked Witch of the West, and others.

Zevon curates a musical gallery of celebrity, a cultural cross-section that includes artists, actors, and athletes; outlaws and explorers; world leaders and spiritualists: Frank and Jesse James, Patty Hearst, Lon Chaney, Dracula's daughter, Calamity Jane, Marilyn Monroe, Elvis, Woodrow Wilson, Jimmy Carter, Mikhail Gorbachev, Mata Hari, Madame Blavansky, Ponce DeLeon, Sinbad, Charlton Heston, Georgia O'Keeffe, and Michael Jackson; couples Billy (Joel) and Christie (Brinkley), Bruce (Springsteen) and Patti (Scialfa); sports figures Boom Boom Mancini from boxing and baseball's Bill "Spaceman" Lee; underwater explorer Jacques Cousteau; and yard work with Liz (Taylor) and Liza

(Minnelli) at Detox Mansion. He also inserts himself with scathing style into the 1970s Neil Young-Lynyrd Skynyrd "Southern Man"/"Sweet Home Alabama" feud.

Zevon's penchant for name-dropping is neither novelty nor non-narrative nonsense in the vein of the radio-friendly Barenaked Ladies 1998 tune, "One Week." Zevon's referencing is imaginative and less glib, with socio-comic commentary, history, homage, and biographical intent, with a smirk of cultural conceit. Peculiar pop pairings proved Zevon to be a jester of juxtaposition reminiscent of the MTV claymation series, *Celebrity Death Match* (1998–2002, 2006–2007) —"Albert Einstein . . . making out like Charlie Sheen," "Jesus and John Wayne at the Marriott." Zevon also masterfully mosaics such incongruent pieces as Smokey and the Bandit, Saddam Hussein, Russell Crowe, and Hafiz Assad into one verse; and in another song on the same album, converges Shelley, Keats, Milton, and Lord Byron gathering for a gunfight outside a Hilton Hotel in East Texas.

TENDERNESS ON THE BLOCK: HEARTACHE SPOKEN HERE

Beneath the vitriol and volatile veneer that mark Zevon's songs lies an "arch-Warren" who portrays vulnerability and yearning as counterpoints to the aggression, desperation, and bravado. Zevon was a romantic renegade "searching for a heart of gold in a four-letter world," composing wistful ballads about what he considered "the most dangerous adventure"—love. Often with a Quixotic outlook, Zevon wrote gracefully and honestly about love lost and longed for; and love that conquers all: "You can't start it like a car, you can't stop it with a gun." Nor could he resist finding a dark lining in love's sweet and silver cloud. With Zevon, it was "Accidentally Like a Martyr," rather than "Accidentally in Love," the Counting Crows' infectious reprise of the Lovin' Spoonful's "Do You Believe in Magic?" on the *Shrek 2* (2004) soundtrack.

His song titles alone were revealing, from the pleading "Reconsider Me," to the pessimistic "Empty-Handed Heart," "Nobody's in Love This Year," and "The Indifference of Heaven"; the self-pitying "She's Too Good for Me," and the promising "Let Nothing Come Between You" and "Never Too Late for Love." Zevon's tone and tactics conjured images of a latter-day Harold in search of a Maude. He frequently found offbeat humor in heartache, lacing loneliness with low self-esteem and self-effacing, if not lacerating, levity: "I could see me bound and gagged, dragged behind a clown mobile"; "And if she won't love me then her sister will"; "If you won't leave me I'll find somebody who will"; "I didn't have to come to Maui to be treated like a jerk." A versatile romantic, Zevon could assume a game show host guise—"maybe you should buy another vowel"—or employ magician metaphors—"make love disappear" and "for my next trick I'll need a volunteer."

Zevon may not have epitomized the sensitive-guy aura of a Jackson Browne, J. D. Souther, or some of the other L.A. canyon confessionalists, but his lyrics, wrapped in lovely melodies and arrangements, routinely revealed the "arch-Warren" to be as sentimental as he was sardonic. The elegant vulnerability in Zevon's romantic compositions and breakup ballads, 13 of which were assembled into the collection *Reconsider Me: The Love Songs* (2006), resonates alongside some of the era's exquisitely emotive and beautiful love songs, including the Lennon-McCartney works, Van Morrison's mystic meditations, the autumnal melancholy of the Left Banke's lush Baroque "Walk Away Renee" and "Pretty Ballerina," Nick Drake's "Northern Sky," Donovan's "Catch the Wind," Brian Wilson and the Beach Boys' "God Only Knows," the Kinks' thankful, endless, sacred "Days," Neil Young's strumming, wailing waltzes, John Hiatt's "Have a Little Faith in Me," Elton John's "Your Song," and Dylan's "To Make You Feel My Love."

FROM A TO ZEVON

The Zevon discography is spread across five decades and multiple record labels, with Imperial, Asylum, Virgin, Giant, and Artemis as the primaries, and Varése Sarabande, Rhino, and New West among the supplementary. His recording arc is marked by several comebacks and prolonged record label exiles, those gaps in part attributed to Zevon's complexities and uncompromising nature as an artist, and a reflection of shifts within the music industry. Despite those interludes, Zevon's catalog is abundant, comprised of 12 studio albums, one "super group" collaboration with members of R.E.M., two live sets, three "best of" anthologies (one a two-disc set), three tribute records, one love song compilation, a rarities collection, and numerous posthumous reissues.

Beyond that ample body of work, Zevon and his songs have surfaced as inspiration, basis, and citations in a markedly wide range of strange and predictable sights, sounds, settings, characters, and presentations throughout the cultural landscape. Though obviously not as vast as the Elvis Presley "mystery terrain," nor of the Beatles, Dylan, Springsteen, Madonna, or Michael Jackson magnitude, the Zevon cultural chronicle is a rich accumulation that includes: a 1960s folk duo; the Everly Brothers band leader and arranger; advertising jingles; B-sides to hit songs for the Turtles; film and television soundtracks, scores, and opening themes; a satellite radio show title and theme; cover versions and instrumental interpretations by an assortment of artists in musical styles and genres; memorial ceremony and Halloween playlists; a baseball "walk up" song; film and novel titles and dedications; characters in *Jurassic Park*; poems, fiction, short stories, and scholarly essays; crossword puzzle clues and answers; writing liner notes; film roles and television comedy cameos; a late-night Letterman *Late Show* legacy; a gubernatorial inauguration; a minor league baseball mascot; a book of rare photographs; bumper stickers; a Congolese ritual sculpture; an animated cameo and song citation in a video for a charity Christmas single; and a best-selling oral history of his "dirty life and times."

Zevon's cultural absence was often as conspicuous as his presence. While Zevon was a centerpiece for the Showtime cable series, *Californication*, his music was not included in other dramas that seemed discernably Zevon-friendly, notably the funeral home setting of Alan Ball's *Six Feet Under* (HBO, 2001–2005) and Vince Gilligan's *Breaking Bad* (AMC, 2008–2013). Though Gilligan and the series music supervisor were consistently pitch perfect with song selections and their scene placement—among the more memorable, "Crystal Blue Persuasion" by Tommy James and the Shondells, and Badfinger's "Baby Blue" in the series finale's closing scene—any number of Zevon songs—"My Shit's Fucked Up," "Model Citizen," "Lawyers Guns and Money"—would have been fitting accompaniment for Walter White's dark and desperate descent from mild-mannered high school chemistry teacher to his terminal diagnosis to meth manufacturing kingpin.

BOB DYLAN'S COFFEE TABLE

Singer-songwriter Steve Earle famously proclaimed with badass brava-do, "Townes Van Zandt is the best songwriter in the whole world and I'll stand on Bob Dylan's coffee table in my cowboy boots and say that." This desperado music biography—written from the viewpoint of a cultural chronicler, obsessive curator, and fan without cowboy boots—is my coffee table case for Warren Zevon as a significant and singular songwriter; one of the brilliant and best in the whole world.

I

JOIN ME IN L.A.

I used to feel more of a Beach Boys, be-true-to-your-school kind of loyalty to Southern California, which has kind of dissolved some—I'm not sure why. I suppose I'm an Angelino, having spent the bulk of my life there.

—Warren Zevon (Fawcett)

In the glow of Hollywood's glimmer, its irresistible self-obsession and the long shadow cast by the film industry's silver screen superiority, Los Angeles and its surroundings attracted, nurtured, and generated some of the most extraordinary songwriting talent on record during the 1960s and well into the 1970s, before disco's dominance during the latter part of the decade. The abundance from the songwriting Shangri-L.A. of the era provides one of popular music's most prolific and enduring playlists, a remarkably rich rotation that is as geographical, cultural, and mythical as it is musical. The discography of the period and place arguably contains as many, if not more, important artists, momentous songs, and masterpiece albums, both commercially and critically, than the other music hubs San Francisco, New York, and London combined. It is within this Southern California setting and the context of the era that Warren Zevon and his songbook came about.

CALIFORNIA DREAMIN' AND SHANGRI-L.A.

During the early 1960s, the music industry began a notable shift in sound and image from its East Coast core in Manhattan westward to Los Angeles. The Left Coast and its climate represented an attractive alternate vibe to New York City's winters and its legendary folk scene along Bleecker Street and in Greenwich Village, with its renowned clubs such as CBGBs and Gerde's Folk City. Los Angeles's canyon communities—Laurel, running from Sunset to the San Fernando Valley, and the more tranquil Topanga, a woodsy pass from Malibu Beach on the Pacific, deep in the Hills, a 20-mile escape from Hollywood—began to blossom as creative colonies of native and migrating musicians. The songwriting sanctuary, with an organic *Brigadoon*-meets-Brill-Building sensibility surrounded by a natural sound baffle, was what Van Dyke Parks referred to on his album *Song Cycle* (1968) as "the seat of the beat." The geo-musical atmosphere was transcendent, a consciousness as much as it was a place. In his history of the legendary locale, Michael Walker writes, "When you hear [Crosby, Stills and Nash's] 'Suite: Judy Blue Eyes,' you're hearing Laurel Canyon, vintage 1969" (xix). Similarly, Neil Young's *After the Gold Rush* (1970) is considered the homegrown consciousness of Topanga.

Outside the canyon settings, coffee houses and clubs proliferated, from the Ash Grove on Melrose to the Whisky a Go Go, Ciro's, and the Roxy along the Sunset Strip, to open mic Hoot Nights at Doug Weston's Troubadour on Santa Monica Boulevard, the hub of the folk-rock scene and a showcase for such influential groups as the Byrds, Buffalo Springfield, and British Invaders such as the Hollies. The membership from that particular trinity of bands splintered into the synergy that became Crosby, Stills, Nash, and sometimes Young. The thriving music culture and industry epicenter, with singles recorded in Los Angeles dominating the charts and radio rotations, reaffirmed the Mamas and Papas punctuating lyric in their allegoric autobiographical 1967 hit, in "Creeque Alley": "And California dreamin' is becomin' a reality."

Many of those dreams dissipated into nightmarish social, political, and cultural realities at the decade's cusp. Despite anticipated troop withdrawals, the Vietnam War persisted into the My Lai Massacre. The festival scene subsided swiftly, its flimsy flower-power foundation fragmented. The innocence, idealism, and utopian vision of anthemic unity that was celebrated during the fabled "Summer of Love" and Monterey Pop Festival in 1967, and in the three days of peace and music at Woodstock on August 15–17, 1969, at Max Yasgur's dairy farm in Bethel, New York, could not be sustained, despite its "half-a-million strong."

Woodstock was bracketed by two apocalyptic happenings in California. One week before the festival, the grisly Tate-LaBianca mass murders committed by the Manson Family cult chilled Los Angeles into lockdown, the evil episode purportedly motivated, in part, by revenge against producer and son of Doris Day, Terry Melcher, who reneged on a recording contract for cult leader Charles Manson. In December, there was an "Armageddon" at Altamont Speedway in northern California. During a free concert by the Rolling Stones, an 18-year-old black youth, Meredith Hunter, was beaten and stabbed to death in the crowd amidst the stage security provided by the Hell's Angels. The dawning of the Age of Aquarius darkened into the decade's end.

Five months later, campus unrest climaxed tragically with "four dead in Ohio" at Kent State when National Guardsmen fired into a crowd of protesters, killing four unarmed students and wounding nine others. "The May 4th Massacre" accelerated the Nixonian descent to Watergate that eventually destroyed the administration. Freak flags flew at half-staff as three of the period's most captivating performers—Jimi Hendrix, Janis Joplin, and Jim Morrison of the Doors—were gone by 1971, a dead-end destiny.

In the parenthesis between Woodstock and Watergate, there was a collective turning inward, particularly within youth culture. "Talkin' 'bout My G-g-generation" morphed into the "Me Generation" as the era's social consciousness transformed into self-absorption. Los Angeles generated the first emblems of the Me Generation manifesto as songwriting reflected the narcissistic slant. Songs and entire albums became soul searching, introspective, and confessional, with artists routinely writing about themselves and others within the songwriter circle. The naval gazing vulnerability of the autobiographical approach struck a chord with the record-buying, radio-listening 20-somethings and Sixties survivors, still wounded, reeling, and recovering from the decade's demystifying events and hippie daze.

"California mellow" further solidified Los Angeles as the undisputed mecca of pop and rock music. James Taylor's *Sweet Baby James* (1970) initiated music's mellow movement. Anchored by the lamenting hit single, "Fire and Rain," the soft rock record remained a Top 40 album for an astounding 54 weeks. The confessional catalog accumulated swiftly, leaving an indelible mark early in the decade. That same year, Joni Mitchell released *Ladies of the Canyon* (followed by *Blue* in 1971), along with *Carly Simon*, Taylor's *Mud Slide Slim and the Blue Horizon*, and the Carole King classic *Tapestry*, its critical views ranging from Robert Christgau's "triumph of mass culture" to producer Lou Adler's "the *Love Story* of the record industry." The ensuing *Harvest* by Neil Young, self-titled *Jackson Browne*, and *Graham Nash/David Crosby* in 1972 were representative of the genre's steady stream that continued past mid-decade.

The emergence of the singer-songwriter style in pop piloted a new L.A. sound. The serene settings of the canyons, a quiet contrast to the Sunset Strip, provided a natural escape where songwriters comfortably reconnected with their folk roots and dabbled with the increasingly hip country music. Rustic and romantic proved compatible. The resulting sound softened into living room soul, with increased acoustic emphasis. Psychedelia, the Spectorian "Wall of Sound," and the Beach Boys' sunshine and surf harmonies receded slightly, eclipsed by strands of the country-folk-rock blend present in Buffalo Springfield, Poco, and Gram Parsons, with both the Flying Burrito Brothers and the Byrds' groundbreaking *Sweethearts of the Rodeo* (1968), which reconfigured the group's sound of Beatles and Bach chimes and Roger McGuinn's 12-string Rickenbacker, advancing to the forefront.

A central swath of 1970s Los Angeles–based artists, including Warren Zevon, relied on a conclave of rarefied sessionists for backing: guitarist Waddy Wachtel, multi- and maxi-instrument stringed wizard David Lindley, and a crew known as "the Section," consisting of guitarist Danny Kortchmar, drummer Russell Kunkel, bassist Leland Sklar, and keyboardist Craig Doerge. This ubiquitous studio nucleus became known as the "Mellow Mafia." The players produced a tastefully understated, gently rocking sound that provided an ideal complement to the songwriting, vocals, and harmonies of the genre. Individually or collectively, the conspicuous instrumentalists could be heard on the majority of the era's defining songs and albums; their names and credits almost as familiar in the record liner notes as the song lyrics. The Mellow Mafia was to the signature sound of the 1970s what the versatile and renowned Wrecking Crew was to the 1960s Los Angeles music scene, backing Phil Spector, the Beach Boys, the Byrds, and others. The Mellow Mafia's significance should not be understated as one of pop and rock music history's most important session crews. "They collectively changed the face of music," said Peter Asher, one of the period's prominent producers and music managers. "They helped in the process of taking singer-songwriters seriously" (Browne, 70).

BORN TO ROCK THE BOAT

Warren Zevon was a misfit within the distinguished class of 1970s singer-songwriters, misaligned with the mellow, self-satisfied strummers, the breezy acoustics of the group America, whose hit "A Horse with No Name" sounded so much like Neil Young, even Young's father thought it was his son's song; or the peaceful, take-it-easy feeling of the Eagles' country-folk-rock school. "Warren was a bit of an unusual character coming out of California because his tone was obviously not a typical Californian unless you went back to maybe Nathanael West," observed New Jersey–born Bruce Springsteen. "He had a cynical edge, which was really not a part of what was coming out of California at the time" (C. Zevon, 147).

Born in Chicago on January 24, 1947, Warren William Zevon grew up on a cultural and psychological fault line of a curious, contrasting union. His father, William "Stumpy" Zevon (original surname Zivotofsky), a Russian-Jewish immigrant, was a boxer, gambler, gangster, and close associate of notorious mobsters Sam Giancana and Mickey Cohen. Warren's mother, Beverly Simmons, was a withdrawn Scots-Welsh Mormon, 21 years younger than her husband. Stumpy was frequently absent from the family, and relocated Warren and his mother from Chicago to the West Coast. Warren spent most of his nomadic childhood and formative teen years in California, primarily between Fresno, where his mother was from, and San Pedro in the harbor district of Los Angeles, where Stumpy opened a carpeting business as a legitimate "front" for gambling activities. The marriage was unstable and family life unsettled, with Warren frequently shuttled back and forth between parents during a continuous cycle of fighting, separations, and reconciliations. When he was nine years old and living with his mother in Fresno, Warren received his first musical instrument: a Chickering piano that his father had won in a poker game on Christmas Eve. Even that occasion sparked discord. Warren's mother was furious and did not want "the headache machine" in her house. Stumpy responded by hurling a carving knife in Beverly's direction, narrowly missing her, with Warren a witness to the disturbing incident.

Perhaps it is too convenient, or too obvious, to infer that Zevon's father and family situation was a primary source that shaped his desperado demeanor. According to Zevon, his friends all saw his father as a "sort of Jesse James character." Zevon considered that a "mixed blessing" that was "neat sometimes," while other times he "would have preferred a Robert Young type," a reference to the idyllic father figure and family in the popular television series *Father Knows Best*, which aired from 1954 to 1960. Zevon was keenly aware of and conflicted by the Youngian father archetype and its incompatibility with creativity and the rock and roll lifestyle. When his marriage to Crystal was unraveling and very close to its end, he accused her of trying to "destroy a great artist and turn Dylan Thomas into Robert Young." Zevon's last words to Crystal as she walked out the door were, "I'll never be your father."

Zevon's parents' marriage was a mystery to him all his life. They divorced when he was a teenager, though he was never sure exactly when their marriage ended because "nobody ever told me anything." Zevon more or less figured out the state of their union when Elmer, the handy man who had been fixing the family's roof, moved in (C. Zevon, 14).

At 13, Zevon began studying music by listening to a piece and following the score. "If you can do that with 'Le Sacre du Printemps,' that's probably the equivalent of ten years academic training—at least if you're as passionately interested in the subject I was," said Zevon (Maslin, 73). Zevon benefitted from his Dana Junior High band teacher, who was also a classical trumpet player who had recorded with conductor Robert Craft. Recognizing Zevon's musical instincts and passion, Zevon's teacher introduced him to Craft and took him to one of his recording sessions that featured Russian composer Igor Stravinsky. Inspired by the meeting, Zevon began teaching himself harmony and counterpoint. He routinely visited Craft at his Hollywood home, bringing the conductor scores that he was working on. According to Zevon, Craft "liked the idea that some young thirteen year old kid in L.A. was so interested in the culture, making an attempt to be a composer" (Fawcett, 150). Craft introduced Zevon to Stravinsky, who lived two doors down, and invited him to the composer's Hollywood home on several occasions. Zevon estimates that he visited five or six times. Together, Zevon, Craft, and Stravinsky listened to recordings, read scores, and talked about composing and conducting. "It was one of the major events of my life. Stravinsky was like Elvis," said Zevon (Tannenbaum, 25). One of his prized possessions was an album inscribed with "Happy New Year's wishes to Warren Zevon from Igor Stravinsky—December 1961."

The visits with the mentors ended when their departure on a concert tour coincided with Zevon's mother's decision to return to Fresno with her son. Over the years, Zevon suggested in interviews that his "unusual" gatherings with Stravinsky have been "always exaggerated," and that he wasn't "above allowing the press to make perhaps a little more of it than there actually was" (Denberg; Roeser). However, Zevon's interest in classical music never waned. The Craft/ Stravinsky encounters left a profound and lasting mark on Zevon that could be traced in his arrangements and compositions throughout his career. "I still hear all kinds of music the same way," said Zevon. "I never thought that bad classical music was better than good rock and roll. What I like about classical music is the same thing I like about Cajun music or country blues or Tony Bennett" (Tannenbaum, 25).

Zevon connected his classical affinity to his other major musical influence, the Beatles, who "totally turned around" Zevon, particularly *Revolver* (1966):

> It was just like classical composers, who would write an opera, then follow it with a little church piece, then do a string quartet and remain the same composer. And here was an album of songs; the first would be Indian-flavored, the next would be country, then it would be sweet pop, then move to hard rock. And through it all, it would stay intact because they were the same composers. (Catlin, n.p.)

Zevon attended several high schools, accelerating through with his high I.Q., a directive to "keep your mouth shut and you'll get an A," and thinking to himself, "I believe you do this act with a cross." School was "not his wire." Zevon was "superstitious about being overeducated," and thought that having gaps in his musical education might leave "some nice areas that I could still stumble around in, as opposed to being Juilliarded to the point where everything can become technological." During his junior year, he dropped out of school to follow his fleeting Bob Dylan folksinger dream to New York. Beyond his classical interests and pursuits, Zevon learned to play guitar from listening to the banjo parts on folk records. Among the most influential were the New Lost City Ramblers and Koerner, Ray and Glover. Zevon's East Coast experience was brief. He admits he was awful and didn't know what he was doing beyond chasing a romantic dream. As evidence, Zevon recounted a pass-the-hat performance at a small club in Greenwich Village, when he dropped one of his finger picks into the sound hole of his guitar and was too embarrassed to continue playing.

Upon returning to California, Zevon was actively paying his dues in and around the Los Angeles music scene where he accumulated songwriting, session, and commercial credits. In 1964, as "stephen lyme," Zevon, along with his Fairfax High School classmate, Violet Santangelo, formed the folk-pop pair, "lyme and cybelle," a lit-hip lowercase nod to poet e. e. cummings. The name "cybelle" is rooted in mythology and taken from the art house French film *Sundays and Cybele* (1962). After listening to the duo sing Beatles tunes in a living room gathering, Michael Burns, a child actor from the television series *Wagon Train*, recommended them to his mother, who worked at White Whale Records. Zevon and Santangelo secured a recording contract with the local label, whose roster featured the popular group the Turtles. Bones Howe, who had worked with the Association and Fifth Dimension, supervised a four-week demo session with lyme and cybelle, recording original ballads, versions of Lennon and McCartney's "I've Just Seen a Face," Jimmy Reed's blues classic, "Peeping and Hiding," and what would become the duo's inaugural single, "Follow Me," a catchy psych-pop tune, with Eastern accents that Zevon described as "raga and roll." The song was "an extremely small hit" that reached number 65 on the *Billboard* charts in April 1966. The single's B-side ballad, "Like the Seasons," was adopted by White Whale label mates Mark Volman and Howard Kaylan, the Turtles' twin fronts, who were determined to give Zevon every songwriter break they could. In an unusual and selfless move, they employed "Like the Seasons" again as a B-side. This time, it was the flip to "Happy Together," a song Volman, Kaylan, and the record company were convinced was going to be a number-one. Their instincts were accurate; "Happy Together" was an enormous hit in 1967, unseating the Beatles' "Penny Lane" from the top chart spot for three weeks, resulting in respectable royalties, or B-side "gravy money," for the promising songwriter. Zevon, who had a publishing deal with Ishmael Music, also wrote "Outside Chance" with Glenn Crocker, a Beatlesque tune that Kaylan recorded and calls one of his favorite Turtles songs of all time. Nearly 40 years later, "Outside Chance" surfaced as a soundtrack obscurity in a 2005 episode of the popular television forensic series, *CSI: Crime Scene Investigation* (CBS).

Despite the chart success of "Follow Me," which was supported by exposure from lyme and cybelle's performance on *The Lloyd Thaxton Show,* a live local Los Angeles teen dance version of Dick Clark's *American Bandstand,* the folk duo never had the opportunity to record and release a full-length album. The lyme and cybelle demos and recordings were not available until 2003 with the compilation *The First Sessions.* White Whale opted to have Howe produce a second lyme and cybelle single, a Dylan cover, "If You Gotta Go, Go Now." The single sales started strong, only to have its momentum stalled when Bill Gavin, a powerful radio industry figure, claimed the song was sexually suggestive. Zevon moved on, briefly turning to composing advertising jingles for Boone's Farm Apple Wine, and with actor Harry Dean Stanton, for Gallo Wine, and Chevy Camaro. Though lucrative, Zevon found the ad experience doing "folky Gordon Lightfoot commercials" awkward, unsettling, and "abrasive to the soul." During a 1987 interview with Rob Tannenbaum, he recalled, "I'd turn on the radio and hear myself wedged between late '60s rock classics. I was wildly financially compensated for it, and it scared the shit out of me. I thought it was bad karma, and I got out as quickly as I could. Insubordination doesn't go far with Madison Avenue" (26). Zevon continued doing session work, including "strumming a guitar somewhere way in the background on Phil Ochs's *Pleasures of the Harbor*" in 1967. Santangelo eventually made it to Broadway as a singer, Laura Kenyon.

Acounts of Zevon's departure and the duo's divide were largely attributed to Zevon's uncompromising artistic vision and excessive drinking, two traits that advanced into career-long shadows of affliction. The transition also triggered the color quirks of Zevon's obsessive compulsive disorder. Zevon abandoned his "lyme" persona and complementary green guise that included tinted glasses and clothing; he believed the duo's breakup meant the color was unlucky. Zevon's palette preference shifted to a blue tint and a surfer-sounding rename, "Sandy."

AN OUTLAW'S FACE: *WANTED DEAD OR ALIVE*

Bones Howe referred Zevon—the "genius who was driving him crazy"—to another colorful character, Kim Fowley, a noted Hollywood hustler and eccentric entrepreneur of the local underground music scene. Fowley, the self-anointed original "Mayor of Sunset Strip," asked Zevon if he was "prepared to wear black leather and chains, fuck a lot of teenage girls, and get rich?" Zevon was in. Together, Fowley and Howe proceeded to convince Imperial Records to sign Zevon to a record deal. Fowley was initially involved in supervising the recording sessions, until Zevon "had a sudden attack of taste" and decided he wanted to finish the album himself without Fowley's studio supervision. In Fowley's view, Zevon "was being an asshole" and "didn't listen to anyone about anything." Fowley had enough and walked away from the project.

Despite the discord, Fowley remained true to his reputation as "master of grease and hype," taking credit for shaping Zevon's image. Fowley "allowed" Zevon to adopt his swagger, telling him that "if he wanted to convince people he was an artist, the way he walked had to make a statement about misunderstanding and adulation at the same time. . . . Be a prick, but be a literate one" (C. Zevon, 31). At best, or worst, Fowley may have instilled in Zevon some awareness of the value of having an image. From his earliest projects, Zevon's inherent idiosyncrasies and torments were palpable; he proved to be averse and unreceptive to mentoring or authority. Santangelo attests to the same during lyme and cybelle, stating that Zevon's "eccentricities were early and fabulous."

Wanted Dead or Alive was released on the Imperial label in 1969, in Zevon's words, "to the sound of one hand clapping." Within its stark production qualities that are at once coarse and cluttered, there lie glimpses of Zevon's noir nature and songwriting preoccupations, among them lost love. Zevon's peculiar identity crisis lingered, with only his last name above the album title. No lower case "stephen" or surfer "Sandy" or even "Warren." Just "Zevon." The album title's "wanted poster" premise inaugurated the dual motifs of desperado and death that became career context for Zevon. There is also a draft-dodging subtext. When Zevon received his draft notification in the mid-1960s in the midst of the Vietnam War, he and his father conspired to alter his suitability for military service. Instead of the common draft-evasion tactics utilized during those turbulent times such as student deferment, conscientious objector, and crossing the Canadian border, Stumpy sent his son to a psychiatrist in his gangster web who provided a letter stating that Warren was homosexual. Zevon actively participated in the ploy, assuming a pacifist hippie posture and consuming multiple doses of LSD, bi-amphetamines, and marijuana before his induction physical. The father-son renegade ruse succeeded as Zevon's classification went from 1-A: Available to 4-F: Unfit. Zevon felt guilty about avoiding the draft, and more explicitly, believed that lying about it created a permanent "bad luck" stain, not only on him, but on active soldiers in the line of duty. The burden of Zevon's evasion triggered some of his earliest obsessive-compulsive behaviors—with "luck," and with not being able to look at or pass in front of an image of "Uncle Sam," the iconic personification of the United States. "Uncle Sam Wants You" was prevalent propaganda during the era, mainly as an armed forces recruiting pitch on signs, billboards, and posters. Zevon went to extreme measures, such as driving around a block, to avoid the finger-pointing patriot pose.

The desperado tone is further reaffirmed by the album's title tune, and the declaration— "I have an outlaw's face"—repeated with various prefixes ("But they say," "My Lord," "My, my, yes," "Sweet God almighty") in each of the last nine verses. Similarly, "Bullet for Ramona" previews the Sam Peckinpah presence and Zevon's gun-slinging side that frequently followed, from "Frank and Jesse James" on his major label debut to echoes in subsequent Western sagas, stretching from "Jeannie Needs a Shooter" to "My Ride's Here" to Dylan's "Knockin' on Heaven's Door" on his final record. "Bullet for Ramona," a letter from Laredo about lost love, begins with the casual bluntness of a bullet— "Oh, today I shot Ramona, Ma." Before the shooter rides across the Rio Grande, knowing he will never live to see another sunrise, he justifies his deed. When he found his love with a drifter, he "knew right then Ramona had to die."

"Tule's Blues" reveals the romantic Zevon, a poetic presence that whispers wistfully on every subsequent record. "Tule" is Marilyn Livingston, who Zevon met in San Francisco while traveling with his father and playing as many Haight-Ashbury folk clubs as would have him. Livingston, an aspiring model, was Zevon's first love. The couple lived together in Hollywood, though they never married. They discovered they were going to have a child while Zevon was occupied with making *Wanted Dead or Alive*. Considering his own unsettled childhood and his parents' rocky relationship, family values, domesticity, and its duties would never be a secure or natural mode for Zevon. When Livingston went into labor in August 1969, Zevon rushed her to the hospital, nobly carried her up the stairs, kissed her, and returned to the studio. "It didn't occur to me that I should be there. At the hospital . . . I don't know how much anybody was into that then," said Zevon. "I had a recording session booked, and all I knew was that it cost me money not to go to the studio" (C. Zevon, 34). When news of the baby's birth reached the studio, Zevon and crew briefly celebrated with a bottle of Boone's Farm wine, cigars, and a toast, and then returned to recording. Zevon did contribute his son's name from the studio session: "I had this Jordan amplifier I loved because it had a great sound. I looked over at the amp, liked the name, so that was it. Jordan" (35).

"Tule's Blues" is "a sad song [Tule and Zevon] seem to be singing to each other." An upbeat country-folk arrangement, in the vein of the Lovin' Spoonful's leaving-you-behind "Butchie's Tune" from 1966, veils the gravity of the fragile relationship. Zevon's poetic prose colors the couple's crossroads as "sweet and slightly out of key, like the sound of a running down calliope." He is weeping, "it's lonesome in my heart's land, as the sands of the desert," and Tule "always sang and played while the green vespers rang in the heart of the hillside." The multiple mentions of Tule's name that lead four verses are all a tacit sigh, "Oh Tule." The quioxtic Zevon sees himself as her "once knight in golden armor, sun behind his hair, his music filling the air with symbols and lightning," but he "is changing like the seasons." And, thus, so is their alliance; "There's no room left in the ark for a lark with a broken wing." He is leaving on account of Tule, the departure more fatefully self-aware than bitter, "Whatever wild worlds I may see, will be empty without you." The pitch of the poignancy deepens with the inclusion of "a child's voice, so tender and out of tune" that "keeps a' praying I'll be singing home soon," the verse a likely expression of the guilt Zevon said he always felt for not being present at his child's birth. The solo piano versions of "Tule's Blues" that were released on posthumous recordings resonate more intimacy and emotion, particularly with the child verse altered to "Does he ask if I'll be coming home soon." Tule Livingston lingered as a subtext of two divergent songs on Zevon's major label debut that followed six years later—"Hasten Down the Wind," a gentler reprise of "Tule's Blues," and the scornful "The French Inhaler."

Wanted Dead or Alive also features Zevon versions of B. K. Turner's country-blues "Hitchhikin' Woman" and "Iko Iko," and James "Sugar Boy" Crawford's 1953 New Orleans Mardi Gras Indian chant originally titled "Jack-A-Mo." In 1965, the Dixie Cups converted an impromptu drumstick-tapping-ashtray studio rehearsal rendition of "Iko Iko" into a girl group standard. Unlike his California colleagues Ronstadt and James Taylor, who, as superior vocalists, routinely interpreted other artists' songs on their albums, Zevon's cover catalog is sparse. His selections, beginning with the two adaptations on *Wanted Dead or Alive*, are intriguing, with New Orleans R & B composer Allen Toussaint, Prince, Judee Sill, Steve Winwood, and French provocateur Serge Gainsbourg among the artists whose songs he has recorded.

Perhaps the most notable obscurity on *Wanted Dead or Alive* is "She Quit Me," which was included in the Academy Award–winning film *Midnight Cowboy* (1969), starring Dustin Hoffman and Jon Voight. In the movie, the song was re-gendered as "He Quit Me" and performed by Leslie Miller and Garry Sherman. The film's soundtrack, highlighted by Harry Nilsson's hit version of Fred Neil's "Everybody's Talkin'" and music by noted film composer John Barry, earned a Recording Industry Association of America (RIAA) gold record. As the composer of "She Quit Me," Zevon received a gold record, an award that he presented to his father.

Despite some career foreshadowing and a few salvageable songs with worthy qualities and promising titles, *Wanted Dead or Alive* had minimal merit as an album. Plans for a follow-up titled *Leaf in the Wind* were abandoned. Nor did the record age particularly well with critics, the most loyal fans, and Zevon, who said the record was "like a terrible John Hammond album, with drums" (Roeser, n.p.). Thom Jurek's assessment of the album as "a shambolic mess of a record, one that wears it excesses everywhere" (n.p.) endures as a prevailing critical view. There has never been significant revisitation, posthumous elevation, or belated auteur acceptance of the album as a "buried treasure," even following its reissue in 1996, with no bonus tracks to enhance the re-mastered package. *Wanted Dead or Alive* remains relegated to first footnote status as a distant anterior debut or "independent release" in the Zevon discography. Zevon's self-titled Asylum album that followed in 1976 is generally regarded as his proper debut. In his review of *Wanted Dead or Alive*'s reissue, Paul Nelson, who was perhaps Zevon's most steadfast advocate in rock journalism, provided a magnanimous summation: "Hey, he just wasn't ready then. Simple as that" (1980, 63).

FOREVERLY

During the 1970s, Zevon continued to showcase his songwriting skills while touring with the Everly Brothers as their musical director, arranger, and keyboard player. Looking back on the role, Zevon said it was "like I was [Paul] Shaffer" (David Letterman's bandleader) (Roeser). At his audition for the piano position, Zevon performed his breakup ballad "Hasten Down the Wind." Phil Everly asked Zevon if he could "play like Floyd Cramer," one of the pioneers of the "Nashville sound" and "slip note" style of playing piano, with an out-of-key note sliding into a correct one. Zevon assured Everly, "You bet I can," and was hired without playing another note.

Brothers Phil and Don Everly were among the most influential acts during rock's formative years, producing 25 Top 40 hits between 1957 and 1964. As country music converged with rock and roll via Elvis Presley and Sun Studios, the Everlys also contributed by introducing the high lonesome harmony sound that chimes sweetly in their hits such as "Bye Bye Love," "All I Have to Do is Dream," "Cathy's Clown," "Wake Up Little Susie" and "'Til I Kissed You." In 1970, they hosted what Zevon referred to as "a really cool little TV show," *Johnny Cash Presents the Everly Brothers.* The summer variety series featured comedy sketches and country-western, rock, and gospel acts, including Neil Diamond, Kenny Rogers, the Carter Family, the Statler Brothers, Jackie DeShannon, Kris Kristofferson, Ike and Tina Turner, and many others. Among the cast of standout guest performers, it was "one of the new guys," Billy Joel, who overwhelmed Zevon. When Joel "sat down and started improvising this massive [Aaron] Copland-esque thing on the piano," Zevon walked off the set, recalling, "Whatever idea I had about myself as sort of like a classical pianist-turned-rock-guy evaporated in one moment of standing behind Billy Joel" (Roeser, n.p.).

Country-rock's roots are a straight line that runs from the Everly Brothers to Rick Nelson to Linda Ronstadt and the Eagles to the David Crosby/Graham Nash harmonies that echo in the rustic Americana of Gary Louris and Marc Olson of the Jayhawks. Rock journalist Bill Flanagan observes that when two singers from rock or country duet, they frequently start with an Everly Brothers song. Robert Plant and Alison Krauss ("Gone, Gone, Gone"), Vince Gill and Sting ("Let It Be Me"), and Carole King and James Taylor ("Crying in the Rain") are among the recent renditions reaffirming Flanagan's premise. The Everly legacy and influence are far-reaching. In the 1950s, among the many teenagers inspired by the brothers were Paul Simon and Art Garfunkel in Queens, and John Lennon and Paul McCartney in Liverpool. When the Beatles formed, Dick Clark initially dismissed them as "Everly Brothers imitators." The brothers also influenced Buddy Holly, who upgraded his style from wearing Levis and t-shirts to the Everlys' Ivy League suit look.

The Everly Brothers gig was a beneficial and sustaining step in Zevon's rock and roll quest, and a period when Zevon notes "the road, booze, and I became an inseparable team." The position paid well, and provided an opportunity for Zevon to hone his performance skills and audition his own songs. It was through the Everlys that Zevon began to grasp pop-rock harmony and learned about being a melody writer. The Everly experience also enriched Zevon's grudging appreciation for country music, which, until then, was a genre he looked down on from his elite literary and classical tastes.

When Zevon assembled the band to revitalize the Everly Brothers sound, he hired Waddy Wachtel, an extraordinary guitarist who was in the group Twice Nicely. The union, though initially prickly, marked the beginning of a 30-year relationship between Zevon and Wachtel, who ultimately cowrote songs with Zevon, coproduced three of his albums, and, as a member of the omnipresent Mellow Mafia session collective, contributed to Zevon's sound. It was also through Wachtel that Zevon met Crystal Brelsford, who had dated Wachtel on and off since 1967 when they met in Vermont. After migrating cross-country to Los Angeles, Brelsford managed the fan club of the family singing group the Cowsills, best known for their hits "The Rain, the Park and Other

Things" and a popular version of the rock musical theme, "Hair." True to the "free love" spirit of the times, when companion crisscrossing was common practice, particularly in the creative and counter culture communities, Zevon and Brelsford struck a relationship and soon moved in together. Zevon had been in constant transition, moving in and out of the place he lived with Tule Livingston and son Jordan, as well as extended stays at the Tropicana and Hollywood Hawaiian motels, two locales that became central settings in his songs. The couple married in 1974, "Hunter Thompson style," driving all night across the desert to Nevada, their trip fueled by acid and vodka the whole way, then drinking Bloody Marys until dawn at a Las Vegas casino until the Chapel of the Bells opened. Crystal was the only woman Zevon ever married, even though she is often inaccurately referred to as his "second wife," a result of Zevon's relationship with Tule Livingston being mistaken as a first marriage. Zevon himself perpetuated the marriage myth, preferring it to be taken for granted that he and Livingston, though staunch anti-establishment Sixties types, were married for his son's sake. Zevon's marriage to Crystal ended in 1979, then officially in divorce in 1981, though he continued to refer to her as his wife during his entire life.

By the mid-1970s, the Everlys were no longer harmonious and as a duo they had disintegrated. "We only ever had one argument, it's been lasting 25 years," said Phil Everly in 1970. Zevon continued to tour and record with both disbanded brothers as they tried to launch post-breakup solo careers. He moved to Berkeley briefly, playing two or three clubs a night, which had been his musical intention for a decade. Back in Los Angeles, Zevon's funds were dwindling, his dissatisfaction with the music industry increased, and his own publishing contract lapsed. His life was further complicated by a drunk driving arrest in front of the Troubadour. Zevon considered his career to be at a crossroads. The magical moments and musical opportunities of the late 1960s and his feeling like the "golden boy" were fading. Disillusioned, he sold his possessions—except for a Martin guitar and Sony stereo cassette recorder—and moved with Crystal to Spain in an effort to redirect his music pursuits. In Spain, Zevon read all the Ross Macdonald novels, and played country and western songs for pocket change in the Dubliner Bar, a small Irish tavern in Stiges, near Barcelona, owned by David "Lindy" Lindell, a former mercenary and *Soldier of Fortune* character who eventually collaborated on a few songs with Zevon. A return to Los Angeles was imminent.

2

THE ASYLUM ICONOCL.A.ST

With a cold eye, a boozer's humor, and a reprobate's sense of fate,
this California rounder put Los Angeles back on the rock and roll
map and nearly blew the Malibu singer-songwriter crowd right off it.
—music/cultural critic Greil Marcus (Hoskyns)

"THANKS ALWAYS TO JACKSON"

In the liner notes of each of Warren Zevon's five albums released during the 1980s, the acknowledgment—"Thanks always to Jackson"—is a floating footnote in the credits. Zevon's recurrent expression of gratitude to fellow songwriter Jackson Browne predates Zevon's major label debut on Asylum Records in 1976. In the summer of 1975, while in Spain, Zevon received a pleading postcard from his buddy Browne: "Warren, Too soon to give up. Come home. I'll get you a recording contract." The correspondence set in motion Zevon's return to Los Angeles in September and a major label record deal.

Browne had been an ardent advocate of Zevon's songwriting since they first met in 1968 in Laurel Canyon. He frequently performed a range of Zevon's songs live, even spelling the virtually unknown Zevon's last name so people would remember it. He also urged fellow artists in the L.A. music circle to record Zevon's material. Browne's contributions to the Eagles debut—"Nightingale" and the country-folk-rock road anthem, "Take it Easy," a collaboration with Glenn Frey—and "Doolin-Dalton," which he cowrote for *Desperado* (1973), came after he unsuccessfully pitched two Zevon songs to the Eagles for their albums. Nor could Browne persuade producer Terry Melcher to have the Byrds record for their "reunion" album on Asylum in 1973. "I didn't think anybody got Warren but me," said Browne. "That's the kind of writer he was—he spoke to your inner cynic. There was a dialogue that went on inside of him that's going on inside of everybody" (Scoppa, 65).

Browne's mentoring of Zevon and his "rough edges" impressed fellow singer-songwriter Bonnie Raitt:

> I always admired Jackson for appreciating Warren. I saw something in the people who appreciated Warren—it says something about the people that he touched, the people who could relate to him. Jackson's appreciation of Warren made me see Jackson in another way. That was another unexpected gift. We had to be truly twisted to be able to get Warren—and I mean that in a good way. (C. Zevon, 117)

Browne, whose primary allegiance was to hearing Zevon sing Zevon rather than outsourcing his songs, was an ideal benefactor. By mid-decade, Browne had established himself as one of the archetypal introspective poets of the Los Angeles songwriter sphere. Though born in Germany, Browne's West Coast residency translated more "native" than other avatars along the sensitive songwriter spectrum such as Joni Mitchell (Canada), James Taylor (North Carolina), Dan Fogelberg (Illinois), and Carole King (New York), who migrated west during music's solid gold rush. Browne also had credibility and contacts as a cornerstone and wunderkind of David Geffen's Asylum Records. The only artist signed from an unsolicited tape, Browne was Geffen's primary impetus for pursuing his own record label after he was unable to secure Browne a record deal anywhere else. The favorite son figure was one of the fledgling label's initial record recruits, along with Greenwich Village folkie David Blue, Judee Sill, Ned Doheny, and Jo Jo Gunne, a Spirit spinoff group that produced the hit "Run, Run, Run." Geffen's instincts, eye, and ear for talent proved perceptive and positive. Browne's first three albums in successive years— the eponymous debut later known as *Saturate Before Using* (1972), *For Everyman* (1973), *Late for the Sky* (1974)— are arguably as impressive a series of recordings and career commencement by any singer-songwriter.

Asylum Records evolved out of a management partnership between Geffen and Elliot Roberts, who founded Lookout Management (named after Lookout Mountain Avenue located in Laurel Canyon). On their way to becoming the most powerful management stable on the West Coast, the duo established a reputation for being shrewd businessmen, and more importantly, they were considered trustworthy, kind, and artist-friendly. Geffen and Roberts paid nominal advances, and effectively controlled every aspect of their artists' careers, including record deals, publishing, gate money, and touring.

Asylum was designed as a songwriter refuge, with Geffen an "excellent father confessor to his artists." Creative freedom was central to the label's musical mission. "Asylum was definitely shelter from the storm," said singer-songwriter J. D. Souther. "There wasn't a huge panic to get us packaged. I think there was a sense of the Blue Note days, where a school of jazzy guys got to play what they wanted and were treated as artists" (Hoskyns 2006,140).

The name "Asylum"—its iconic logo an incongruent image depicting a heavy wooden door with barred window floating on a clouds and blue sky backdrop—reflected the unique corporate philosophy of "benevolent protectionism" that buffered artists from the snares of the media and music industries. The symbolic insinuation of the "inmates running the asylum" is rooted in old Hollywood, when silent film star Charlie Chaplin, Mary Pickford, Douglas Fairbanks, and director D. W. Griffith, frustrated with restrictive financial and creative policies, boldly, if not insanely, took back control of their films from the major studios.

Geffen astutely merged the local music scenes of the Troubadour and Laurel Canyon into a formidable Asylum subculture and enterprise. Decades later, in 1994, Geffen's ascension as a major media mogul culminated when he teamed with Lawrence Katzenberg and film director Steven Spielberg to form the multimedia DreamWorks SKG studio empire.

Asylum prospered; its artists were prolific, with most on a strikingly steadfast album-a-year release pace throughout much of the decade, before the age of multimedia market synergy arrived in the early 1980s. The Eagles' string of albums between 1972 and 1976—*Eagles, Desperado, On the Border, One of These Nights, Hotel California*—featuring a radio-friendly Crosby, Stills, Nash, and Gram Parsons country-rock harmony sheen, was emblematic of the quality, consistency, and productivity of the Asylum roster. With its 22 million copies sold, the Eagles' *Their Greatest Hits (1971–1975)*, released on Asylum in 1976, has long maintained its place as the best-selling compilation of all time. The record is also tied for top selling U.S. album with Michael Jackson's *Thriller* (1982, Epic), which received a significant spike following his death in 2010, and ranks among the top albums with international sales at 42 million.

Browne negotiated a contract with Geffen and Asylum for Zevon. The deal was minimal, with no money up front and a limited recording budget. Browne would be the producer for the project:

> The last thing on my mind was how to make a hit record; I just thought people needed to hear him. So we'd make the best versions of his songs we could. Geffen had the feeling I was just making a record for a friend—doing somebody a favor. It wasn't until after the LP was done that he really heard it for what it was, especially when the critics hailed it (Scoppa 65).

Zealous and protective, Browne proved a fitting, if not ideal, production partner for the obsessive Zevon, who had been steadily working on songs before, during, and after *Wanted Dead or Alive*. The photographer hired by Imperial to shoot Zevon's cover for that album, Richard Edlund, the inventor of the portable Pignose amplifier and an Academy Award–winning cinematographer who worked on *Star Wars* and with George Lucas's motion picture visual-effects company, Industrial Light and Magic, witnessed Zevon's writing routine. Edlund strongly suggested that Zevon "needed a producer who would literally wrench the material out of his hands before it became too rarefied." Zevon would write a song, get bored with it, and "then there'd be an allusion to that song in another song. The songs became so esoteric that nobody could understand them unless you saw the whole progression" (C. Zevon, 38). Browne successfully got Zevon to stop overwriting and record his material before it got out of control.

Browne recruited an impressive cast of singers and sessionists from the L.A. sphere to contribute instrumental backing and vocal harmonies on Zevon's 11 piano-driven compositions. The lineup included Mellow Mafia members Waddy Wachtel and David Lindley, who had become Browne's symbiotic sidemen; Phil Everly; Fleetwood Mac's Stevie Nicks and Lindsey Buckingham, who Zevon had roomed with and recruited to play rhythm guitar for the Everly's touring band; Bonnie Raitt; Beach Boy Carl Wilson; Billy Hinsche of Dino, Desi and Billy—

his participation perhaps attributed, in part, to his sister being married to Carl Wilson; Rosemary Butler; J. D. Souther; Eagles Glenn Frey and Don Henley; Jorge Calderón; Bob Glaub; Bobby Keys; Jai Winding; Ned Doheny; and the Sid Sharp Strings.

For the first recording session with Sharp's string unit, Zevon prepared jokes to tell the "wrung out jaded musicians who had been on every *Lassie* date since 1957" (C. Zevon, 111) with the hopes that the humor would get the elderly troupe to play well. Everyone was easily accessible, frequently responding to early morning phone calls to show up at the studio once Browne determined whose skills among the core group were best suited for a song, sentiment, or sound. With Browne's good standing in the L.A. music circle, and Zevon's name circulating for years, the singers and musicians were delighted and flattered to participate in the debut project.

Recorded between October 1975 and February 1976, the resulting self-titled album was released in June, months before Zevon turned 29 and the birth of his daughter, Ariel, in August. Browne was chosen to be her godfather. By debut record standards, Zevon's age was conspicuous, a "late bloomer" or mature mark among newcomers who commonly arrive or "burst on the scene" with their first album when they are in their early twenties. The album itself was atypical Asylum, its Zevonian view and tone blatantly divergent from the label's brand and its notables such as Browne, Ronstadt, the Eagles, Mitchell, Souther, solo-Poco Richie Furay, and Byrd Chris Hillman. The lone exception was perhaps street Beat poet, hobo-hipster Tom Waits, whose work aligned more with Hollywood's Jazz Age.

The disparity struck a chord. "It sounds as though Zevon is out to demolish every cliché in the Asylum bin," wrote *Newsweek*'s Janet Maslin. "Zevon is that refreshing rarity, a pop singer with comic detachment" (72). Music historian and British rock critic Barney Hoskyns observed, "It was as if a Laurel Canyon version of Elvis Costello had suddenly surfaced amidst Asylum's pervasive complacency"; what Zevon "really did for Asylum was provide a kind of bridge between the old singer-songwriters and the emergent Angry Young Men of new wave rock and roll" (2009, 281).

Beyond Zevon's writing perspective and his resistance to L.A.'s prevalent melodic musical modes, even his appearance was a contrast to the canyon casual of the Laurel and Topanga troubadours. On the covers of his first four studio albums for Asylum, Zevon appeared dressed in suits. Whether his debut album cover pose aside a searchlight outside the Palladium, an uninvited guest to the Grammy ceremony taking place inside, or the Asylum Records publicity photo of him reaching into his suit coat pocket, presumably for a firearm, Zevon's look—described by Ronstadt in her 2013 memoir, *Simple Dreams*, as a "complicated gaze"(62)—was deadpan, that of a nocturnal sophisticate and bespectacled intellect, attired in a black banker suit, a one-size-fits-all fashion statement that concurrently conveyed pianist, poet, historian, detective, and undertaker.

MIDNIGHT IN TOPANGA: "A SLUMMING ANGEL"

Raymond Chandler wrote like a slumming angel and invested the sun-blinded streets of Los Angeles with a romantic presence.
> —crime fiction writer Ross Macdonald

Zevon's literary hero Ross Macdonald's above characterization of Zevon's kindred detective-fiction muse, Raymond Chandler, was equally fitting for Zevon and his Asylum debut. Both writers' works were deeply ingrained into Zevon's noir outlook, particularly Chandler's 1939 novel, *The Big Sleep*, and its first film adaptation in 1946, directed by Howard Hawks, its screenplay cowritten by William Faulkner, and starring Humphrey Bogart as detective Philip Marlowe. The influences in *Warren Zevon* were distinct. In his June 21, 1976, review of the album, *Village Voice* critic Paul Nelson wrote that Zevon "takes us . . . tenaciously and triumphantly . . . through several elegiacally angry and corrosively funny episodes which take place in a Los Angeles so acutely drawn that we can practically smell the sweat inside the fedoras of Philip Marlowe and Lew Archer" (21; Avery 359–360).

In a comprehensive interview with Steve Roeser, published in *Goldmine* in 1995, Zevon offered a factual fictional perspective on his city:

> [T]here's something so general and generic about Los Angeles itself, that I think it's hard to . . . [identify it]. Unless there's a Los Angeles that we think was in that movie version of *The Big Sleep*. That's the Los Angeles that we *pretend* is like we grew up in, or is still there. Some kind of late-Chandler/early-Ellroy Los Angeles, that really

none of us live in. . . . So, I think the city, and the growing up in it, or living in it, is such a broad experience, that it gets to the point where if you're not talking about *The Big Sleep*, I don't know what you are talking about. (n.p.)

In the view of producer/manager Peter Asher—late of the 1960s pop duo, Peter and Gordon (Waller), who were known as "the English Everly Brothers" with harmony-rich hits such as "A World Without Love," "I Go to Pieces," and "Lady Godiva"—Zevon was conspicuously clever, well read, literary, and clearly writing about "a different L.A." (Hoskyns 2009, 246). His was not Tinsel Town, nor a palm tree paradise. There was no jingle jangle morning, good vibrations, or California girls. Zevon's tones countered neon with noir, glamour's glow with gloom, and shimmer with shadows. He preferred the loneliness of locals, down-on-their-luck losers, and low-lifes to the lifestyles of the luminaries. Zevon's tragicomic chronicle of excess in the City of Angels reflected a Fitzgeraldian vision of hedonism, hidden desperation, and the dissolution of dreams.

Warren Zevon is, in part, a geomusical neighborhood *noir*vella, a misguided tour that restlessly roams an Angelino axis of undercurrents and depraved destinations, from the Whiskey a Go Go to the Rainbow Bar and Grill where the Sunset Strip ends, to the notorious Continental Hyatt House—a rock-star refuge referred to as the "Riot House." On to Echo Park and the Pioneer Chicken stand on Alvarado Street, then from hippie haven in Topanga Canyon to the Tropicana Motel on Santa Monica Boulevard, an extended-stay bohemian hideout for actors, artists, writers, poets, directors, sports figures, film and music producers, and musicians, among them Zevon and Modern Folk Quartet founder-turned-iconic-rock-photographer Henry Diltz. Richard Edlund contended that Zevon "had this thing about the Tropicana because it fit into this image he had of what a rock star was supposed to look like and live like. He was all kind of Bukowski-esque" (C. Zevon, 52). Owned by Los Angeles Dodgers Hall of Fame pitcher Sandy Koufax, the Tropicana was what Iris Berry branded "the Chelsea Hotel with poolside Astro-Turf," referring to New York City's landmark artist, musician, writer lair. The East Coast hangout attracted Leonard Cohen, Janis Joplin, Iggy Pop, Bob Dylan, Patti Smith, and Allen Ginsberg, among others, and is where Arthur C. Clarke wrote *2001: A Space Odyssey*; Dylan Thomas was staying when he died of pneumonia; and Sex Pistol Johnny

Rotten's girlfriend, Nancy Spungen, was stabbed to death. At the Tropicana, parties sometimes lasted for months and often ended in mayhem. In addition to the artists and celebrity clientele, there was a constant parade of groupies, photographers, pimps, hookers, and drug dealers, intermingled with innocent tourists on their Hollywood vacations. Word on the street was that anything anyone desired—no matter how bizarre, kinky, sleazy, or unsavory—could be had at "the Trop" for an extremely low nightly rate. From the debauched boulevard, Zevon's 11-song excursion ends at the Hollywood Hawaiian Hotel on Yucca and Grace before exiting down Gower Avenue.

Zevon's point of view is double vision; he is both detached observer and passionate participant. He shapes an antihero atmosphere brimming with outlaws and outcasts on the outskirts, a desperado thread that extends from the late 1880s American West frontier to 1970s Hollywood haunts and hangouts on the strips and boulevards. Musically, the album is bracketed by the same melody. The piano notes that open "Frank and Jesse James" reprise ten songs later in a string arrangement on the closing "Desperados Under the Eaves." Cinematic, but short of epic, the two comprehensive bookend narratives are the album's longest at 4:33 and 4:45 minutes, each demonstrating Zevon's dexterous piano proficiency with allusions to his classical training. The compositions are inspired by the cowboy choreography of Aaron Copland's 1942 ballet, *Rodeo*. "Frank and Jesse James" features a sophisticated do-si-do bridge, with David Lindley's banjo and fiddle adding authenticity.

The bandit brother piano ballad summons a specter of the Allman Brothers' Southern rock classic "Midnight Rider" from earlier in the decade, as well as more obvious Old West outlaw echoes, from Billy Joel's "The Ballad of Billy the Kid" on *Piano Man* (1973) to the conceptual Western Americana–themed albums—Elton John's *Tumbleweed Connection* (1971) and the Eagles' *Desperado* (1973), with the title tune and "Doolin-Daltons" among its gunslinging songs. The facial resemblance between Zevon and the young Elton John *Tumbleweed* image is mildly intriguing. There is also a Peckinpah presence that evokes the dissident director's films *The Wild Bunch* (1969) and *Pat Garrett and Billy the Kidd* (1973).

Zevon's "cowboy mini-epic" is allegorical, written for and about the Everly Brothers. The well-informed chronology begins on a small Missouri farm where the boys learned to rope, ride, and be handy with a gun. They "joined up with Quantrill" (Confederate guerilla leader William Clarke Quantrill) when the Civil War broke out; learned to kill in Clay County; after Appomattox, were on the losing side with no amnesty granted; ending with Jesse the victim of Robert Ford the gunman. As outlaws, Frank and Jesse "rode against the railroads, the banks, and the governor," and as Zevon points out, "never did they ask for a word of thanks." Zevon is sympathetic, portraying the antiheroes as well-intentioned and, like many of the fringe dwellers he writes about, "No one knows just where they came to be misunderstood." In the end, "the poor Missouri farmers knew that Frank and Jesse do the best they could." The chorus is heartening, encouraging Frank and Jesse to "keep on riding, riding, riding across rivers and range, prairies and plains, 'til they clear their names." Forty years later, Zevon's version of the sibling legend would have been a suitable soundtrack theme for the film *The Assassination of Jesse James by the Coward Robert Ford* (2008). While the song is a kindred historical homage that links two legendary pairs of brothers—the James and Everlys (Phil sings harmonies on the song)—it also announces the arrival of the Hollywood desperado Zevon, the Midnight Writer, writing/riding off beat into the Sunset Strip shadows.

Zevon's lyricism maintains an oblique biographical or self-referential undercurrent throughout the album. "Mama Couldn't Be Persuaded," livened further by Lindley's fiddle, is a parental portrait from Zevon's perspective as a kid "stuck in the middle" of the precarious relationship between his withdrawn, repressed Mormon mother and gangster father. There is a significant grandparent subtext in the song. Much of Zevon's attention focuses on his mother's parents, who tried to warn, reason, and plead with their daughter not to marry that gambling man. They were the ones who "never kept their disappointment hid" and "all went to pieces when the bad luck hit." In a 1976 *Village Voice* interview speckled with therapy session–speak, Zevon revealed to Paul Nelson that he considered his mother's relationship with her parents to be a "tremendously destructive factor" in the lives of both himself and his father. Zevon's "very senatorial grandmother" ran the family. His recollection was empathetic and begrudging; he said how "terribly uncomfortable" his grandparents made it for his father by treating him "like a vagabond and roustabout," so he was frequently absent from the family. Zevon concluded, "I wouldn't have been there either if I had a choice."

"Backs Turned Looking Down the Path" is also personal, though more positive; Zevon's reflection on being "caught between the years/ cost me nearly all my tears" and getting his "outlook fixed" after abandoning California dreaming for Spain. He completed the song in Madrid. The upbeat ode is charming, conveying the sensation of the first flush of a love affair: "People always ask me what's the matter with me/ Nothing matters when I'm with my baby." Zevon is content among those who "may have" and those who "may not;" he is "thankful for what he's got." The understated, overlooked song prompted Zevon to suggest "wait and see if they don't figure out that was the best song I ever wrote."

The warmth of "Backs Turned Looking Down the Path" eases into tenderness on "Hasten Down the Wind," ostensibly a more mature sequel to "Tule's Blues" from *Wanted Dead or Alive*. Zevon renders a withering dialogue, a he/she seesaw that begins with a proverbial premise: She thinks she needs to be free; he doesn't understand. Nothing is working out as they planned. The gentle ache of Lindley's slide guitar, Phil Everly's sweet harmony, strings, and a twinkling piano complement the emotional state with an appropriate tone and texture for the waning relationship. The love song establishes another steadfast strand of Zevon's versatile songwriting, evidence that he could do West Coast mellow, melancholy, and maybe even maudlin, and be as sensitive and poetic—"hanging on to half a heart/ he can't have the restless part"—as any of the L.A. songwriting romantics, from Browne, Mitchell, and James Taylor to Karla Bonoff and J. D. Souther.

The tender tone twists into darker shades and debauchery, beginning with the hedonistic excess in "Poor Poor Pitiful Me" and continuing through to the album's completion. The song is loosely inspired by Desmond Dekker and the Aces' 1968 international reggae hit "Israelites," of which Zevon sang an odd folk version in Berkeley coffeehouses. Zevon's unruly Sunset Strip saga portrays a self-indulgent, self-pitying rock star bemoaning "these young girls won't let me be." Frequently alleged that Zevon wrote the song with Browne and his cover-boy good looks in mind, the account is mischievous, highlighted by one of Zevon's signature clever couplets rhyming "gender" with "Waring blender." The Rainbow Bar cruising climaxes at the infamous if not notorious den, the Hyatt ("Riot") House, in a night of masochistic "sexcess." Zevon refuses to reveal the dirty details. Instead, he delivers an ad-libbed, silencing run-on merciless mutter—"I don't want to talk about it," with an exclamation, "Hut!"—to end the song in pitilessly waggish fashion. Ronstadt's hit version of the song from *Simple Dreams* (1977), which Zevon considered "vastly better than mine," inverts the gender and modifies Zevon's Rainbow Bar and casual S&M sex at the Hyatt to "the Vieux Carré down in Yokohama . . . please don't hurt me Momma." In her memoir Ronstadt, who learned to sing "Poor Poor Pitiful Me" from Browne, "wonder[ed] why Jackson didn't record it himself, because he sang it better than I did" (63). In addition to his frequent live renditions, Browne recorded a version of "Poor Poor Pitiful Me" with Bonnie Raitt on the *Enjoy Every Sandwich* posthumous Zevon tribute in 2003.

"The French Inhaler" echoes Dylan's "Positively 4th Street," though the tone of Zevon's mean streak far surpasses Dylan's nasally "you've got a lot of nerve." Zevon provides a poor, poor pitiful "Piano Man" portrayal of the late-night-into-early-morning miseries at a Hollywood bar, except there are no "la-la-la diddy-das" of Billy Joel's East Coast lounge loser lament. These are friends, phonies, and wannabes "with no home to go home to." The song builds to Zevon's last-call observation that is beyond brutally blunt. When the lights come up, he catches a glimpse of the pretty face, now wasted, devastated, looking like "something Death brought with him in his suitcase." The simile is stunning, a wicked lyrical punch with fatal blow impact that instantaneously transforms the song from a kiss-off to a fuck-off. The elegant texture of the Sid Sharp Strings and immaculate harmonies from Henley and Frey are enthrallingly incongruent with the acerbic scene. Though soothing, the melodies do little to alleviate the pain, loneliness, futility, and frustration. The choral fade into "So long, Norman" conveniently infers literary hero Mailer, and his failed marriage to Marilyn Monroe, an interpretation Zevon rejected for years. It was not until 2004 that Zevon's son Jordan revealed that the spiteful song was about another Marilyn—his mother, Marilyn Tule Livingston. Tule confessed on her deathbed on March 3, six months after Zevon's death, that "The French Inhaler" was a bitter farewell to her from Zevon after learning of her tryst with a fellow musician after their relationship ended. The shift in tone in the trilogy of "Tule tunes" is so striking a progression, extending from the poetic imagery of "Tule's Blues" on *Wanted Dead or Alive* to the gentle prettiness of "Hasten Down the Wind" before descending into the vindictive "The French Inhaler," the songs separated only by "Poor Poor Pitiful Me" on the album's sequencing.

"Mohammed's Radio" is a Halloween hymn. Despite its refrain— "Don't it make you want to rock and roll/All night long"—the song is, in the view of *New York Times* music critic John Rockwell, a "dirge like anthem, a rolling, inexorable attestation to the darker, more passionate side of life" (in Marcus, 1979, 218). That said, Rockwell preferred the Ronstadt version on *Living in the U.S.A.* (1978) to the Zevon original, citing the production values, hard-edged, weighty ferocity of the arrangement, and Ronstadt's illuminating vocalism. The ambiguous spiritual subtext of the song approaches hymn, heightened by the Buckingham/Nicks harmonies that crescendo in the chorus. The "someone singing, sweet and soulful on the radio" signals deliverance for the restless and desperate. The song originated, in part, from Zevon's predictably peculiar observation of a Halloween parade in Aspen in 1973. Among the costumed locals was a developmentally challenged man dressed in Arab sheik garb holding a radio up to his ear. "I remember exactly the look on Warren's face watching that—something changed in his face, and what it was is he was making mental notes and writing 'Mohammed's Radio' in his head," said studio drummer Eddie Ponder (C. Zevon, 79). Zevon translated the surreal scene into one of his typical remarkably bizarre lines: "In walks the village idiot/And his face is all a-glow/He's been up all night listening to Mohammed's radio." Zevon's longtime aide-de-camp George Gruel offers a counter-mythology to the meaning of "Mohammed's Radio," suggesting that Zevon simply "loved the sound of those two words together . . . the mellifluousness. That's it" (110).

Zevon's sardonic sensibility and bravado are in full display in the raw and deranged two-note, piano-pounding oath, "I'll Sleep When I'm Dead." Wielding fierce defiance, Zevon charges into that single fact of life—death. The song materialized during a dawn in Spain as his wife Crystal was trying to get the up-all-night Zevon to bed. He disobediently snapped, "I'll sleep when I'm dead." The retort defused the situation into laughter, and ignited an impromptu songwriting session. Together they proceeded to generate a litany of anomalous lyrics around the hook line, most of them referencing Zevon fixations—prescription medicine, a .38 special, and "drinking heartbreak motor oil and Bombay gin." The catchy title became Zevon's self-sabotaging signature, as evidenced in its fitting designation of the posthumous chronicle of conversations compiled by Crystal. The song was also distant grim foreshadowing of Zevon's diagnosis-to-death "Deteriorata Trilogy" from 2000 to 2003. The phrase has been appropriated into songs, from rock (Bon Jovi, 1992) to country (Jason Michael Carroll, 2007), as well as a British crime noir film in 2004. It has also slipped into the popular culture vernacular, uttered occasionally as a line of often insomnia-related dialogue by television and film characters, from novelist Hank Moody (David Duchovny) in cable television's *Californication* to James Bond villain Gustav Graves in *Die Another Day* (2002).

The character study in "Carmelita" is detailed and casually despairing. The heroin addict, strung out on the outskirts in Echo Park, is sinking to the depths. With no methadone or welfare check, the desperate junkie is "playing solitaire with a pearl handled deck." The suicidal junkie pawns his Smith Corona typewriter and goes to meet his dealer, who is hanging out at the Pioneer Chicken stand on Alvarado Street. Perhaps paying homage to the firearm aficionado Zevon rather than honoring one of his preferred writing devices, Ronstadt's version on *Simple Dreams* (1977) substitutes "Smith and Wesson" for "Smith Corona." Zevon, too, uses "Smith and Wesson" is some of his live and demo versions of the song. The Tex-Mex acoustic arrangement reflects the "Mariachi static on the radio," its tubes glowing in the dark, while the chorus implores "hold me tighter." The song's title derived from the name of the avenue that was a shortcut through Beverly Hills. Zevon considered the frequently covered "Carmelita" his "personal calling card," as it was always among the first songs he auditioned early on for peers, among them Waddy Wachtel and Crystal Zevon (Mehr, 11–12).

"Join Me in L.A." is a sinister antecedent to Randy Newman's sun-kissed satire, "I Love L.A.," from *Trouble in Paradise* (1983). Zevon's treatment of "Join Me in L.A." as a shadowy Babylonian invitation rather than a slogan promoting tourism is blatant in the song's ominous leading lyric—"Well, they say this place is evil." The black-magic mood conjures a canyon cult with Manson whispers. At "midnight in Topanga" the DJ warns, "there's a full moon rising," and a voodoo vibe befitting the HBO vampire series *True Blood* (the "L.A." conveniently converts into the abbreviation for "Louisiana"). Despite the foreboding nature, Zevon is staying. He's at the Tropicana on a "dark and sultry day." Zevon engraves the noir narrative with a resounding précis on the soul-selling illusion of the Hollywood dream—"'Cause I found some-thing that'll never be nothing." The music and vocals provide a super-natural silhouette for the nocturne. Bobby Keys's saxophone wails in unison with Bonnie Raitt's and Rosemary Butler's soulful vocals that resound in the chorus, whispering "wake up, wake up" and moaning "Ohhhs" of pleasurable pain that solely sustain the song's final minute.

The album's song cycle builds to a magnificent finale, "Desperados Under the Eaves," a striking composition, both lyrically and musically, that is unquestionably Zevon's magnum opus. "Warren was obsessive, so he worked on the order of the songs, how it would sound, how it would come off, for a long time," offers Crystal Zevon. "The ideas of what it needed to be were almost part of the writing. He was classically trained so he always thought of things more in terms of finished work" (Mehr, 7).

The outlaw spirit of the James brothers rides full circle from the album's frontier overture through its underbelly travelogue into its con-clusion. An orchestral echo of the piano melody that commenced the album sets a melancholy tone for the doomed protagonist holed up at the shabby Hollywood Hawaiian Hotel, the embodiment of Nathanael West's "dream dump" from *The Day of the Locust*, a junkyard where all dreams eventually end up. Singer-songwriter J. D. Souther heard the song as Biblical, a sketch of Barabbas the traitor-thief who sold out Christ to the cross. The hotel/motel (Zevon uses both in the lyrics) scene is biographical, giving a glimpse of Zevon's struggles with alcohol-ism—"still waking up with shaking hands," "staring in an empty coffee cup," determined to "drink up all the salty margaritas in Los Angeles." The view is bleak, a glowering gaze—"the sun looks angry through the trees" and "the trees look like crucified thieves"; the fatigue is heavy—"trying to find a girl who understands me"; and the spirit relinquished—"except in dreams you're never really free."

The song features what may be Zevon's definitive quatrain—"And if California slides into the ocean/like the mystics and statistics say it will/I predict this motel will be standing/until I pay my bill." Zevon's emble-matically droll dread is fatalistic foreshadowing of the Eagles' iconic "Hotel California" lyric: "You can check out any time you like/but you can never leave." Though Zevon's view is faintly merciful: "Heaven help the one who leaves." Again, the verses are a slice of Zevon's life. During a stay at the Hollywood Hawaiian, he left without paying his bill, exiting via a fire escape to an awaiting getaway car. Guilt-ridden, he eventually returned to settle his debt, with management requesting only autographed albums.

The final verse finds him deep in solitary "listening to the air conditioner hum." He describes the sound: "It went mmmmmmmm . . ." The hypnotic humming continues, then flows into a concluding sea chantey choral arrangement by Beach Boy Carl Wilson, a hymn-like murmuring medley of "Dixie" and "Battle Hymn of the Republic." The wondrous whirr of the Gentlemen Boys—Wilson, Hinsche, Winding, Browne, and Zevon—harmonizing in unison with the Sid Sharp Strings is no purring precursor to the Crash Test Dummies' clumsy cute single "Mmm Mmm Mmm Mmm" in 1993. Instead, the haunting coda is a sublime songwriting moment, one that is a stunningly acute and astute arrangement, an anthemic drone that rises to sheer orchestral and harmonic splendor as the record's fading processional, looking away down Gower Avenue, equal parts New Orleans parish jazz funeral and Western Big Sky ride off into the sunset.

DESPERADO UNDER THE EAGLES: "SOMETHING THAT'LL NEVER BE NOTHING"

Warren Zevon was a premonition of the decadent zenith for the unrelenting vagaries and self-gratification in the West Coast music scene. Zevon's sordid seclusion under the eaves of the Hollywood Hawaiian captures the mood of the panicked rock fraternity in the mid-1970s. His scene, though solitary, is a vision of desperados turned vagabonds, like everyone else, huddled together in apocalyptic dread of the seismic shift from Eden to dystopia, "thinking that the gypsy wasn't lying."

"Despair was ubiquitous in Los Angeles in 1976," writes historian Hoskyns. "The first epoch of rock and roll was drawing to a close. An inertia had set in just as a new generation was rising up to slay its musical fathers" (2006, 248). Bob Dylan, Neil Young, Joni Mitchell, Eric Clapton, Muddy Waters, Van Morrison, and others gathering to perform on Thanksgiving Day for the Band's *The Last Waltz*, the San Francisco Winterland wonder event chronicled in a concert documentary by film director Martin Scorsese, marked a symbolic spectacle exalting the exiting golden age of rock. Songwriter Ned Doheny, who had been with Asylum since its inception, observed that "The whole scene got a lot more desperate," the artists increasingly uncomfortable with the personal and professional outcomes of their immense successes. Hints surfaced in song. The sweetness in the Eagles' hit "New Kid in Town" veiled its star paranoia subtext. "We were writing about our own replacements," revealed J. D. Souther, who cowrote the song with Henley and Frey.

In the face of this foreboding, the centennial year marked a pinnacle for the melodic, country-folk-rock genre distinguishing the 1970s "California sound" that had become synonymous with Asylum Records. *Warren Zevon* initially sold 80,000 copies, slipping into *Billboard*'s Top 200 at number 189, its sales figures far surpassed by several albums released the same year by his fellow Asylum roster mates. Browne's *The Pretender* charted at number five; *Hasten Down the Wind* became Ronstadt's first platinum record, a crossover that reached number three in rock/pop and number one in country; and the Eagles' *Hotel California* remained at number one for eight weeks, well into 1977, and subsequently rose to multiplatinum sales, Grammy recognition, and rock classic eminence. Among the *Hotel California*'s many distinctions, several are in the top 100 of *Rolling Stone* magazine's "500 Greatest" lists, where the album ranks number 37 and the song is at number 49.

Zevon was allied with all three records, perhaps most obviously as a continuing song source for Ronstadt and producer Peter Asher. Browne, having gone directly from producing *Warren Zevon*, which ended on February 28, 1976, to his own recording sessions for *The Pretender* on March 1, acknowledged that his atypical lyric on the title song, "The Pretender—"I'm going to be a happy idiot"—was influenced by Zevon.

The most curious correlations surface when juxtaposing *Warren Zevon* with *Hotel California*. Beneath the albums' thematic resemblance, there are intriguing distinctions between the two that are more subtle shades than stark contrasts of Southern California culture. Released in December 1976, six months after Zevon's debut, the Eagles present a last-resort rendition of the privileges and pitfalls of paradise and its pretty people as prisoners of their own device. While Henley, Frey, Don Felder, Randy Meisner, and Joe Walsh were thinking to themselves, "this could be heaven or . . . hell," Zevon's interpretation is a purgatory of pity and penance, an elegiac premonition of the desolate, haunted hotel in Stephen King and Stanley Kubrick's *The Shining*, where ghosts gather for Unhappy Hour.

Hotel California is clearly more conceptual than *Warren Zevon*. The album embodies the romantic rock-and-roll mythology and fast-lane lifestyle—the land of blue jeans and cocaine, mirror shades reflecting palm trees, blond hair flowing from convertibles on freeways leading to the ocean. In Henley's view, it was a love/hate existence that was "a whore" and "a fertile mother."

While the Eagles were living it up—going from take it easy to take it to the limit— Zevon was living it down. The noir narratives on *Warren Zevon* are infused with more desperation and less contemptuous coked-out arrogance that characterized the Eagles' manner and method, their extravagance encouraged by their manager and Geffen nemesis, Irving Azoff. Despite dealing with his own demons and disorder, Zevon still swerved from the starlight, spotlight, and sunlight, refusing to grant California's rock-and-roll mythology little, if any, credence at all.

The extent of creative reciprocity between Zevon and the Eagles, whether deliberate or inadvertent, is limited to their commonalities of desperado themes and collaborations with Browne. Decades later, Crystal Zevon described Warren's relationship with Don Henley as "strange." While discussing whether or not he wanted a funeral following his mesothelioma diagnosis in 2003, Zevon said, "I just don't want to spend my last days wondering whether Henley will show up" (C. Zevon, 439). Henley participated in *The Wind* requiem, but did not attend Zevon's memorial ceremony. The typical imbalance between sardonic and serious in Zevon's comment is difficult to decipher, further perpetuating the mythology. However, the timing of their 1976 records is noteworthy. The Eagles began recording *Hotel California* in March, one month after *Warren Zevon* was completed. Zevon loiters like a phantom presence in *Hotel California*. The Eagles' sprawling 7:30 minute closing denunciation of artificial paradise, "The Last Resort," echoes Zevon's "Desperados Under the Eaves." Perhaps more conspicuous is the string arrangement on *Hotel's* succinct (1:22) "Wasted Time (reprise)." Whether blatant borrowing, trendy orchestration, or resourcefulness, the Eagles recruited Sid Sharp, who had contributed significantly to *Warren Zevon*, as their own *Hotel* "concert master." Considering Henley's and Frey's participation in the Zevon sessions, the intersections between their albums, though negligible, may be dually construed as mere coincidence or subconscious, curious carryover. The parallels and proximities invite whispering intimations of influence, homage, creative conspiracy, and a competitive undercurrent, which, though counter to the canyon's community ideals and values, was common in the L.A. songwriter circle.

A subtle sense of "squatter's rights" lingered over the two albums' mirroring similitudes. The back cover notes on the digitally remastered version of *Hotel California*, reissued in 1999, perpetuate the mythology. The tone is as territorial as it is self-congratulatory, as if the Eagles appear to be staking their claim as the key chroniclers of the L.A. scene: "Meticulous craftsmanship of all phases of the recording was preceded by more than a year and a half of reflection and writing." The passage boasts that the album's three thematically unified number-one singles—"Hotel California," "Life in the Fast Lane," and "New Kid in Town"— "contributed to the group's growing reputation for writing masterful editorials on the singular state of mind called Southern California."

Bob Mehr makes a similar case for *Warren Zevon* in his liner note essay for the album's remaster(piece)ed, double-disc reissue on Rhino Records (2008), more than 30 years after its initial release. Mehr boldly broadens the discussion beyond the Frey and Henley *Hotel*, declaring that Zevon "should rank among Southern California's greatest chroniclers, placing him in a continuum somewhere between early L.A. historians like Carey McWilliams and contemporary sociologists such as Mike Davis" (13).

Warren Zevon was not destined or designed to rival the Eagles. "Zevon is on Asylum, a famous home for self-pitying narcissists; [including] Don Henley and Glenn Frey of the Eagles," wrote critic Greil Marcus in the *Village Voice* in 1978. "The people who inhabit the commercial context in which Zevon makes his music aren't merely integrated into the system [they were] out to fuck up, they are the system" (quoted in Eliot, 145).

Asylum's limited investment in Zevon's debut record translated into minimal commercial expectations. Sales were secondary, at least on the surface, to Browne's primary purpose of exposing Zevon's songwriting talents. While there is certainly merit in Bonnie Raitt's view that there was "no way the mainstream could be hip enough to appreciate Warren Zevon," there were other factors that may have subtly sabotaged the album's wider appeal and accessibility. Musically, Zevon was a mutineer who resisted fully committing to the predominant country-rock genre resounding in L.A.'s idyllic canyons, strip, and boulevards. He preferred to remain on the fringe with a piano-fighter presence rather than deliver an album that conformed to a melodic, radio-friendly "70s sound."

Nor was Zevon's voice a prominent feature. In Browne's view, Zevon had "a limited instrument as a singer;" his vocals a basic baritone at best, occasionally boisterous, with an Eric Burden (of the Animals) bent, but without the gravelly allure of Tom Waits. Zevon could be self-deprecating about his voice, saying he "sounded like Nick Nolte trying to sing the national anthem," perhaps a self-aware one-uppance of the *People* magazine critic who callously commented that Zevon sang like "Swamp Thing." Yet Zevon's songs, no matter the voice, were inseparable from him, as they bear the indelible stamp of his writing voice, his point of view and personality, and depth, complexity, and honesty of his conflicted character.

SONGWRITING STATE OF THE ART

The superior record sales and status of Zevon's songwriting peers, and the subsequent success of his next album, *Excitable Boy*, may have deflected from *Warren Zevon*, but they did not diminish the lasting significance and singularity of his Asylum Records debut. The *noir*-narratives that comprise *Warren Zevon* imparted an incisive, inimitable shadowy observation of the underside of an era, a locale, and lifestyle. The album was an iconoclastic triumph that displayed masterful maturity and composition, and powerful literary attributes devoid of pretension.

More than any quality, it was the writing that distinguished *Warren Zevon* from the Asylum Records catalog, more broadly from the prolific 1970s L.A. soft-rock songwriter sphere, and more specifically from the classic *Hotel California*. The debug album revealed an abundant songwriting palette and lyrical depth that that was sophisticated, intelligent, detailed, dark, romantic, poetic, psychological, geographic, historical, sly, and sardonic. *Warren Zevon* facilitated a precedent for vivid literary locality, a songwriting seam that eventually stretched to regional rock chronicles such as Springsteen's somber acoustics on *Nebraska* (1982) and *The Ghost of Tom Joad* (1995), the abiding drawl of Lucinda Williams's Louisiana-Mississippi essay, *Car Wheels on a Gravel Road* (1998), and the Heartland snapshots in *Too Long in the Wasteland*, a 1989 album by James McMurtry (novelist Larry McMurtry's son).

Within Zevon's own catalog and the splendid 1970s Los Angeles singer-songwriter discography, *Warren Zevon* endures as a masterpiece, the quintessential document of Zevon's brilliance as a songwriter, composer, and noir whisperer. Renowned music manager and producer Jon Landau, perhaps best known for his prophetic anointing of Bruce Springsteen as "the future of rock and roll" in an article in the *Real Paper* in 1974, was an interested bystander who witnessed the Zevon work in progress. Though not directly involved in the recording process, Landau, in anticipation of producing Browne's *The Pretender*, frequented the *Warren Zevon* sessions, his presence enough to earn an honorary "shadowboxing" credit on the album. Browne was scheduled to play Zevon's completed record for Joe Smith, head of Elektra/Asylum. However, when Browne's wife suddenly died, he asked Landau, who knew Smith, to present the record to the company chief, which Landau did. Landau's firsthand observations provide further commanding, credible testament to the virtuosity of *Warren Zevon* as a debut: "As the record was going by, I kept thinking to myself, once again, how masterful it was. The songwriting was just state of the art. It is in reality, one of the truly great first albums. I don't know how many artists ever creatively kicked off things like Warren did" (C. Zevon, 114).

3

KNEE DEEP IN GORE WITH GLEE

The further these songs get from Ronstadtland, the more I like them.
—critic Robert Christgau, review of *Excitable Boy*

Warren Zevon was well received across the journalistic reviewscape, from *Rolling Stone* and the rock press to the *New York Times* and *Village Voice*. There was even coverage in the national weekly news magazines, *Time* and *Newsweek*, both devoting two columns to the album in their August 2, 1976, issues. The critical consensus, no matter the source, was that Zevon's major-label debut was a triumph and a refreshing rarity, with descriptions that included intelligent, enlightening, imaginative, beguiling, terrifying, infectious, romantic, and funny. Paul Nelson deemed the auspicious debut "good and gritty, one of the best records of the year," while unapologetically declaring Zevon "a major artist" whose "talent can be mentioned in the same sentence with Bob Dylan, Jackson Browne, Randy Newman, Neil Young, Leonard Cohen, and a mere handful of others" (1976, 21).

The symmetry of the *Time* and *Newsweek* reviews was particularly notable. Ten months earlier, the covers of the October 27, 1975, issues of both magazines heralded Bruce Springsteen and his *Born to Run* breakthrough. The dual portrayal was unprecedented for a rock artist. The multiple cover distinction was ironically more frequent with sports figures—Joe Namath, Reggie Jackson, Olympic gymnast Mary Lou Retton, race horse Secretariat, the 1980 U.S. Olympic men's hockey team, O. J. Simpson's murder case and trial in the mid-1990s, and 1999 Women's World Cup soccer—than with political, religious, military, and world leaders. Some of the athletes completed a same-week trifecta by simultaneously appearing on the cover of *Sports Illustrated* in addition to the news magazines. Though the pair of Zevon articles was minor-scale magnitude compared to the parallel Springsteen covers, the concurrent column space devoted to the Los Angeles newcomer songwriter in the national news weeklies was nonetheless impressive and spoke to Zevon's promising presence.

The reviews were marked by their similar slants, with the journalists drawn to the angle of "rock songwriter with ambitions to compose a symphony." Both pieces were echoes of each other, emphasizing Zevon's classical background as much as they focused on his album and aura as music's "Hollywood Desperado," the title of the *Time* article. Zevon willingly contributed to his myth-making, readily admitting that he liked making people aware of his classical training and aspirations. He frequently steered the interviews in that direction without deflecting, telling *Newsweek*'s Janet Maslin, "Whereas one of my songs may come off sounding like a satire on the Eagles, it may actually be homage to Bartók." Likewise, in *Time*, Zevon talked about experimenting with atonality, while invoking the names of composers Berg and Bartók again. Reading between the lines of the two interviews and Zevon's responses, he came across as a rare rocker, one who reveled in taking the high (culture) road, and assuredly wore his intelligence and sophistication on the sleeve of his three-piece suit. In discussing his next record, he told *Time*, "I'm not about to make a concept album of Hamlet playing guitar. I just want to work on my symphony, in the early mornings," while the *Newsweek* column closes with this: "my next album's going to be musical comedy based on the life of [painter] Mark Rothko."

BERSERK QUALITIES

Jackson Browne continued to be Zevon's ardent mentor. In November 1976, following the release of *Warren Zevon* and Browne's *The Pretender*, Browne invited Zevon to open for him during a nine-country European tour. Some of their performances and interviews from that circuit surfaced in a widely bootlegged Dutch radio program recording that featured songs and interviews packaged as *The Offender Meets the*

Pretender. Browne would also return to the studio with Waddy Wachtel to coproduce Zevon's next album for Asylum, *Excitable Boy*, released in 1978. "Jackson figured that the way Warren and I related to each other would really help him," said Wachtel of his coproducing role (Hoskyns 2006, 259).

The symbiosis between Zevon's first two albums is significant. Many of Browne's decisions that shaped *Warren Zevon* also influenced the follow-up, *Excitable Boy*. There were a number of songs Zevon had written that were available for his first album, among them the cavorting "Werewolves of London" and the unruly, macabre "Excitable Boy." Both displayed the strand of Zevon's writing that Browne characterized as a "berserk quality." As the debut producer, Browne insisted those two songs be saved for Zevon's second album rather than be included on *Warren Zevon*, fearing that if they replaced the more fitting "Frank and Jesse James," "The French Inhaler," and "Desperados Under the Eaves," those three songs might become lost and never recorded later. He explained, "There was a literary quality to those songs and I felt it was better to get them established and out there first and then come out with the record that had 'Werewolves' and 'Excitable Boy' on it. On the other hand, his first album might have been a much bigger hit had it had those songs" (Scoppa, 65; C. Zevon, 112).

Browne's instincts not to compromise Zevon's compositions for commercial appeal on the Asylum debut proved wise. *Warren Zevon* would have been a dramatically different record had there been any song substitution. The lone exception may have been Zevon's misbegotten, broken-down-car lament, "Studebaker," which counters the Beach Boys' "fun, fun, fun in Daddy's T-Bird" sunny California mythology, and was never released until the posthumous *Preludes* (2007). The booklet that accompanies the deluxe edition of the *Warren Zevon* reissue (Rhino, 2008) contains a photograph of a notebook open at a page with a hand-written set of songs neatly printed in capitals, presumably being considered and sequenced for Zevon's debut album. "Studebaker" is on the list, along with three eventual *Excitable Boy* songs and "Working Man's Pay," also released on *Preludes*. Zevon's son Jordan eventually recorded "Studebaker," first on the tribute record *Enjoy Every Sandwich: Songs of Warren Zevon* (2004), and then as a family heirloom on his own debut, *Insides Out* (New West, 2008).

In retrospect, Jordan Zevon endorsed Browne's judgment regarding song selection. He also expanded the case, suggesting that his father's subsequent success with *Excitable Boy* two years later ironically undermined the brilliance of *Warren Zevon*:

> I have such affection for that record because it does have so much of Dad in it. If none of his other records had done anything or if it was the only record he made and he pulled a Nick Drake and kicked off early, I think it would have been hailed as genius. But he had the success of "Werewolves of London" hanging over his head on his next album, and I think that overshadowed how great this record really was. (Mehr, 13)

Just as Browne chose not to include certain completed songs on *Warren Zevon*, Wachtel exercised similar influence as the coproducer of *Excitable Boy*. He eliminated the attempted reintroduction of "Tule's Blues" from *Wanted Dead or Alive* and a succinct acoustic "Frozen Notes," which was never released until after Zevon's death as a bonus track on reissues. Wachtel considered the two songs to be folkie and boring. He also insisted that Zevon write two additional songs to complete the album, expanding the running time past the mere 24 minutes they had. Zevon complied, providing "Tenderness on the Block" and "Lawyers, Guns and Money." Wachtel considered the response "one of the best things Zevon ever did for him."

As with *Warren Zevon*, the producers employed an impressive cast of musicians on *Excitable Boy*, anchored by The Section and vocalists that included J. D. Souther, Karla Bonoff, Linda Ronstadt, and Jennifer Warnes.

THE SECRET OF RUGGED INDIVIDUALISM

Two-thirds of the songs on *Excitable Boy* were collaborative writing efforts. The proportion is somewhat conspicuous, considering that Zevon's songwriting was one of the most distinctive merits of his Asylum debut. Among those who contributed verses, phrases, ideas, and characters to the *Excitable Boy*'s songs were coproducers Browne and Wachtel; David Lindell, who Zevon befriended while in Spain; guitarist LeRoy P. Marinell; and musician Jorge Calderón. Zevon was particularly comfortable working with Calderón, who became an indispen career-long collaborator and faithful friend. "Veracruz" was the first 18 songs Zevon and Calderón would work on together over the next 25 years. In addition, the versatile Calderón accumulated a range of credits that included vocalist, musician, and producer on each of Zevon's post-1976 albums except *My Ride's Here* (2002). Calderón's wife, Yvonne, suggested that one of the main reasons Zevon was drawn to her husband as a collaborator was because of his patience and natural temperament, which enabled him to tolerate Zevon's "crazy, self-serving self."

Browne, who perhaps related to Zevon and understood his complexities as well or better than anyone, recognized the intricacies of the songwriting interactions, saying that "the selectivity who Warren was engaged with is very important in understanding Warren because there was certain chemistry that produced 'Werewolves of London.' That song wouldn't have happened with Warren and me" (C. Zevon, 69). Browne teamed with Zevon to compose one of the album's gentler songs, "Tenderness on the Block."

The collaborations on *Excitable Boy* established a precedent for Zevon's subsequent records, with his songwriting evolving into notable literary alliances. Zevon liked the creative energy derived from exchanging stories, ideas, phrases, lyrics, and observations with fellow artists and writers, and shaping them into songs, stating later in his career, "I've had a lot of help from my friends. That's the secret of rugged individualism" (Sutcliffe, 124).

While convenience, conversations, and chemistry were among the factors that led to Zevon's songwriting partnerships, there was also a sense of urgency stirred by the inevitable heightened expectations that follow a critically acclaimed debut. Whereas the songs on Zevon's first album had been years in the making, the time frame was more narrow for the follow-up. Zevon felt that pressure and was furiously trying to come up with enough material for his next record in addition to the songs he had written that were not included on *Warren Zevon*. He was driven to deliver a follow-up that would equal, if not exceed, the literary, musical, and lyrical qualities of his preceding album.

THE TERROR TRILOGY

43

...ɔrs, that scares me. Not violence—helplessness. That's
...violent stories.

—Warren Zevon (Dansby)

Excitable ... was neither conceptual Hamlet nor comic homage to an abstract expressionist artist, as Zevon suggested his next album might be in the *Time* and *Newsweek* interviews. There was musical comedy, albeit in noir tones. And Zevon did borrow from a German opera in the lead song. Asylum's ads promoted *Excitable Boy* as "Sam Peckinpah meets the Rolling Stones." The album's nine narratives included historical fiction, international intrigue, thinly veiled political observations on occupational foreign policy, tender ballads, disco noir, and a three-chord rock anthem. The songs revealed Zevon's incendiary imagination and a sophisticated sense of violence, highlighted by an arresting cast of characters, some who appeared to stray for the pages of pulp fiction. Among them were a decapitated mercenary, werewolves, a sociopath at the Junior Prom, revolutionaries, and innocent bystanders, appearing in global settings such as the Congo, Mombasa, Havana, and Honduras. In his 2003 article, *New York Times* critic Jon Pareles characterized the song cycle as "terse, action-packed, gallows-humored tales that could sketch an entire screenplay in four minutes and often had death as a punch line." The assessment was not exaggerated, considering that one of the love songs uses "martyr" as a metaphor.

Even the album's accompanying images hinted at what lay ahead in the songs, subtly reinforcing the motif. The album cover close-up of Zevon on a red background, photographed by Waddy Wachtel's brother, Jimmy, conveyed a misleading choir boy innocence. Mirroring the werewolves that he sang about, Zevon's "hair was perfect" and his wire-rimmed glasses indicated a stereotypical honor-roll student. At Zevon's request, the photo was repeatedly retouched to erase his bad complexion. In Wachtel's view, the polished portrayal "always looked like a cadaver with makeup to me, but he liked it." Wachtel, along with the creative company he formed, Dawn Patrol, was the era's preeminent album art designer, particularly within the West Coast music scene. *Excitable Boy*'s inner jacket contained a small cutout image of Zevon in his piano-playing undertaker black suit and tie, seated, arms propped on raised knees. More prominent was the full-sleeve color photograph of a .44 Magnum resting atop a plate of vegetables, a tribute to Zevon's firearm fascination. The composition, "Willy on the Plate," was arranged by Crystal Zevon.

Zevon was unflinching about violence, stating that "there are things more insidious than violence, like hypocritical optimism" (Alfonso, 24). He did not consider his songs to be particularly violent, especially when placed within the context of one of his favorite writers, Aeschylus, the "father of Greek tragedy"; Shakespeare; and contemporary culture from film to cable television. He viewed popular music as being somewhat "limited" to love songs, and that wasn't exactly, and exclusively, what he was doing as a songwriter.

Zevon's high-culture leanings prefaced *Excitable Boy*'s prevalent undercurrent of chaos. The title character in the album's easing lead song, "Johnny Strikes Up the Band," was widely interpreted as referencing a renowned Johnny—Carson, Rotten, or Lennon. The phrases "keeper of the keys, put your mind at ease, guaranteed to please, back by popular demand," and the resulting jubilation and "rocking in the projects" from Johnny's presence, also implied the local drug dealer. The "Freddie get ready/rock steady" only muddled the mystery. The range of alleged allusions included Carson's longtime *Tonight Show* producer Freddie de Cordova, Curtis Mayfield's "Freddie's Dead (Theme from *Super Fly*)" in 1972, and the flamboyant Freddie Mercury of Queen. The most likely "Freddie's" being referenced are blues guitarist Freddie King and musical instrument and equipment expert Fred Walecki at the legendary Los Angeles guitar shop, Westwood Music (Gruel, 110). Popular interpretations aside, Zevon appropriated the title from Ernst Krenek's 1927 opera, *Jonny Spiet Auf*, about a jazz violinist and "the problem of freedom." *Mojo* magazine's Phil Sutcliffe considered the modest song a product of Zevon's "Tin Pan Alley side, a sort of overture" in old showbiz musicals that stated the obvious, "Here we are and we're going to play" (124).

What followed in the album's core was a ghostly, ghastly three-song sequence brimming with abandoned amusement—a terror trilogy comprised of "Roland the Headless Thompson Gunner," "Excitable Boy," and "Werewolves of London." "Roland the Headless Thompson Gunner," a joint writing effort with former mercenary Lindell, is a global saga of double-crossing and revenge set in the aftermath of the Nigerian civil war and the Congo crisis of 1966–1967. Over his stately piano,

Zevon's delivery is resolute, as if reading from the pages of adventure pulp fiction by the campfire. He tells the tale of Roland, a warrior from the Land of the Midnight Sun, who sets off for Biafra to "join the bloody fray, fingers on their triggers, knee deep in gore." Roland's motives are self-serving and altruistic—"They killed to earn their living and to help out the Congolese." The most skilled of the Thompson submachine gunners, Roland is betrayed by his comrade, Van Owen, who under direction of the CIA, blows off the head of Norway's bravest son. The Gentlemen Boys (Browne, Wachtel, Calderón, J. D. Souther, and Kenny Edwards) salute the fallen soldier in a chorale homage that conveys heroism and is layered with subtle political sarcasm at the suppression of the unofficial conflicts in foreign countries—"Time, time, time for another peaceful war."

The action shifts into shadows of *The Legend of Sleepy Hollow*. Snare drum flutters pat gallows-march textures, as the headless ghost of Roland searches the continent, stalking the son-of-a-bitch who done him in. Roland finds him in Mombasa in a bar room. As the tale rises to a climactic moment, with Roland aiming his Thompson gun to even the score, Zevon adroitly employs the oblique off-rhyme literary device: "he didn't say a word/But he blew Van Owen's body from there to Johannesburg." Triumphant, the eternal Thompson gunner continues to "wander through the night, keeping up the fight," haunting various conflicts during the next decade, among them Ireland, Lebanon, Palestine, and Berkeley. Zevon dangles the final note in "Berke-leyyy . . ." before proceeding to the concluding verse. There, he merges his historical fiction with a bizarre incident that became one of the major media events of the era: "Patty Hearst heard the burst of Roland's Thompson gun/And bought it." Zevon's contemporary reference is heightened by Wachtel's production touch, "a real specific little thing at the end" designed to "blow Warren's mind." Russell Kunkel's drumming crescendos into eruptions that echo in unison with Zevon's pounding keys. Together they sound "the burst," clustering the last line into a choppy, emphatic vocal delivery before descending into the ta-da finale: "And-bought-it." The verse, particularly the multiple meaning of "bought it," is a wry caption for the notorious, nationally published photographs from surveillance camera images depicting the newspaper heiress Hearst holding an assault weapon during a 1974 bank heist plotted by the Symbionese Liberation Army. Two months earlier, the left-wing guerilla group kidnapped Hearst, the granddaughter of renowned publisher William Randolph Hearst, from her Berkeley apartment. While captive, Hearst allegedly converted to the cause, changing her identity to "Tania"—inspired by the girlfriend of socialist icon Che Guevara. Hearst was apprehended for participating in the bank "fundraiser" with the SLA revolutionaries. She was convicted of robbery in 1976 and imprisoned for almost two years before her sentence was commuted by President Jimmy Carter. Zevon casts Hearst as a James Brothers' sister spirit, a desperado who projects ahead to the circumstance of "an innocent bystander, between a rock and a hard place" in "Lawyers Guns and Money" that closes the album.

The song's Headless Gunner legacy lingered improbably into character adaptations in director Steven Spielberg's *The Lost World: Jurassic Park* (1997) as "Nick Van Owen" (Vince Vaughn) foils a plan by famous animal hunter "Roland Tembo" (Pete Posthelwaite) to kill the Tyrannosaurus Rex.

The album's title tune was instigated during a post–pot roast dinner exchange between Zevon and LeRoy Marinell. Zevon wondered why "nobody ever lets me play lead guitar." When Marinell diplomatically explained that it was because he "gets a little too excited," Zevon replied, "Well, I'm just an excitable boy." According to Marinell, he and Zevon extracted the phrase into a song 15 minutes later (C. Zevon, 102). Joni Mitchell was not impressed. When Zevon banged out an impromptu version of the song at a celebrity party in Malibu in 1975, the Queen of the Canyon songwriters sneered, "How amusing." The lofty disapproval did not deter Zevon.

"Excitable Boy" chronicles a sociopathic pattern of bad-boy behavior that begins innocently enough with rubbing pot roast all over his chest while dressed in his Sunday best (a real-life Zevon self-reference); descends to biting the usherette's leg in the dark during a 4 a.m. show at the Clark Theater; then raping, killing, and taking home his Junior Prom date, "Little Suzie"—an homage to the Everly Brothers' song, "Wake Up Little Suzie." Then, ten years later when they let him out of "the Home," digging up her grave and building a cage with her bones. There were widespread assumptions that the graphic verses were Charles Manson references, perhaps a frolicking follow-up to Neil Young's sinister "Revolution Blues" from *On the Beach* (1974), when they were merely a "goofy kid thing" with no social significance. According to Marinell, many of the lines were simply recalled from harmless boyhood schoolyard exchanges: "Eat shit." "What will I do with your bones?" "Build a cage for your mother."

The explicit inventory in the title song might have earned the album an "Advisory" sticker had the Parents Music Resource Center, initiated by Tipper Gore and other senators' wives, been in place before 1985. The tone of "Excitable Boy," however, is not totally terror. Every horrendous episode is dismissed as mere mischief by an enabling, coddling chorus who collectively shrug in denial or simply ignore the warning signs: "Well, he's just an excitable boy," they all say. The underlying brilliance of "Excitable Boy" partly lies in its incongruent bubbly piano-driven melody that creates a carefree, sing-along backdrop that renders the heinous acts almost unnoticeable. The graphic "Then he raped her and killed her" followed by "then he took her home" is seamless sociopathic songwriting. Any offensiveness defuses into a harmless cartoon condition, a musical precursor to Seth McFarlane's off-color animated television series *Family Guy* or Cartoon Network's *Adult Swim* program block. The playful manner was further amplified by Zevon's defiantly casual delivery, backed by doo-wop girl-group harmonies from Linda Ronstadt and Jennifer Warnes cooing "oooh wah-oooh, ooh, excitable boy," and a spirited saxophone in the bridge.

"I'D LIKE TO MEET HIS TAILOR"

The trilogy's thread of sophisticated unruliness continues in "Werewolves of London," another "literally 15-minute song" that none of its cowriters—Zevon, Marinell, and Wachtel—took seriously. The spontaneous composition, referred to by Zevon as "a dumb song for smart people," defied the conventional attributes of songwriting such as labor, craft, and agonizing. The idea originated with Phil Everly who, after watching the movie *Werewolf of London* (1935) on late-night television, suggested to Zevon that he adapt the title for a song and dance craze. When Wachtel heard the idea, he mimicked a wailing wolf—"Aah-oooh"— which became part of the howling chorus. The trio frivolously alternated verses, beginning with what may be one of the all-time opening lines: "I saw a werewolf with a Chinese menu in his hand/Walking down the streets of Soho in the rain." The romp is comic noir, featuring a stylish werewolf on his way to Lee Ho Fooks for a "big dish of beef chow mein" and another "drinking a piña colada at Trader Vic's." There is a warning of "the hairy handed gent who ran amok in Kent"; alleviated with nifty alliteration—"little old lady got mutilated late last night"; droll fashion statements—"his hair was perfect"; characteristic celebrity name dropping—Lon Chaney, and Lon Chaney Jr. walking with the Queen; the dance endeavor Everly had hoped for, "doing the Were-wolves of London"; and an "Aah-oooh" chorus. Zevon effortlessly sprinkled verses with punch lines: "You better stay away from him/He'll rip your lungs out, Jim/Heh, I'd like to meet his tailor." He drolly punctuates the prance with a salivating, "Draw blood."

Fortunately, Crystal Zevon was present to transcribe the lively lyric exchange onto a steno pad that she always carried. The following day in the studio with Browne, who was cutting some Zevon demos to solicit to the Eagles and Ronstadt to possibly record before the *Warren Zevon* sessions began, they mentioned the "new song" and recited the "Were-wolves" lyrics. Browne responded favorably. One listen was enough to prompt him to occasionally perform the song live as early as 1975— three years before it was recorded. Bootleg recordings of those performances, notably the Main Point show, frequently circulated, creating expectations from Asylum that Browne was going to record the song.

Recording "Werewolves" was a contrast to its hasty composition. Wachtel compared his struggles during the studio sessions to the challenges that director Francis Ford Coppola faced during the production of the Vietnam War epic, *Apocalypse Now* (1979), as chronicled in the documentary *Heart of Darkness: A Filmmaker's Apocalypse* (1991). Though the comparison of a three-minute song to a three-hour film may be a bit disproportionate, Wachtel nonetheless considered "Were-wolves" the hardest song to get down in the studio that he ever worked on. The song was built around a lick that Marinell had been carrying around for years. Wachtel used seven bands and endless combinations of musicians, before recruiting Fleetwood Mac members Mick Fleetwood and John McVie, who finally executed the drum and bass parts to best fit the song during an all-night session. Most of the *Excitable Boy* budget went into recording "Werewolves of London" due to the disproportionate number of attempts to get the song done.

When the record label chose "Werewolves" as the album's single, Zevon and Wachtel were insulted from an artistic stance. They were perplexed by Asylum's logic in taking "that piece of shit." Their preferences for the single were "Tenderness on the Block," the tune cowritten with Browne that they considered exceptional, or the mid-tempo lead cut, "Johnny Strikes Up the Band." Whether luck, intuition, or music marketing savvy, to the label's credit, "Werewolves of London" became an overnight hit, reaching number 21 and remaining in the Top 40 for six weeks. The single was also issued in a limited-edition, 12-inch picture disc featuring a werewolf close-up and Zevon sitting in the sleeve's bottom-right corner in his three-piece suit.

Zevon conceded that "Werewolves of London" was a novelty, though "not a novelty the way, say, Steve Martin's 'King Tut' is a novelty" (Alfonso, 24) Zevon's hairy-handed hit contained qualities that, had it been recorded five years later, might have settled somewhere between a Weird Al Yankovic parody and the John Landis epic 13-minute music video of Michael Jackson's "Thriller" in 1983, with werewolves replacing zombies in the horror choreography. Surprisingly, Landis did not include the song in his film *An American Werewolf in London* (1981). Similar to "Excitable Boy" in its lyrical dexterity, surprising hooks, merry piano melody, and guilty pleasure sing-along aura, "Werewolves of London" possessed a novelty nature and abandoned amusement that translated well beyond a Halloween standard as a song that was as sardonically smart as it was savage. Browne, an unwavering acolyte, gives the song more credit than Zevon does. Browne told *Rolling Stone*'s David Fricke that when someone inevitably made reference to "Werewolves of London" at Zevon's memorial service in 2003, Browne came away with a new perspective on the song 25 years later, with one of Zevon's patented comes-out-of-nowhere lines his focal point. Browne's incisive "Werewolves" reading reveals him to be one of those "smart people" Zevon's "dumb song" was written for:

> It's about a really well-dressed, ladies' man, a werewolf preying on little old ladies. In a way it's the Victorian nightmare, the gigolo thing. The idea behind all those references is the idea of the ne'er-do-well who devotes his life to pleasure: the debauched Victorian gentleman in gambling clubs, consorting with prostitutes, the aristocrat who squanders the family fortune. All of that is secreted in that one line: "I'd like to meet his tailor." (Fricke, 2003, n.p.)

"WEREWOLVES OF LONDON AGAIN." AND AGAIN . . .

I don't think it was as big a hit as people think it was. People remember it from year to year more—it's been in movies and it gets trotted out regularly—but it's not as if it sold four million copies, like a Paula Abdul single, you know what I mean?

—Warren Zevon (Newton)

Listen, I don't want to be a prick, but every single show I do, I play "Werewolves of London" and it's driving me fucking crazy.

—Warren Zevon, scene from *The Larry Sanders Show* (HBO),
September 15, 1993

"Werewolves of London" was "trotted out regularly." The hit song's 15-minute conception, prompted by a horror film and a dance-crazed Phil Everly, progressed into a lineage of assorted and unusual cultural citations. In addition to the song's signature "Ahh-ooh" chorus howl and idiosyncratic "I'd like to meet his tailor," the opening lyric has been abstracted with recognition. In 2004, "Werewolves of London'" won the BBC Radio 2's "Greatest Opening Song Line" vote, finishing ahead of Bill Haley and the Comets' "Rock Around the Clock"; "Hey Joe" by the Leaves, Jimi Hendrix, and others' Little Richard's "Tutti Frutti'" and Lynyrd Skynyrd's "Freebird." The first part of the opening line—"I saw a werewolf with a Chinese menu in his hand"—has also been appropriated as a bumper sticker, with the verse catchy but confounding to those not familiar with Zevon.

The most common conveyance of "Werewolves of London" is as a Halloween standard. Beyond the annual October playlist, the song has been used widely in television, including *Californication, Community, Grimm, Glee, Hawaii Five-O,* and *Dancing with the Stars*; and in film, notably Martin Scorsese's *The Color of Money* (1986). Cover versions range from the Flamin' Groovies, David Lindley, and Magnolia Electric Co., to actor Adam Sandler. Masha Shirin's sultry rendition provides a striking divergence from the original within the ironic setting of a noirish musical featuring a stylish lupine ladies' man that was part of an ad campaign for Three Olives vodka in 2014. There is also ironic juxtaposition in Kid Rock's "All Summer Long," a huge hit that reached number one in eight countries in 2008. The song samples the "Werewolves" piano hook, mashed up with Lynyrd Skynyrd's "Sweet Home Alabama," a song Zevon satirized in "Play It All Night Long" in 1980.

"Werewolves of London" surfaced in several rather uncommon settings. During the gubernatorial inauguration ball in 1999, Minnesota governor Jesse Ventura growled his way through an organic live performance of a tailored version, "Werewolves of Minnesota," guided by Zevon who shared the stage on piano. In major league baseball, Washington Nationals outfielder Jayson Werth includes "Werewolves of London" in his rotation of walk-up tunes played over the stadium PA system as he approaches the batter's box. The personal theme was presumably selected to correlate with Werth's beard and shaggy hair. The song also circulated to the spirited atmosphere of minor league baseball. In 1999, when the independent Frontier League team Kalamazoo Kodiaks relocated from Michigan to London, Ontario, their name change to "Werewolves" seemed an oddly obvious choice. The team mascot, a harmlessly howling wolf dressed in top hat and tails, named "Warren Z. Vaughn," erased any doubt as to the source of the team name. The caricatured Zevon homage was weirdly transcendent, an Elvisian distinction and a rarity for rockers that highlighted the song's cartoon qualities and novelty party mythology.

In cameos on two 1990s cable comedies on HBO, *The Larry Sanders Show* and *Dream On*, Zevon advanced his own "hit song torment" counter-mythology. Zevon displays deft, unaffected, and edgy comic timing in hilarious scenes in which he expresses his ire at the endless requests, whether from fans or television show hosts, to play their favorite Zevon song, "Werewolves of London."

PRETTY IN PAIN: TERROR TO TENDERNESS

Zevon continued to demonstrate his two sharply divergent songwriting personalities on *Excitable Boy*, a contrast he attributed in part to his mismatched parents and their personalities. The album's rampant thread of macabre mayhem and noir elements were steadied by the sensitivity and emotional depth in songs of parting and longing: "Accidentally Like a Martyr," "Veracruz," and "Tenderness on the Block." According to Zevon, several people believed he wrote "Accidentally Like a Martyr" about them. The lament of lost love represents one of

Zevon's touchstone themes that was ostensibly self-referential. Steered by a pondering piano, the mood is somber—"the phone don't ring and the sun refused to shine"; the lingering loneliness devastating—"Never thought I'd have to pay so dearly for what was already mine/For such a long time"; and the regret wearisome—"should have done, should have done, we all sigh." In the chorus, Ronstadt protégé Karla Bonoff's harmonies with the Gentlemen Boys recount a litany of love's many variations—mad, shadow, random, and abandoned—followed by Zevon's agonized summary: "the hurt gets worse and the heart gets harder."

While the emotional gravity of "Accidentally Like a Martyr" is self-sustaining, its placement on the album following the sinister sequence of the ghostly Roland, grisly excitable boy, and stylish mutilating werewolves, provides calming contrast that magnifies the song's pretty pain and Zevon's songwriting versatility. More subtly, the positioning of "Accidentally Like a Martyr" was further classical influence, as Zevon explains, "giving the album a structure like Bartók, with the most important songs dead center, sending out waves" (Fawcett, 152).

Vulnerability, heartbreak, home, and homeland converge in "Veracruz," a poignant historical vignette set during the U.S.–led invasion of the Mexican seaport in 1914. The idea for the song emerged after Zevon viewed a documentary about General Emiliano Zapata, who, along with ally Pancho Villa, was a key figure in the Mexican Revolution. Zapata straddled the protagonist/antagonist duality, embodying the desperado complexities that both intrigued and personified Zevon. Characterizations of Zapata were conflicting, among them bandit, barbarian, womanizer, and true revolutionary who worked for peasants during the U.S. occupation of Mexico. Rather than painting a "Frank and Jesse James" type portrait of the populist rebel, Zevon references Zapata in the song—singing that he will take those left behind after the American troops withdraw. Zevon's choice not to do a biographical ballad may have been awareness that Zapata's assassination—an elaborate betrayal and ambush at the hands of a fellow general and his aide—was too similar to the headless Roland saga.

Zevon instills grace into heritage amidst tragic circumstances. The recorder that opens the song sets a solemn tone, while Spanish vocals combine with traditional Mexican instrumentation to augment authenticity. Zevon assumes a first-person point of view within a family forced to flee their home during the rebellion. The account is subtly striking as an exclusively aural progression: "I heard Woodrow Wilson's guns, I heard Maria crying . . . I heard the news, that Veracruz was dying." The technique creates a visual drift, intensifying a cinematic atmosphere of fear, hiding, darkness, and helplessness. There is uncertainty: "someone calls Maria's name, I swear it was my father's voice." And urgency; they have no choice, they must leave now or they will be slain. A profound and haunting directive for refuge follows, instructing them to ride west, and "Keep the child close to your chest." Calderón completes the account of the fateful event with a stirring passage sung in Spanish, swearing to return, where "in Veracruz I shall die."

"Tenderness on the Block" provides yet another revealing glimpse into Zevon's writing approach. According to Crystal Zevon, Warren needed "to create his own drama for the sake of a song" (140). Zevon candidly admitted to being envious of fellow artists such as Browne and Neil Young, who were among those who had people close to them die, as the firsthand painful experience of their losses provided material for great songs. Browne's *The Pretender* followed the suicide of his wife, Phyllis Major, in March 1976. And Young's dark masterpiece, *Tonight's the Night*, recorded in 1973 but not released until 1975, confronts drugs and the rock-and-roll lifestyle in the wake of the overdose deaths of Crazy Horse guitarist Danny Whitten and roadie Bruce Berry.

The sweetness of "Tenderness on the Block" emerged, in part, out of such self-inflicted disorder. The night the song was written, Zevon had pulled a banister off a staircase in a drunken rage. Browne, responding to a call from Crystal, came to their residence. The domestic situation was settled, though Zevon had no recollection of the banister incident. In the immediate aftermath, Browne became an expedient writing partner, working with Zevon on the song while the drinking continued into the late night. Browne eventually passed out, and when he woke up, the song was finished. "Tenderness on the Block" conveys the youthful quest for true love, with emphasis on the growing pains of letting go as a parent, as their wide-eyed daughter is growing up, "trying to run before she can walk." The advice to Daddy is, "don't you ask her when she's coming in, and where she's been; let her have her day." Though composed amidst chaotic circumstances, the song is centered in Zevon's own fatherly frame of reference as his daughter Ariel was two years old, and in Browne's view as her godfather. Four years later, Browne's teen dating tune, "Somebody's Baby," featured on the *Fast Times at Ridge-*

mont High (1982) soundtrack, echoed as a pop companion to "Tenderness on the Block."

DESPERATION ROCKLAMATION

The album's alternating arc of menacing motifs and sentimental strands ignites into a blazing conclusion in the amplified call to arms, "Lawyers, Guns and Money." The three-chord rock anthem originated during an adventure from a cocktail lounge through a sugarcane field in Hawaii with Zevon, Asylum Records A&R rep Burt Stein, and a waitress acquaintance en route to a friend's plantation house. When the three learned that nobody was home and they would have to break in, they imagined a telegram they would send to record company president Joe Smith: "please send lawyers, guns, and money." With the escapade abruptly ended, Zevon returned to the lounge where he expanded the telegram phrase into a down-on-my-luck account sketched out on two cocktail napkins. The series of unfortunate events begins harmlessly, "I went home with a waitress, the way I always do." A bewildering twist of fate follows: "How was I to know she was with the Russians too?" The expression is more than a naïve shrug at the pick-up blind spot. The line is idiosyncratic, suspending itself outside the verse. Like many Zevon lines, it leaves a listener wondering where a phrase like that comes from. The calamities escalate to taking a little risk gambling in Havana, begging "Dad, get me out of this" (a Stumpy Zevon allusion). There is an undercurrent of spy-boy privilege, with no accountability, only a self-proclaimed "innocent bystander" who "somehow got stuck between a rock and a hard place." Hiding in Honduras, a desperate man, Zevon delivers a last-ditch declaration with valedictory verve, hollering: "Send lawyers, guns and money. The shit has hit the fan!" As the song fades, Zevon grunts his trademark "Huh!" and "Hah!" while repeating the three-part request. The album-ending rocklamation naturally became an ardent audience sing-along-in-unison line at Zevon's live shows.

DEATH BEFORE DISCO

Situated within *Excitable Boy*'s intermingling triplets of bloody havoc, menacing merriment, and tenderness, "Nighttime in the Switching Yard" was conspicuous as the album's least complex song lyrically, and ironically its longest at 4:15 minutes. Stylistically, the song was a super-fluous attempt at a requisite danceable track to coincide with the late 1970s disco phenomenon, which was the likely rationale for its strategic spot as the lead cut on side two of the album. The minimal, repetitive lyrics (with Calderón, Wachtel, and Lindell cocredited) were backed by a forced funk groove, thumping bass line, and syncopated "doot dat doot dat doot dadoot," simulating the train on track at midnight running both ways. Based on a Lindell story about a switch operator in the railroad yard who was a junkie, thus the lyric—"get it out on the main-line, listen to the rhythm of the train go by"—the pulsating song was Zevon doing disco noir, more shadow than strobe, boogie, or mirror ball.

In January 1978, the month *Excitable Boy* was released, the sound-track to the film *Saturday Night Fever,* starring John Travolta, reached number one, joining Chic, the Village People, A Taste of Honey, and other purveyors of dance music permeating the charts. The disco era's touchstone film and soundtrack were a Robert Stigwood enterprise. The entertainment impresario's music, theater, and film credits ranged from founding and managing RSO Records to producing *Hair* and *Jesus Christ Superstar.* The music and film industries' interdependence on full display in *Saturday Night Fever* was at the forefront of the synergy that would become the standard marketplace mode with the arrival of MTV three years later in August 1981. Stigwood reshaped the Bee Gees, transforming the brothers Gibb sound from their Beatlesque be-ginnings with songs such as "New York Mining Disaster 1941," "To Love Somebody," "Holiday," "Words," "Massachusetts," and "I've Gotta Get a Message to You" to falsetto dance tracks that became a string of hit singles—"How Deep Is Your Love," "More Than a Woman," "Stay-in' Alive," "Night Fever," "If I Can't Have You." The previously re-leased "Jive Talkin'" and "You Should Be Dancing" were also included on the soundtrack. Released in November 1977, the *Saturday Night Fever* soundtrack supplanted Fleetwood Mac's grand and glossy *Ru-mours,* which had been at number one for an astounding 31 weeks. The double album of disco stayed at the top spot for 24 weeks, from January until July. The Grammy-winning soundtrack remained on the charts for 120 weeks until March 1980.

"Disco fever," a hallmark of 1970s American popular culture, was not without backlash. "Disco Demolition Night," a riotous radio promotion gone awry, was the climactic moment of the anti-disco crusade. The infamous event, rampant with "Excitable Boy" misbehaviors and disorder, took place on July 12, 1979, at Comiskey Park in Chicago in between games of a twi-night doubleheader between major league baseball's Chicago White Sox and Detroit Tigers. Popular radio personality Steve Dahl was the mastermind behind Disco Demolition Night. Dahl had lost his job with WDAI when the opportunistic station changed their format to "all disco." Dahl was quickly hired by WLUP, "The Loop," where he mischievously established an anti-disco advocacy organization called "The Insane Coho Lips" (the name "Coho" borrowed from a Great Lakes fish). The mock organization gained notoriety through Dahl's on-air hype. Dahl and his on-air sidekick Garry Meier plotted a "98" (WLUP's location on the radio dial) promotion where fans who brought disco music records to the ballpark were admitted for the fee of 98 cents.

The event attracted atypical baseball fans. Attendance, estimated at 50,000, exceeded expectations, and many people were turned away at the gates. Inside the park, banners draped in the bleachers and upper deck facades proclaiming "Death before Disco," "Disco Sucks," and "Down with Disco" provided a backdrop for the riotous atmosphere that included beer and firecrackers. Vinyl LPs sailed through the stands like frisbees, often striking spectators. Throughout the game White Sox broadcasters, the legendary Harry Carey and Jimmy Piersall, commented upon the "strange people" wandering aimlessly through the stands.

The infamous moment occurred between games of the doubleheader. Dahl, his sidekick Lorelei, and bodyguards proceeded to center field for the Disco Demolition ceremony. The disco records used for admission were gathered and placed in a bin rigged with explosives. When the bomb detonated, shards of vinyl scattered and a hole was ripped in the outfield grass surface. Chaos ensued. A mob poured out onto the field, lighting fires, burning banners, and engaging in mini-riots. The infield bases were stolen (not by players) and chunks of the field's turf were torn up for souvenir sod. Other fans on the field casually milled, observing the surrounding disarray.

Carey and White Sox owner Bill Veeck, who was known for his P. T. Barnum–like showmanship and suspected to be behind the promotion, used the public address system to urge fans to return to the stands. When this failed, police in riot gear cleared the field. There were reportedly many minor injuries and nearly 40 people arrested for disorderly conduct. The White Sox were forced to forfeit the second game of the doubleheader. Tigers manager Sparky Anderson refused to allow his team on the field due to safety concerns with the fans and playing surface. The poor field conditions from the demolition debacle lingered throughout the remainder of the baseball season.

"Disco Demolition Night" is listed as one of the worst ideas in sports history, ranking with "10 Cent Beer Night" and glow pucks designed to make fast-paced hockey games easier to follow during telecasts. In popular culture discussions, the event is commonly recognized as an emblematic moment, the unofficial "day disco died." Though disco as a cultural phenomenon and fad was peaking by mid-1979, Dahl's dubious "Disco Demolition Night" hastened its demise.

THE END OF AN ERA?

Disco's popularity was only one indicator of the continual shift in the music industry and its culture during the mid- to late 1970s. Glenn Frey of the Eagles, whose recognition and success from *Hotel California* was proportional to any of the period's biggest artists and records, told *Rolling Stone* he believed the music business and its bottom-line focus had grown out of touch with rock and roll. Frey specifically mentioned Zevon and the 1977 Grammy Awards to support his point: "There's a credibility gap, Debby Boone wins Best New Artist, and Warren Zevon and Karla Bonoff aren't nominated" (Eliot, 170). Teen idol Andy Gibb, Shaun Cassidy, Foreigner, and soft-rock songwriter Stephen Bishop joined Boone as nominees in the category. Boone, daughter of singer Pat Boone, had a huge hit with "You Light Up My Life." The Joe Brooks ballad, which had been performed by Kasey Cisyk for the soundtrack to the film of the same name, was awarded a Grammy for Song of the Year. Boone's version became the most successful single of the 1970s, staying at the top spot on the charts for ten weeks. Frey's disappointment extended to fellow artists David Crosby and Stephen Stills, who appeared at the Grammy ceremony dressed in black tie and tails. "Rock and roll does not belong in a tuxedo," chided Frey. "When we saw [Crosby and Stills] walk out there, my fuckin' heart sank. It was like the end of an era" (Eliot, 170).

Rolling Stone also personified the shifting sociopolitical, cultural, and economic values. Jann Wenner's rock and political publication emerged from San Francisco's fabled "Summer of Love" in November 1967, with its lead story on the Monterey Pop Festival. Ten years later, the journal of record for the 1960s progressed from counterculture to corporate as a pop-culture money-making machine.

The markers were not confined to West Coast culture. In New York City, the punk subculture began to diversify, fragmenting into subgenre strands, while in L.A. the mainstream record business barely acknowledged the Ramones. Among the more notable of the "New Wave" were the Cars, Devo, and Debbie Harry and Blondie, whose eclectic style blended disco, pop, punk, and reggae. On television, the late-night satire *Saturday Night Live*, which premiered on the NBC network in 1975, fulfilled a similar role that music had for youth culture in the late 1960s, with comedy displacing protest anthems and socially conscious lyrics. Created and developed by Canadian comedy writer-producer Lorne Michaels, the show's "live" presentation had a counterculture undercurrent. With no editing or ten-second delay, there was nothing the network establishment could do if a performer "went too far." Even the ensemble's name—"The Not Ready for Prime-Time Players"—reflected the show's nonconformist tone. Each week, a guest host joined the irreverent comedy troupe in sketches, parodies, and a "Weekend Update" news segment that commented on mainstream culture, sociopolitical affairs, and current events. A musical guest also performed two songs in Rockefeller Center's Studio 8H garage-band setting. Considering the acclaim that accompanied Zevon's first two albums, his song noir and antihero demeanor, which seemed a natural fit for *Saturday Night Live*, it is somewhat surprising that he was never booked to perform on the late-night satire. On May 9, 1980, Zevon did appear on *Fridays*, the ABC network's late-night, comedy-variety version of *Saturday Night Live*, performing "Johnny Strikes Up the Band" and "Gorilla You're A Desperado" from his 1980 release, *Bad Luck Streak in Dancing School*.

RONSTADTLAND

Critic Robert Christgau's appraisal of *Excitable Boy* was accurate, albeit rather obvious; the record was not "Ronstadtland." Though Linda Ronstadt contributed harmonies on the album, she and producer Peter Asher chose not to cover any of its songs, unlike the four she recorded from Zevon's debut. The majority of *Excitable Boy*'s songs were not as amenable to adaptation and gender translation as those on *Warren Zevon*. Perhaps the most perceptibly appealing of the album's nine songs, "Tenderness on the Block" was eventually covered by Shawn Colvin on *Fat City* (1992). Dave Marsh circuitously reaffirmed his fellow critic's Ronstadt resistance in *Rolling Stone*, pronouncing Zevon "one of the toughest rockers ever to come out of Southern California."

Zevon's sophomore album, however, did resemble Ronstadt in its popularity and hit song presence in FM radio's rotation. The prevalent "berserk qualities," comic noir, and the macabre nature of Zevon's songwriting on the album, did not hinder the record's popular reception. As Browne and Jordan Zevon suggested, those songwriting attributes that may have overshadowed the brilliance of *Warren Zevon* correspondingly benefitted his follow-up album. *Excitable Boy* exceeded Asylum's cautiously optimistic expectations, going gold, and ascending to number 8 on the *Billboard* Pop Album chart in 1978. And the album's designated single, "Werewolves of London," rewarded its skeptical producers and Zevon with a hit that reached number 21 on the *Billboard* Pop Singles. The commercial achievement was impressive, if not a triumph, for a singer-songwriter within the corporate rock climate of the late 1970s. *Excitable Boy* endured as Zevon's career best-selling album, and "Werewolves of London" his most popular, persistent, and pervasive song.

With the success of *Excitable Boy*, Zevon's insecurities surfaced in conjunction with his artist anguish. "And, believe me, the man was tormented," said Marinell (C. Zevon, 143). Zevon began to distance himself from many of the album's collaborators. Among them, Marinell and Wachtel speculated that Zevon was concerned that *Excitable Boy*'s shared credits might diminish his individual acclaim. Zevon was keenly aware of his fellow artists' successes, particularly the Asylum label mates, and of his own rising status within the L.A. music scene. He did not want there to be the perception that somebody other than he was responsible for the music and songwriting talents displayed on his first two albums. Thus, Zevon felt the need to disassociate. Wachtel was not slighted, accepting the detachment as part of Zevon's artist temperament: "Warren and I were shattered after working on that record, and it's one of the best things he ever did as far as I'm concerned" (C. Zevon, 139).

Wachtel's view was not totally tinged with coproducer partiality. *Rolling Stone* called *Excitable Boy* one of the most significant records of the 1970s, and placed Zevon alongside the songwriting trinity of Jackson Browne, Neil Young, and Bruce Springsteen as one of the four most important new artists to emerge in the decade. The commercial success of *Excitable Boy* following the critical acclaim for *Warren Zevon* combined to further validate and singularize Zevon among the era's prolific songwriting pantheon.

4

ROCK BOTTOM: THE CRACK-UP AND RESURRECTION

Somehow I got the songs written for Excitable Boy. I thought my days were numbered in fractions. . . . Clearly, I had carried this F. Scott Fitzzevon thing too far.

—Warren Zevon (Nelson, 1981)

Warren knew he was an alcoholic, and he never pretended otherwise, but rather than look upon his alcoholism as a scourge, or acknowledge it as a disease, he found ways to flaunt it like a badge of honor. He used his drunken episodes to build a reputation on and as material to write songs about. Warren believed that alcohol fueled the fire of his creativity.

—Crystal Zevon (63)

The '70s were like a decade-long Lost Weekend that a lot of people were devoured by. My dad was one of them.

—Jordan Zevon (Jones, 2014)

"**E**xcitable Boy, they all said," was a prophetic Warren Zevon verse. The tag became instantly and permanently affixed to Zevon as person and persona, and foundation for his mythology. The brand was convenient, fitting, and well-earned, as Zevon's notorious and relentless wild lifestyle routinely reinforced the designation. The motif became part of the showmanship of Zevon's live shows. Road manager and live-in aide-de-camp George Gruel would lead Zevon on stage, handcuffed to each other. "We're going to unleash the excitable boy this evening," warned

Gruel, as he unlocked the shackles. "I'm going to cut him loose for you. Rock and roll!"

THE DANGEROUS DEAN MARTIN

In the wake of *Excitable Boy*'s rowdy success, there was a notable shift in emphasis in the increasing press coverage of Zevon. The focus on his song noir and classical composer aspiration that attracted credible news publications following *Warren Zevon* diffused into footnotes, with story slants on Zevon's rock and roll wreckcess moving to the forefront. Even celebrity sources were enticed. The May 22, 1978, issue of *People* magazine improbably cast Zevon deeper into mainstream popular culture. *People* was in its fourth year of publication, launching March 4, 1974, with the premiere issue's cover featuring actress Mia Farrow, at the time starring in *The Great Gatsby* with Robert Redford. The slick weekly magazine advanced celebrity coverage beyond newspaper gossip columns and sensational tabloids such as the *Globe* and *National Enquirer* into a more credible "personality journalism" accented with human-interest stories.

People perpetuated the bourgeoning riotous Zevon mythology, from its front cover to the article title, subheadings, photos, and captions, and the content of Sue Reilly's profile in the "For a Song" section. Zevon was complicit, telling Paul Nelson that "*People* magazine—with my help—made me into the dangerous Dean Martin of my generation" (1981, 34; Avery, 382). The issue's cover, featuring comic actor John Ritter, who ironically died four days after Zevon's death in September 2003, included the unimaginative spin-off cover line—"Rock's Excitable Boy, Warren Zevon"—further evidence of the moniker's opportune, widespread adoption. While the repeated usage was inherently promotional and effective branding, which no doubt delighted Asylum's executives, Zevon's name seemed oddly out of place amidst the *People* cover's other showbiz tags promoting the issue's features: "John Ritter, the cuddly stud of *Three's Company* . . ." "Erma Bombeck, even her name sounds funny," and "The hottest seat in the Cabinet."

Inside, the tiring thesis was reiterated in the article's lengthy title: "The Next Big Quake Has Already Rocked L.A.; It's the Excitable Warren Zevon." Above, a full-page image by L.A. photographer Julian Wasser depicted Zevon in archetypal writer pose, hovering behind a small typewriter, elbows on desk, hands posed in explaining gesture, cigarette dangling from his mouth, and his partially legible *Star Wars* t-shirt providing a casual Hollywood fashion statement, acknowledging the George Lucas epic that premiered in May 1977, seven months before *Excitable Boy*. Zevon's occupational hazards and necessities were aligned like props in the foreground next to sheets of paper: a pack of cigarettes, ashtray, and half-empty bottle of vodka, which was the focal point of the photo's caption: "The creative juices that make Warren Zevon a hot rocker are bottled up inside him—and his omnipresent fifth."

The title, image, and caption could have stood by itself in encapsulating Zevon. The thin portrayal that continued over two subsequent pages offered a "family man" glance, but primarily underscored, if not overplayed, Zevon's "excitable boy" image. A concert photo depicted Zevon as desperado—arm extended, with one hand propping the other, his finger pointing like a gun as he sings—with the caption: "Zevon gunned down critics at a gig last month at L.A.'s Roxy." A subhead in bold type—"the boozy poet of weirdo rock"—prefaced the lead in the text: "L.A. rock's newest darling desperado. . . likes to start his day with a screwdriver." Zevon corroborated journalist Reilly's account of his drinking routine, admitting with casual indifference, "I used to get lots of drunk-driving tickets. So I knew it would come down to drinking or driving. So I picked drinking, I don't drive anymore" (98).

"DOWN ON MY KNEES IN PAIN": THE JETT RINK TOUR

The flavor of Warren was dark. . . . On the other hand, the guy's out of his mind.

—guitarist David Landau (C. Zevon)

From the recording of *Warren Zevon* through *Excitable Boy*'s release and tour, Zevon's drinking escalated dramatically, from "morning to night, turning his moods from dark to way past midnight" (C. Zevon, 134). Turning 30, becoming a father, and the critical and commercial successes of his Asylum albums only intensified Zevon's self-destructive manner rather than improving his abysmal condition and outlook.

Zevon admitted that "much of 1977 was a nightmare," and that the following year, he "crashed completely" as he was "seriously into the noir lifestyle—vodka, drugs, sex" (Nelson 1981, 33–34). He considered himself "a walking advertisement for chaos and disorder"; the excessiveness was stunning. In 1982, during the first of Zevon's many appearances on *Late Night*, host David Letterman engaged Zevon in a polite discussion about Zevon's "continuous celebration" and "bottoming out." When Letterman asked Zevon specifically about the amount of alcohol he consumed during the tumultuous period, Zevon appeared a little taken back. "Really?" he replied, before candidly estimating "a couple of quarts of vodka a day."

Zevon's behavior during what he referred to as his "cowboy days" inevitably took its toll on his marriage. He and Crystal lived apart for several months and their relationship steadily unraveled through separations into an eventual divorce. The drunken episodes became more frequent and frightening, with many accompanied by violent and abusive behavior, blackouts, and loaded guns from Zevon's collection, which had accumulated to arsenal proportions. Among the stupefied scenarios involving firearms were Zevon, with no recollection, waving a pistol in the face of fellow songwriters LeRoy Marinell and J. D. Souther; and him shooting at a Richard Pryor billboard on Sunset Boulevard from his window at the Chateau Marmont. No one ever knew what to expect from Zevon. His drunken postures, as characterized by music journalist and friend Paul Nelson, ranged from "outrageous, falling down drunk, to a courtly but inebriated Tennessee Williams–style 'gentleman caller,' to a desperately sick man who felt that death was just as close as the corner bar" (Avery, 368–69). Crystal Zevon's view of her husband's deteriorating condition was direct and distressing: "He's dying," she told Nelson in a phone conversation (Nelson 1981, 31). Nelson was convinced that had it not been for the saintly devotion of Crystal Zevon, Warren "would have been dead ten times over" (32).

Crystal and the tour managers and crew often struggled to get Zevon up and dressed, and from place to place, without falling over. At times, Zevon was lucid while drunk and managed to perform sets, though in most instances his live shows were descending to outrageous and embarrassing levels. He frequently forgot lyrics, and was prone to falling off his piano stool. During a show in Chicago, Zevon fell off the stage and injured his leg. For the rest of the tour, he was in a wheelchair, on crutches and gimping about. Exhibiting his erudite knack even in the most miserable circumstances, the droll Zevon referred to the subsequent shows as "the Jett Rink Tour," in honor of James Dean's character passing out in the middle of a drunken speech in *Giant* (1956), the last of the rebel hero's three films.

The exhaustive tales of Zevon's excesses and the accompanying chaos, particularly those painstakingly chronicled in the best-selling posthumous oral history, *I'll Sleep When I'm Dead* (2007), were as astonishing as they were disconcerting even by the wildest sex, drugs, and rock-and-roll standards. The firsthand stories from friends, family, and associates further reaffirmed most of the versions that preceded them in the rock press throughout Zevon's career. An eyewitness account by guitarist David Landau (brother of producer/manager Jon) of the disastrous Excitable Boy Tour was representative of the candid testimonials to the turmoil that engulfed Zevon: "I'm not sure what the psychological classification of Warren would be. When someone who is alcoholic plays at being a sociopath, it's hard to know when playtime is over. . . . The only thing that I ever saw that came close to how Warren drank was Nicolas Cage in *Leaving Las Vegas*" (C. Zevon,153–54).

As part of Crystal's constant quest for solutions, she, Warren, and daughter Ariel relocated north to the lavish coastal community of Santa Barbara, specifically Montecito, where Ross Macdonald lived, hoping that the distance from L.A.'s noir enticements would make a difference. The move inevitably failed; the idyllic setting was not compatible with Zevon's restless nature. At his own housewarming party, a drunken Zevon began target practice with his .44 Magnum in his guest cottage/ writing studio at two o'clock in the morning, firing three shots into his portrait on the *Excitable Boy* album cover that was propped up on the couch. The rock-bottom behavior triggered a prolonged cycle of drug and alcohol rehabilitation, counseling, and treatment programs for Zevon, who roller-coastered between recovery and relapses. The pattern extended into the recording of his next records and beyond, continuing until 1986, when Zevon began a sustained period of sobriety that lasted until 2002 when he was diagnosed with mesothelioma.

A BLOOD BROTHER MASTERPIECE

This guy's just weird enough to be my friend.
                    —Warren Zevon, on critic Paul Nelson, 1976

I think the Zevon cover story in Rolling Stone *is worth any 150—any thousand—record reviews by anyone else.*
                         —critic Charles M. Young (Avery)

In the midst of Zevon's mayhem during the late 1970s and into early 1980, Paul Nelson emerged as a redemptive figure. Nelson was a pioneer of rock criticism and one of its most talented, influential practitioners. While at the University of Minnesota in the early 1960s, Nelson and his buddy John Pankake cofounded a seminal folk music criticism magazine, the *Little Sandy Review*. "We could not afford to buy records and folk music was getting reasonably popular so we decided to start our own magazine just to get records for nothing," said Nelson (Ward, n.p.). A forerunner to the fanzine, the mimeographed pamphlet, brimming with youthful, unrestrained, witty idealism, cost 30 cents per issue and initially had three subscribers. That number grew to 1000 by the time the publication ended 30 issues later in the mid-1960s.

With the *Little Sandy Review*, Nelson was at the forefront of the music journalism movement as it took shape in the 1960s and into the 1970s, spawning publications such as *Creem, Crawdaddy*, and *Rolling Stone*, along with an impressive (anti) establishment of writers of which Nelson said, "Nobody ever took us seriously" (Ward). Among that core of eminent critics were Ralph J. Gleason (who cofounded *Rolling Stone* with Jann Wenner), Lester Bangs, Robert Christgau, Richard Meltzer, Nick Tosches, Greil Marcus, Jon Landau, Dave Marsh, Bill Flanagan, Chet Flippo, John Rockwell, Ben Fong-Torres, Jon Pareles, David Fricke, Kurt Loder, Charles M. Young, Mikal Gilmore, and 15-year-old Cameron Crowe, whose career trajectory from teen rock journalist to film director was the basis for the coming-of-age film, *Almost Famous* (2000).

Described by his colleagues as "subterranean" and "quixotic," Nelson wrote for *Sing Out!, Circus, Village Voice*, the Boston alternative weekly the *Real Paper*, and *Rolling Stone*, where he was one of the most influential record review editors. He was one of the few critics to defend Dylan when he went electric at the Newport Folk Festival in 1965.

Nelson also worked with Mercury Records in publicity and A&R. Of Nelson's overarching influence, Christgau stated, "It was Paul, more than anybody else, who made rock criticism cross disciplinary about certain off-center strains of American, putatively popular culture" (Ward).

Nelson and Zevon met for the first time in 1976 at the Bottom Line in New York City after Zevon's initial performance during the "I'll Sleep When I'm Dead Tour" that followed the release of his Asylum debut, which Nelson loved. The two "hit it off right away." Nelson, who was freelancing at the time, found Zevon to be "a very serious guy," while Zevon was reciprocally drawn to Nelson's enigmatic nature. The pair connected as kindred aesthetes who lived in the world of literature, movies, and music, and as writers who wanted to get their words right. Much of their initial conversation centered around their mutual admiration for the hardboiled trinity of crime writers, Raymond Chandler, Dashiell Hammett, and in particular Ross Macdonald, whom Nelson had met and was scheduled to interview. Later that summer, days before Ariel Zevon was born, Nelson took Crystal and Warren to Santa Barbara to meet Macdonald. "It was like I'd invited them to meet God," said Nelson (1981, 30).

During the next four years, Nelson and the Zevons kept in touch and frequently saw each other on both the East and West Coasts. Nelson's relationship with Warren evolved from mutual professional admiration into a close friendship. In late summer of 1978 while in New York, Nelson and Zevon swore a corny, albeit genuine and emotional, "blood brother" oath during a dialogue until dawn in which they shared life stories, successes, failures, and the future. Fear was a major theme: Zevon's deep-seated fear of not being able to write another album, and of losing his central writing aesthetic—conflict—if he did not drink. Shortly thereafter, following the album cover assassination incident which "was enough to make everyone who knew Zevon nervous" (C. Zevon, 367), he reluctantly agreed to check into Pinecrest, a private hospital in Santa Barbara, to begin treatment for alcoholism.

Nelson flew to the West Coast to participate in an intervention, joining Jackson Browne, LeRoy Marinell, Jorge Calderón, Jimmy Wachtel, and Zevon family members. Over the course of the next two and a half years, Nelson crafted an extraordinary account of his relationship with Zevon, framed around his role before, during, and after Zevon's intervention. The Nelson narrative was epic—a 45-page, 20,000-word manuscript without a single typo. Beyond sheer volume, the scope was singularly striking for Nelson who, by choice, almost exclusively wrote record reviews. He struggled with broader writing assignments, particularly with arriving at their endings. The more meaningful the subject to Nelson, the more difficult it was for him to condense. He never completed features on his heroes Ross Macdonald and Clint Eastwood, despite an extensive accumulation of recorded interviews.

The resulting feature, Nelson's fourth and final Zevon-related piece, became the cover story of the March 19, 1981, issue of *Rolling Stone*. Zevon, dressed in a gray suit and tie, his customary obsessive color, was sprawled across the magazine front, with the main cover line —"The Crackup and Resurrection of Warren Zevon"—referencing *The Crack-Up*, F. Scott Fitzgerald's collection of letters, notes, and essays on the pressures of fame. Zevon's spread-eagle pose, an X-configuration composed by renowned portrait photographer Annie Leibovitz, simultaneously conveyed snow angel and crucifixion, rescue and torture, with hands grasping Zevon's arms and limbs, stretching them to each of the four corners of the frame.

Inside, Nelson's feature, "Warren Zevon: How He Saved Himself from a Coward's Death," was transcendent—"the Mona Lisa of rock profile writing," in the view of critic Charles M. Young (Avery, 356). Nelson's comprehensive exploration of Zevon's journey encompassed the physical, intellectual, emotional, spiritual, and musical, projecting beyond individual biography to broader universal connections with the artist condition and spirit, the creative process, and the agony of genius. In the process, Nelson infringed on traditional professional codes of journalistic objectivity. He became part of the story, and his deep personal affinity with Zevon was evident. In critic Young's view, "Paul knew he had the subject of his life in that piece: an artist that he was in a position to understand better than anyone else"; Nelson had mastered Hunter Thompson's gonzo journalism approach of an "intense, total demented involvement" with the subject being written about (Avery, 356). Nelson had established Zevon's trust, which allowed Zevon to open up to him a way that was rare in such profiles.

The intimate, intense chronicle was a stark contrast to the *People* magazine profile of Zevon. Nelson adroitly wove empathy with unflinching candor. The forthright lead—"Alcoholism. That's what this story's supposed to be about" (28)—culminates eight pages later in a redemptive tone with Zevon's recollection of Ken Millar (Ross Macdonald) visiting him at his home at Nelson's request following another post-Pinecrest setback: "Ken Millar made me realize that I wrote my songs *despite* the fact that I was a drunk, not *because* of it. It was like a dream come true. At the lowest point in my life, the doorbell rang. And there quite literally was Lew Archer (Millar's fictional private detective character) on a compassionate mission, come to save my life" (Nelson 1981, 70).

In between, Nelson's detailed chronicle of Zevon's week in hell at Pinecrest and subsequent soul searching in and out of sobriety was brimming with cultural touchstones—Stravinsky, Hemingway, Fitzgerald, Clint Eastwood, Ingmar Bergman, Frank Capra, Billy Wilder's *The Lost Weekend* and *Sunset Boulevard*, Ken Russell's *The Devils*, Neil Young's "Powderfinger," T. S. Eliot's *Four Quartets*—and anchored by penetrating passages with meditative qualities. Whether Nelson was expressing his uneasiness as a participant in Zevon's intervention at Pinecrest:

> The very word suggests such a cold and exact, sanctioned and yet sinister interference with another person's life that I still get the shakes whenever I say it out loud . . . *In-ter-ven-tion.* Is it a Nixonian noun for some act of official pornography, a euphemism for gang rape by governmental robots? No, in a way it is what Pinecrest has instead of God. While an intervention can seem as harsh and fear-provoking as eternal damnation, it's also kindly and forgiving. An intervention is an execution with a happy ending. (31)

Or describing Zevon's hotel room after another relapse:

> There were empty bottles everywhere. Full ones, too. . . . To me, the room reeked of death. I can't really describe it. The closest I can come is Van Gogh's description of his painting, *Night Café at Arles:* 'The most violent passions of humanity . . . blood red . . . dark yellow . . . in an atmosphere of pale sulfur, like a furnace . . . I tried to show a place where a man can ruin himself, go mad, commit a crime. (34)

The *Rolling Stone* article was Nelson's crowning achievement and a definitive profile in the rock journalism archive. The acclaimed version became part of the immense manuscript's mythology that carried significant professional and personal implications for Nelson. By the time the feature was published in *Rolling Stone*, the manuscript was dramatically reduced from its original vastness to slightly longer than a standard cover-story length, from 67 pages to 40. Brief discussion of making the article a two-part series quickly diminished. *Rolling Stone* publisher Jann Wenner, who after witnessing Zevon's obnoxious, falling-down drunken state firsthand at a Springsteen concert in New York in 1978, swore he would never print another word about Zevon, claimed that Nelson knew from the outset that "we were never going to publish this at that length":

> But there was no talking him out of it. He was going to write an opus on the subject and that was going to be the end of it. He was really writing for his own purpose. And I suppose at the end—of him writing that perfect piece that he wanted to write about Warren that got it all and explained all where Warren stood in the West Coast literature of the dispossessed or whatever the fuck—that in his mind that was so perfectly clear it should be published as is. (Avery, 357)

Years later, Wenner remained true to his word. In 1986, Merle Ginsberg, a *Rolling Stone* contributor and Zevon's girlfriend at the time, approached the editor about running her interview with Zevon and story about his mid-decade recovery and comeback. Wenner adamantly refused, saying Ginsberg was "full of shit" and that "he's not sober. I've known him for years and it ain't happening. We're not running that bullshit" (C. Zevon, 208).

The abridged version of Nelson's story that was published maintained its brilliance and was a great read. Nelson, however, was distraught, and never recovered from what he considered an evisceration. His fellow music critics, notably Young, were sympathetic and saddened by the toll the editing episode took on Nelson:

> I never saw a writer more angry and more devastated than he was by that edit. But for Paul it was like taking the Mona Lisa and ripping it in half. His masterpiece was ruined. . . . He was traumatized by that edit. That was a turning point in his life. The fact that he didn't write about rock and roll for a long time, or wrote about it only in kind of sporadic and fitful ways, it's kind of like Greek tragedy. There was an inevitability about it. I think Paul expected—and had a right to ex-

pect—that the Zevon article would be given truly special treatment. . . . For that article not to be recognized as a masterpiece, I think it demolished him. (Avery, 357)

On September 7, 2006, two months after Nelson's death at age 69, the crowd that attended his memorial service at a church in Lower Manhattan's East Village exited to Zevon's "Lawyers, Guns and Money" playing on the public address system. Three months later, Neil Strauss's intriguing profile of Nelson, "The Man Who Disappeared," was published in *Rolling Stone*'s year-end edition. Kevin Avery compiled Nelson's works into *Everything Is an Afterthought: The Life and Writings of Paul Nelson* (2011), with a foreword by Nick Tosches and insightful critical commentary. The volume features the complete unedited Zevon manuscript. Nelson's singular piece, whether the original or the *Rolling Stone* edit, sustains as the most important and revealing written work about the life, mind, and tormented soul of Warren Zevon this side of the posthumous oral history assembled by Crystal Zevon.

5

SWEAR TO GOD I'LL CHANGE

I said, you're not a fucking boy, *and you're not a fucking* werewolf,
you're a fucking man, *and it's about time you acted like it.*
—Warren Zevon (to himself) (Nelson 1981)

Warren Zevon had confronted his excitable, howling, finger-on-the-trigger mythology, a Fitzgeraldian two-fisted drinker, writer, adventurer identity and image that he himself cultivated in conjunction with the media. As he continued to wrestle with whether to stay or not "stay the wild age," Zevon channeled an intense self-awareness, healing, and a more mature outlook into his music, both in the studio and on stage. In 1980 Zevon released two albums: *Bad Luck Streak in Dancing School* in February, and a live-in-concert set, *Stand in the Fire*, in late December, a few weeks after John Lennon was shot to death outside the Dakota Hotel in New York City. The recording output was notable. Zevon had made himself a difficult act even for him to follow, considering his personal struggles and the promise generated by his first two Asylum records. Despite a fairly standard two-year span between records, some critics treated Zevon's 1980 recordings as a "comeback," mainly in reference to his alcohol rehabilitation following *Excitable Boy*. The "comeback" marked the first of several, both personal and professional, throughout Zevon's career.

The dedications in both 1980 albums further reaffirmed Zevon's literary and film inspirations. The one for *Bad Luck Streak in Dancing School*, "For Ken Millar *il miglior fabbro*," was a direct appropriation of T. S. Eliot's dedication to Ezra Pound in *The Waste Land*. The quote is from *Purgatorio*, the second cantica of *The Divine Comedy*, where Dante defines a troubadour as "the best smith of the mother tongue." *Stand in the Fire*'s dedication, "For Marty," recognizes director Martin Scorsese, whom Zevon met in New York. Scorsese apparently loved Zevon's music, and was particularly fond of "Accidentally Like a Martyr," which helped get him through a difficult time (Avery, 389).

Bad Luck Streak in Dancing School came together primarily in Hollywood following Zevon's rehabilitation at Pinecrest. Zevon recorded as he wrote, with Greg Ladanyi coproducing. Bruce Springsteen, T-Bone Burnett, and Jorge Calderón collaborated on songs, while Los Angeles loyalists from Zevon's first two records contributed instrumentation and vocal backing—Calderón, Browne, Ronstadt, Wachtel, and J. D. Souther; Eagles Henley, Frey, Joe Walsh, and Don Felder; David Lindley; Section bassist Leland Sklar; Rick Marotta; and Sid Sharp, concertmaster. Neil Young's steel guitarist, Ben Keith, whose lengthy credits include Patsy Cline's "I Fall to Pieces" in 1961, also guests on the album. The expanded sound, anchored by Zevon's piano arrangements and standard, often edgy rock guitar, also incorporated string synthesizers, pedal and lap steel, strings, and classical flourishes. Pleased with the content of his first two records, Zevon's main preoccupation with his third album was "unifying the realms of classical music and popular song," and "changing and experimenting with the form of the songs" (Fawcett, 151).

The album, from its title, cover images, and dedication, and through its 12 songs, is discernably self-referential, with an outlook and tone that are self-revelatory, repentant, vulnerable, and satirical. The Jimmy Wachtel photograph on the album cover depicts Zevon, again dressed in suit and tie, in a stance with one arm on hip, the other propped against a bright balcony window frame of an open dance studio. He is surrounded by ballerinas in various warm-up poses on the floor, in front of wall mirrors, and at the barre. Among the dancers is actress Kim Lankford, a regular on the popular prime-time television drama series, *Knot's Landing*. Lankford and Zevon began a relationship and lived together in 1980 following his split from Crystal. The cover image and album title embody multiple inferences, among them Zevon's obsession with "luck"; his post-rehab study of dance with choreographer JoAnn DeVito, who had also coached actor John Travolta; and "dancing school" as a euphemism for brothel, dating back to the seventeenth century. The back cover's striking juxtaposition of an Uzi machine gun, pointe ballet shoes, and bullet casings on the studio floor reprise the Magnum vegetable plate composition on *Excitable Boy*'s inner sleeve. The ballet-and-bullet image was tailored onto tour t-shirts despite stirring mild controversy over its evocative association.

The high culture and gun incongruence presented on the cover image lingers into an emblematic Zevon moment in the first 20 seconds of the album's opening and title track. A graceful classical string overture is punctuated by the pop of two gunshots, which cue an edgy guitar lead. The progression is Zevon's idiosyncratic method of inferring the dance master's handclaps. The echoing substitute sound for the hand claps originated from a Smith and Wesson .44 Magnum revolver fired into a trash can filled with gravel. Zevon conceived the sequence as part of a music video for the song, but could not garner financial support for the production, as music video did not begin to emerge as a viable form until the following year with MTV.

The dance imagery and title song's orchestral prelude contextualize the album's pair of classical compositions by Zevon. The succinct arrangements—"Interlude No. 1 (25 seconds) and "Interlude No. 2" (1:07 minutes)—are sequenced as the fifth song on side one, and second song of side two. While the pieces solicited critical responses ranging from ambitious and grandiose to pretentious and stylistically intrusive, the miniatures accumulated importance as the only audible traces of meticulously annotated notes from Zevon's unfinished symphony, which Nelson observed, "hanging like a stone around his neck" (1981, 30).

From the outset in "Bad Luck Streak in Dancing School," Zevon confronts his failings with confessional grace, establishing a contrite demeanor that threads the album. He is "down on my knees in pain," which not only signifies pleading for forgiveness (though he asks "don't make me beg"), but also pertains to being falling down drunk. Zevon admits to "acting like a fool" and "breaking all the rules," and vows repeatedly, "Swear to God I'll change."

The bouncy version of Naomi Neville's (Allen Toussaint's songwriting pseudonym) "A Certain Girl" that follows the title track ensures that the album will not wallow. The sly and shy R&B tune features the question, "What's her name?" and an answer, "I can't tell you," then a disappointed sigh—"Awwww." Along with "Iko" on *Wanted: Dead or Alive*, the song further confirmed Zevon's affinity for curious cover choices with R&B tendencies. "A Certain Girl" was popularized by Ernie K-Doe, best known for the hit "Mother in Law" in the early 1960s, and also recorded by the Yardbirds as a B-side to their first single in 1964, "I Wish You Would."

"Jungle Work" could be considered reworked Roland, a do-or-die sequel to the warrior's mercenary mission on *Excitable Boy*. Despite a familiar ominous tone and a guns-and-violence motif, the song seems out of place among the album's narratives and sound, and is far less engaging than Zevon's headless gunner tale. One review cited the song as a "failed experiment" (DeCurtis and Henke, 802). Cowritten with Calderón, "Jungle Work" depicts the midnight run of a Lear jet S.W.A.T. team, parachuting in, screaming "death from above," descending "to battle in hell," where the pay is good, risk is high, and the gun is law, from Ovamboland to Nicaragua. Zevon arms the verses with the M16, the Ingram, stun guns, and "a little M10 sent 'em running to the huts," underscored by a disciplined chorus chant, "Strength and muscle and jungle work" and droning incantations layered with aggressive electric guitar as the song wanes. During the album's accompanying Jungle Tour, "Jungle Work" translated into a highly theatrical live rendition that utilized a smoke-filled stage, strobe lights, and prerecorded gunfire for special effects, with Zevon dressed in camouflage fatigues, crawling, tumbling, hiding behind amps and flaunting martial arts moves he learned from private training sessions that Kim Lankford arranged with actor Chuck Norris's younger brother, Aaron. The histrionics climax with two uniformed roadies carrying the wounded soldier-of-fortune Zevon out on a stretcher.

Zevon's most intense reflection on past mistakes and future possibilities lies in "Empty Handed Heart," a parting piano ballad in the vein of "Accidentally Like a Martyr" and "Hasten Down the Wind," tinted in shades of Joni Mitchell's *Blue*. Following the Pinecrest rehab, the core of the Zevons' relationship changed, with Crystal and Warren never able to redefine their roles and find fresh compatibility that would allow them to move forward together. A little over a year after the intervention, the couple's serial separations descended to the inevitability of divorce. In this farewell love letter to Crystal, Zevon is as desperate as he is honorable as he tries to explain his "heart-jinxed condition" and why their marriage would not work. Aware of time "rolling like a rockslide down a hill," Zevon remains torn, wondering about falling in love again while also acknowledging that "no one will ever take the place of you." Linda Ronstadt graces the song's heartache with a gorgeous descant, a haunting reminiscence of love left behind that coincides with Zevon repeating, "Then I've thrown down diamonds in the sand." Zevon offers a final line of advice to his wife, "Leave the fire behind you and start," as he will "be playing it by ear, left here with an empty handed heart." Profoundly personal and its circumstances universal, "Empty Handed Heart" is certainly among the most poignant songs in Zevon's body of work. Curiously, Crystal was initially upset at critic Jay Cocks' interpretation of the song in his review of the album, even though he called it a "centerpiece" and "classic." Crystal wrote an emotional letter which she intended to send to *Rolling Stone*, though Paul Nelson convinced her not to follow through.

SOUTHERN CULTURE ON THE SKIDS: REDNECKS, HIPPIES, REBELS

If "Empty Handed Heart" is one of Zevon's most intimate songs, "Play It All Night Long" is among his most idiosyncratic and caustic. Zevon trespasses on the "Songs of the South" subgenre with his noir viewpoint, and he is whistling the dueling *Deliverance* theme more than he is "Dixie." "Play It All Night Long" echoes Tony Joe White's swampy "Polk Salad Annie," recorded at legendary Muscle Shoals in 1968; it fills in a bizarre blank halfway between satirist Randy Newman's *Good Old Boys* (1974) and rebel Tom Petty's *Southern Accents* (1985); and foreshadows James McMurtry's "Choctaw Bingo" in 2002. More specifically, Zevon bizarrely triangulates the 1970s mythical feud between Neil Young and the band Lynyrd Skynyrd.

As the turbulent 1960s climaxed into a new decade, Young turned his ragged hippie vison from campus unrest at Kent State and "four dead in Ohio" toward the South. His distant gaze resulted in one of his best-known songs in an extraordinary body of work, "Southern Man," on *After the Gold Rush* (1970), and "Alabama" on *Harvest*, the best-selling album of 1972. With the two songs, Young unknowingly fired the first resounding shots in what became a lyrical Civil War. The vivid backdrop in "Southern Man" conveys contrast: cotton and black, tall white mansions, and little shacks. Young confronts the regions' misplaced morality, segregationist practices, and racism. Amidst the screaming, bullwhips cracking, and crosses burning fast, the question "Southern man when will you pay them back?" evolves into a wailing plea, "How long? How long?" The indignation becomes a more reasoning visitor's voice in "Alabama." The images may be more "down home," with "banjos playin' through the broken glass" and "old folks tied in white ropes . . . shaking hands, making friends," yet the troubled undercurrent persists— witness the "Cadillac with a wheel in the ditch and a wheel on the track." Young's previous plea, "How long?" now asks, "What's going wrong?" frustrated at the ruin and lack of progress despite the Union's efforts to help.

Young's condemnations struck a chord. To some, he represented the worst kind of outsider—a hippie from California who was not even a natural-born American, but an outsider from Ontario, Canada. In 1974 Lynyrd Skynyrd, a Jacksonville, Florida, rock band led by Ronnie Van Zant, defended Dixie with "Sweet Home Alabama," an editorial-like response to Young's denunciations and stereotypes. Lynyrd Skynyrd was a central part of the emerging Southern rock subgenre, a loud, aggressive, and occasionally crude guitar-driven sound with roots in country-western, gospel, rhythm and blues, and often incorporating swamp, boogie beat, and jazz-length improvisations. The fiercely provincial music voiced unwavering faith in Southern culture, perhaps best embodied in the Charlie Daniels Band's fiddle-driven anthem, "The South's Gonna Do It Again."

The movement received its impetus from Phil Walden, manager of the late Otis Redding, when he began Capricorn Records in Macon, Georgia. The first act Walden signed was the Allman Brothers, whose fleeting reign as pioneers of the sectional strand of music diminished following Duane Allman's motorcycle death in 1971. New bands arose to carry the Confederate cause, among them the Charlie Daniels and Marshall Tucker bands, Elvin Bishop, the Outlaws, and Wet Willie. Lynyrd Skynyrd was perhaps the only band who came close to living up to the Allman Brothers' guitar-frenzy legacy. They also one-upped the brothers by utilizing a three-piece lead guitar section which helped popularize such songs as "Free Bird," a tribute to Duane Allman. The song's legacy sustains in part as a humorous universal concert encore shout, "Free Bird!" no matter who is on stage performing.

"Sweet Home Alabama" was Lynyrd Skynyrd's biggest hit; the title was eventually adapted as the state's license plate slogan in 2009. The widely interpreted regional homage to a way of life embraces patriotism, working class and family values, comin' home, and loving the governor. It was also a "response record" or "answer song" aimed at Young and his condescending view of the region. Van Zant expresses more Southern hostility than hospitality toward Young. Having "heard Mr. Young sing about us" and "ol' Neil put us down," he scolds, "Well I hope Neil Young will remember, a Southern man don't need him around anyhow," punctuated with "Sweet Home Alabama." The progression is mildly amusing, going from formal address ("Mr. Young") to Southern politeness ("Ol' Neil") to a stern "no trespassing" warning to "Neil Young" that conjures a hackneyed image of Van Zant rocking cautiously contented on his front porch with a loaded shotgun, filled with Southern pride.

The fabled feud accumulated a rich mythology, both personally and musically, with their sectional strife perhaps most completely chronicled in the enshrining "Ronnie and Neil" on the Drive-By Truckers' two-act *Southern Rock Opera* (2001). Lyrics from Young's "Walk On" from *On the Beach* (1974), released the same year as "Sweet Home Alabama," were interpreted to be as much about Van Zant as they were about Young's parting with Crosby, Stills, and Nash: "I heard some people been talkin' me down/Bring up my name pass it round. . . . They'll do their thing, I'll do mine." The animosity between Young and Van Zant was overstated. The two were mutual admirers. There were rumors that after hearing that Lynyrd Skynyrd was interested in recording one of his songs, Young sent an early demo of his nihilistic ballad "Powderfinger" to the band, thinking they might record the song before his version appeared on *Rust Never Sleeps* (1979). On the cover of the Lynyrd Skynyrd's fifth album, *Street Survivors* (1977), featuring hits "That Smell" and "What's Your Name," Van Zant is wearing a Young *Tonight's the Night* t-shirt, one of several he owned and frequently wore during concerts. On October 17, 1977, three days after the album's release and only two months after Elvis Presley's death, the band's private plane crashed en route to Baton Rouge, Louisiana, killing the pilot, copilot, the group's road manager, and three band members, including Van Zant. The legend was magnified in the tragedy, with proliferating speculation that Van Zant was buried wearing a Neil Young t-shirt.

"PLAY THAT DEAD BAND'S SONG"

With "Play It All Night Long," Zevon joins the fray, a mocking mediator who taps into the Young-Skynyrd mythos with a twisted third-party perspective on their exchange. Van Zant likely would not have taken kindly to Mr. Zevon's vision of the Deep Dark South. David Lindley, whose signature slide guitar accentuates Zevon's derisive family portrait, and who has covered "Play It All Night Long" along with numerous other Zevon works, considers the song one of Zevon's strangest and best. Zevon reciprocates, stating in the liner notes of his 1996 anthology that "Lindley's guitar parts make it one of my favorite tracks." He also divulges that "Play It All Night Long" "was written really fast on marijuana around the synthesizer ostinato."

The symphony selection, "Interlude No. 1," is a misplaced and misleading prelude that bridges "Empty Handed Heart" with "Play It All Night Long." The three-song sequence cascades from a purposeful piano ballad to the classical sophistication of the interlude to a fluttering snare drum and stomping Scottish jig melody that provide a musical bed resembling a funeral or execution march.

The literary influences shift south, with Zevon borrowing a page from the gothic and grotesque strands of Flannery O'Conner and William Faulkner. Zevon's creepy kinfolk eclipse Randy Newman's cast of rednecks, crackers, freaks, a Birmingham steel worker, and "the famous Naked Man" in *Good Old Boys*. He even dashes the lyrics with regional dialect proclivities such as "ain't" to accent authenticity and magnify the stereotype, while rattling off each peculiar trait with methodical delight. The opening couplet may be as salient a lead line as there is anywhere: "Grandpa pissed his pants again/He don't give a damn." A lurid descent into dysfunction and rural degeneration swiftly ensues. There is post-traumatic stress—Brother Billy, with "both guns drawn, he ain't been right since Viet Nam"; incest—"Daddy's doing Sister Sally"; suffering and disease—"Grandma's dying of cancer now/ The cattle all have brucellosis." The line was informed by Zevon's recent reading of the Newton Thornburg novel, *Black Angus*, about a family farm in the Missouri Ozarks in danger of foreclosure. Despite the clan's hardship, there is hope—"We'll get through somehow," and a means of coping—"going down to the Dew Drop Inn, see if I can drink enough." As if reporting the discoveries during a cultural anthropological case study, Zevon delivers his disdainful pronouncement on rural simplicity—"There ain't much to country living/Sweat, piss, jizz and blood"—his pitch ascending on each syllable to emphasize the backwoods idiosyncrasies.

The chorus, an irreverent abstraction of the Lynyrd Skynyrd anthem, kinks the cornerstones of family, community, and blaring music into an odd nocturnal ritual: "Sweet Home Alabama/ play that dead band's song/Turn those speakers up full blast/play it all night long." Zevon sardonically references Lynyrd Skynyrd's inevitable demise following their plane crash three years earlier. He is more subtle in his allusion to Van Zant's famous studio utterance, "Turn it up," that was unintentionally recorded at the beginning of "Sweet Home Alabama."

Zevon depicts an implicit Alabama that is comparable to the southern state that Young witnessed. The chorus's weird invocation of the Skynyrd song in an endless loop repeating all night may be interpreted as another metaphor for the depraved South that is analogous with the broken-down Cadillac that Young observed. However, unlike Young, Zevon doesn't vent, accuse, ask any questions, plead for explanations, or deliver judgments. There may even be a scant trace of empathy in his scorn, with Zevon relating to aspects of the family's debauchery, particularly the guns and drinking. As the closing track of side one, amidst the album's healing and heartache, the backwoods noir of "Play It All Night Long" is a sneering reminder of Zevon's berserk brilliance. In an ironic twist of fate, Zevon and Lynyrd Skynyrd's "Sweet Home Alabama" were reunited in 2008, their song samples mashed up in Kid Rock's "All Summer Long."

A SHOOTER, SPACEMAN, AND BIG GORILLA: "STAY THE WILD AGE?"

A desperado undercurrent pervades the album's entire side two sequence, beginning with "Jeannie Needs a Shooter," a song instigated by Zevon's interest in a Springsteen title. Springsteen was a Zevon fan from his first encounter with Zevon at a New York show in which Zevon performed a version of Muddy Waters's "I'm a Man," spelling out his own name—Warren—instead of "M-a-n." "It was one of those classic things that told you everything you needed to know about him," said Springsteen (C. Zevon, 156). Springsteen admired "the beautiful stuff Warren came up with," observing that Zevon "had the ability and gift of beautiful voicings that he orchestrated his records with—a lot of what was Coplandesque in different parts. He had a beautiful head for arrangements, and the types of arrangements he used were always creative" (156).

Zevon was aware of the "Jeannie Needs A Shooter" title through Springsteen's manager Jon Landau, who "really wanted Warren and Bruce to get some kind of relationship going because they were two of the most talented people I knew" (C. Zevon, 148). Zevon's persistent interest over time prompted Springsteen to suggest Zevon supply the lyrics for the tuneless title. The resulting song, which adroitly employs a string arrangement and a Joe Walsh guitar solo, was a Freudian Western saga. The Shooter, "born down by the river where the dirty water flows," yearns for Jeannie from Knightstown, despite her father, a lawman, "swearing he'd shoot me dead." The love-at-first-sight, had-to-make-her-mine bravado ends on a cold and rainy night down by the border. While riding hard to meet Jeannie to fulfill their getaway vow, "a shot rang out behind." As the fallen suitor lay there in the darkness with a pistol by his side, "Jeannie and her father rode off into the night."

Prefaced by his classical "Interlude No. 2," Zevon's ode to major league baseball pitcher Bill Lee is not the typical hero ballad within an "America's favorite pastime" backdrop. Lee's iconoclastic qualities made him a usual suspect for one of Zevon's pop portraits. The wily left hander with the Boston Red Sox (1968–1978) and Montreal Expos (1978–1982) was one of professional sports all-time free spirits. Lee was a jock rarity—socially conscious, well read and informed, and philosophical. His psychedelic Zen-vernacular and cosmic ponderings of life's contradictions and meanings earned him the label "Spaceman." The witty nonconformist was not one for sport speak and clichés. He routinely cited Thoreau, Mao, Vonnegut, Chief Joseph, Einstein, Russian esotericist P. D. Ouspensky, and rockers such as Zevon. Lee played Zevon's music around the clubhouse, explaining, "Most ballplayers like music they can hit or fuck to, I was into more lyrical things" ("Random

Notes," 1979, 34). Interviews with Lee were not confined to sports outlets, with his musings ranging from reincarnation to the Coriolis effect on how a curve ball spins.

Zevon was as drawn to Lee's anti-establishment values as he was to Lee's intellect, world awareness, and humor. During spring training in 1979, Lee casually remarked that he used marijuana, though he was careful never to state that he *smoked* it, but sprinkled it on his buckwheat pancakes in the morning because it made him impervious to the bus fumes when he jogged six miles to the ballpark each day. Baseball commissioner Bowie Kuhn fined Lee for the statement. After engaging in a legal battle with Kuhn, Lee eventually paid the fine, sending the $250, plus an extra dollar, to the charity of his choice, an Indian mission in Alaska. Lee had the last word on the incident when he appeared on the cover of the July 1980 issue of *High Times*, a monthly magazine devoted to cannabis. A large-font interview excerpt filled the cover space, with an image of Lee with a devilish grin in the lower right corner: *HIGH TIMES: "What would happen if Bowie Kuhn levied a $250 fine against every player in baseball who smoked dope?" BILL LEE: "He'd be a rich man."*

In July 1979, Zevon invited Lee to his Hollywood Hills house while the Expos were in town for a series with the Dodgers. *Rolling Stone's* "Random Notes" column provided a brief account of the mutual fans' Dos Equis–fueled all-nighter, highlighted by an exclusive preview of the songs Zevon had been working on for *Bad Luck Streak in Dancing School*. Lee commented that the seven songs Zevon auditioned "had a lot of classical feeling." As a parting gift, Zevon presented Lee with the collected works of T. S. Eliot. On the August 2, 1982, *Late Night*, Lee discussed the Zevon get-together with David Letterman, wryly revealing that he talked with Zevon about staying in shape, suggesting "he walk down the hill to get his vodka."

Zevon's rebel-hero homage to Lee is succinct at 1:35 minutes, and simple with piano, harmonica, and trace of a Glenn Frey harmony. The opening lines that convey Lee's individualist dilemma within baseball's institution and traditions echo the R. P. McMurphy character played by Jack Nicholson in the 1975 film adaptation of Ken Kesey's *One Flew Over the Cuckoo's Nest* (1962): "You're supposed to sit on your ass and nod at stupid things/Man that's hard to do," followed by the no-win realization that "if you don't, they'll screw you, and if you do, they'll screw you too." The deft duality of "standing in the middle of the diamond all alone" depicts an isolated insurgent within the solitary sphere of the pitcher's mound. Zevon cleverly salutes Lee's outspokenness: "And sometimes I say things I shouldn't, like . . ." followed by a harmonica refrain, as if to fill in the blanks with one of Lee's quotes. The line repeats, as does the harmonica, receding into a bluesy fadeout.

Personal transformation persists in "Gorilla, You're a Desperado," with Zevon changing places with a big gorilla at the Los Angeles Zoo, who snatched his glasses and keys to his BMW. According to son Jordan, gorillas and skulls were among his father's obsessions. His earliest album, *Wanted Dead or Alive*, contained the song "Gorilla," with "Leave My Monkey Alone" (1987), "Monkey Wash, Donkey Rinse" (1995), "Porcelain Monkey" (2000), and stirring with a "monkey's paw" in "Genius" (2001) to follow. The tenor is light and self-satirizing, with a playful nod to the Eagles' 1972 album and hit title song. Ironically, good sport Don Henley provides harmonies. Zevon remains penitent—he's even sorry his apartment is a mess—though he is skeptical of his replacement, or the new version of himself. "Most of all I'm sorry I made you blue/ I'm guessing the gorilla will too." The self-references are thinly veiled as the ape divorces, gets depressed, goes through Transactional Analysis, plays racquetball, runs in the rain, and is "laying low at L'Ermitage," a chic Beverly Hills hotel. The most telling line points to the perils of record industry success: "Still he's shackled to a platinum chain."

Earnest self-assessment is also present in "Bed of Coals," cowritten with T-Bone Burnett, whose career evolved from guitarist in Bob Dylan's "Rolling Thunder Review" in 1975 to the Alpha Band and solo singer-songwriter, eventually becoming one of popular music's most prolific producers during the past 30-plus years. The Grammy-winning Burnett's mark is particularly ingrained in the Americana roots amalgam, a genre that he helped shape with the soundtrack to the Coen brothers' (Joel and Ethan) film, *O Brother, Where Art Thou?* (2000). Ben Keith's pedal steel laces Zevon's deliberate piano pacing and world-weary delivery, evoking a Western saloon confessional in which Zevon contemplates his self-inflicted pain. He is not the typical firewalker scampering across the bed of hot coals. Zevon rolls and tumbles, and is more fixed than fleeting, lying there, crying out of control. Nor is the bed of nails magic; instead it is torturous with Zevon bleeding, feeling every needle that pierces through his heart. His life has been misdirection, "through the smoke behind the veils." The allusions to Zevon's rock bottom, rehabilitation, and redemption are palpable—"lying on a bed of stone . . . dying all alone, I pray for the power to turn it around"—arriving at the pronouncement, "I'm too old to die young and too young to die now/And I can't play the part."

The awareness of death carries over into the final song, with a view more fatalistic than averting. The album's pervasive self-reflection arrives at a conclusion that counters the opening song's vow, "swear to God I'll change." "Wild Age" is an anthem to recklessness with a slight cautionary undercurrent. The third-person point of view may project more broadly to a universal rebel, but does not obscure the self-portrait. The dissident "leaning on the street light listening to some song inside" is Zevon. Defiance and destiny conspire to deflate, if not defeat, the rehabilitation efforts: "Well, they tried so hard to hold him, heaven knows how hard they tried /But he's made up his mind/ He's the restless kind. And, "The law can't stop him; no one can stop 'em. . . . He's the wild age." As in "Bed of Coals," Zevon is aware of the fatal consequences: "Mostly when the reckless years end/Something's left to save/ Some of them keep running/'Til they run straight in their graves." The refrain's extended fade lingers for the final 2:30 minutes, with "stay" a telling word choice. As the Henley and Frey harmonies soothingly sway, "Stay the wild age, Stay the wild age," escorted by Lindley's guitar, Zevon frequently interjects his emphatic "Hah!" and a raucous "Wild age!" as an expression of resistance to a redemptive alternative and acceptance of his reckless fate.

Bad Luck Streak in Dancing School reached number 20 on the *Billboard* Pop chart, while its single, "A Certain Girl," settled in at number 57. Reviews were slightly mixed. Critics were generally positive about the album, admiring Zevon's focus, maturity, and how he demonstrated more bravery than bravado in addressing his failings. There were others who viewed the third Asylum record to be a "step down" from his two previous recordings, with the most common critique directed at the music. Some found Zevon's ambitious attempts to expand his sound flawed and overextended, resulting in a stylistic mess (Erlewine, Bogdanov, and Woodstra, 850). Despite some unevenness, *Bad Luck Streak in Dancing School*'s best qualities further validated its predecessors,

Warren Zevon and *Excitable Boy.* Not only did the album provide a sampling of Zevon's classical ambitions, it revealed a glimmer of redemption in Zevon's gaze into the dark mirror of his distinctive songwriting.

ROCKING AT THE ROXY: "DRUNK ON RESURRECTION AND GRATITUDE"

Any critical wavering about Zevon diminished later in 1980 with the release of the duly titled *Stand in the Fire*, a live album gleaned from five nights of rousing performances at West Hollywood's legendary club, the Roxy on Sunset Boulevard.

After a year in the studio and working at his personal recovery, Zevon was eager to tour. Instead of enlisting the steadfast L.A. sessionsists, the Mellow Mafia, and singers who had backed his first two albums, Zevon, seeking a fresh start and clean slate, broke band rank and opted for a new lineup for the road. The only familiar player was East Coast lead guitarist David Landau, a survivor of the *Excitable Boy* tour debacle. When Zevon approached Landau about joining the tour again, he re-introduced his new self, saying, "David, I'd like you to meet Warren Zevon. You've never met him before, you know" (Avery, 388). Zevon recruited Boulder, a band from the Colorado club circuit led by Stan Bush, who were also Asylum label mates. The compatibility initially seemed suspect. Boulder's version of Zevon's "I'll Sleep When I'm Dead" on their debut album in 1979 aligned more with Survivor's "Eye of the Tiger" than it did Zevon's sound. However their audition, which consisted of a spirited rendition of "Johnny B. Goode," convinced Zevon there was a roughhouse chemistry with him fronting that would translate well to a live setting and an in-concert recording. He audaciously hit the road with the relative unknowns. Zevon titled his newfound group and the tour, "The Dog Ate the Part We Didn't Like," borrowing the line from *Panama* by his friend, novelist Thomas McGuane. The epigram also appears on the album's inner liner note sleeve.

The compact ten-song set draws from Zevon's first three albums, with predictable emphasis on songs such as "Poor Poor Pitiful Me" and "Lawyers, Guns and Money" that were suitable for hard-rocking, no-holds-barred live renditions. Though predominantly consisting of Zevon's better-known songs, the album averts "greatest hits live" exclusivity with the inclusion of new material. Two are aggressive Zevon compositions: the stomping title tune extolling the virtues of electric guitarists and redheads that opens the album; and "The Sin," a stark punk homily about war crimes against friends and lovers which builds to Zevon's primal scream in the final chorus, "How am I gonna pay for the sin?" The third is a rousing closing cover medley, "Bo Diddley's a Gunslinger/Bo Diddley." Zevon said he fulfilled one of his greatest artistic ambitions in recording "Bo Diddley," his all-time favorite song: "Lyrically and musically, I consider it the apotheosis of the rock and roll song. It's a whole world view." Of the performance, Zevon added obtusely, "We did it very Lorca," presumably a reference to Spanish poet and dramatist Frederico García Lorca.

Zevon's compulsion to tour with a spontaneously assembled band paid off. The group rocked loud, hard, and tight, bringing Zevon's sharper edges to the forefront and complementing his kinetic stage presence. During concerts on the tour at larger venues such as the Palladium, Zevon's performance was so dynamic and physical that some reviews criticized him for exhibitionism. Zevon acknowledged there was a "lunatic quality" to the Roxy shows, complicated in part, by medication he was taking. Though he had for the time being banished his falling-down-drunk self-saboteur, Zevon strained a nerve while "doing some James Brown wanna-be dance in rehearsal," and was using painkillers and steroids supervised by a doctor recommended by members of the Eagles. Jackson Browne referred to the phase as Zevon's "karate on speed period" (Fricke 2007, 7).

The physically and mentally fit Zevon was as focused as he was frenzied. There was a jubilant intensity in his performance, from the Elvisian shiver in his delivery to his Jerry Lee Lewis–like piano-pounding exuberance to frequent sparks of spontaneity and unruliness. During "Poor Poor Pitiful Me," Zevon asks: "Where's George Gruel, my road manager, my best friend?" He shouts a command to Gruel to "come on out here. Get up and dance or I'll kill ya. That goes for the rest of you, too." In a photo in the album's inner sleeve, Gruel is wearing an "ALL HELL IS BREAKING LOOSE" t-shirt, a likely remnant from the Excitable Boy tour. The album cover image of Zevon, center stage in a pelvic thrust, six-gun slinger stance, arms bent at the waist with both hands pointing finger guns, is fittingly blurred, implying kinesis and unbridled energy.

Zevon's vigorous delight is further evident in his sly lyric alterations that invoke and shuffle fellow artists, weapons, and world leaders. The name dropping is particularly prevalent in "Werewolves of London." In the alliterative couplet "Little old lady got mutilated late last night," Zevon injects "Brian De Palma again" rather than "Werewolves." The substitution is fitting, as the director is known for psychological thrillers and graphic violence in his films, among them *Carrie* (1976), *Dressed to Kill* (1980), *Body Double* (1981), and *Scarface* (1983). Zevon also pays playful homage to fellow songwriters, cleverly converting, "I'd like to meet his tailor," into a gleeful shout, "And he's looking for James Taylor." And to the song's "I saw . . ." litany, he adds, "I saw Jackson Browne 'walking slow down the avenue' (a cunning insertion of a Browne verse from "Farther Along" on *Late for the Sky* [1974])—You know his heart is perfect" (rather than "his hair is perfect"). And in a subtle, self-referential nod to sobriety, Zevon rephrases into a "werewolf drinking a Perrier at Trader Vic's" rather than a Piña Colada.

Zevon also veers from the verbatim on "I'll Sleep When I'm Dead," with "the .38 special up on the shelf" upgraded to "a .44 Magnum," and a reassuring growl, "And I don't intend to use it on myself." The revisions turn political on "Mohammed's Radio," the (original) album's lone restrained rendition. Instead of "The sheriff's got his problems, too," Zevon inserts "Ayatollah," nicely setting up the Iranian leader substitution with a dramatic pause, followed by a compassionate, "Even Jimmy Carter's got the highway blues," in reference to the president's failed bid for re-election in 1980. Carter's defeat to Ronald Reagan was mainly attributed to a lingering international hostage crisis. The episode was pivotal in U.S.-Iran relations, marked by the 52 American diplomats and citizens held hostage for 444 days, from November 4, 1979, to January 20, 1981. They were released minutes after Reagan's inauguration as the new president.

Zevon's paraphrasing was not a ploy exclusive to the recorded Roxy shows. The citations were frequent and freewheeling, a showmanship signature of Zevon's live performances, no matter the venue. As representative examples, during a May 15, 1985, concert at the State Theater in Kalamazoo, Michigan, Zevon's alterations to "Werewolves of London" included references to "On Broadway" and "Born in the U.S.A.";

notorious convicted murderer Gary Gilmore, who demanded and received his own death sentence—an execution by firing squad—in Utah
in 1977; and actor "Jeff Bridges buying a used car." Musically, Zevon
seamlessly spliced the Rolling Stones' "Start Me Up" into a piano prelude to "Poor Poor Pitiful Me," and he covered "Wild Thing" playing an
acoustic guitar behind his back. Months later, on November 14, at the
Moonshadow Saloon in Atlanta, Georgia, Zevon complied with his requisite tour-town substitution for "London," singing "Werewolves of Atlanta." With "Mohammed's Radio," Zevon further freshened the "sheriff's got his problems, too" line from *Stand in the Fire*'s "Ayatollah's got
his problems, too," tweaked into (Ford and Chrysler CEO Lee) "Iacoc-
ca's got his problems, too." Zevon also enhanced the version with a nifty
swerve into a snippet of the Commodores' 1985 hit, "Nightshift." The
peer-conscious name dropping was also evident in Zevon's droll preface
to his performance of the Springsteen cowrite "Jeannie Needs A Shooter:" "Bruce, I think he's gonna make it." Zevon closed the show with a
rousing version of "Not Fade Away" that leaned toward the Rolling
Stones' Bo Diddley beat version slightly more than the Buddy Holly
original.

Commercially, *Stand in the Fire* charted at number 80, while critically accumulating five-star reviews. Perhaps the album's most obvious
shortcoming was just that—it was short. The ten-song set seemed an
insufficient sampling of the series of Roxy shows, particularly considering the high level of performance. When *Stand in the Fire* received the
Rhino Records reissue treatment in 1986 (for the first time on compact
disc) following a lengthy and unfortunate out-of-print exile, the edition
included four previously unissued tracks—"Johnny Strikes Up the
Band," "Play It All Night Long," "Frank and Jesse James," and "Hasten
Down the Wind." The appended placement of the songs at the end of
the original sequencing of the album evoked the feeling of an encore.

David Fricke, who contributed a wonderful essay in the liner notes
of the record's reissue, and Zevon advocate Paul Nelson were the van-
guard among the music writers who considered *Stand in the Fire* a
transcendent in-concert album, comparable to Lou Reed's *Rock and
Roll Animal* (1974), Jackson Browne's *Running on Empty* (1977), and
Neil Young's two-record set *Live Rust* (1979). More specifically, Fricke
suggested that *Stand in the Fire* was Zevon's first real rock and roll
record, and "a portrait of the artist as a tightrope walker, defiantly

dancing the hairline between emotional exorcism and mass entertainment" (2007, 4).

The "entertainment" endpoint in Fricke's poetic characterization of Zevon as an artist is intriguing. Browne once asked Zevon if he considered himself an entertainer, to which Zevon replied, "Yeah, absolutely." Zevon's answer, and his certainty, surprised Browne, "because I've always regarded the people whose work I love the most to be beyond that, above entertainment." Browne's idealist skepticism made sense. On the surface, it was perplexing that the elitist, cultured Zevon purportedly considered himself an entertainer just as much or more than he thought of himself as an artist or writer. Yet Zevon's perspective ricochets to the East Coast and his piano man contemporary Billy Joel's "The Entertainer" on *Streetlife Serenade* (1974), a misanthropic look at fleeting fame, public tastes, and the music industry. Zevon's rationale to Browne's query was simple: "If you're not entertaining, you're not doing anything" (Fricke 2007, 5).

Zevon was true to that maxim on *Stand in the Fire*. The noir songwriter, composer, sardonic humorist, and desperado that had been varyingly established as attributes of Zevon's artistic identity on his preceding records, and that certainly contributed to his entertainment appeal, were all present on stage at the Roxy. But perhaps as much as any Zevon persona, it was Warren Zevon, the entertainer and rocker, who emerged front and center. *Stand in the Fire* faithfully captures Zevon's notorious vivacity and dynamic presence that distinguished his live performances throughout his career, whether electric or acoustic, solo or with a band, drunk or now sober. On his later concert recording *Learning to Flinch* (1993), Zevon's solo acoustic performance displayed a similar vitality as *Stand in the Fire*'s full band rave-up.

Stand in the Fire is more than a riveting sound souvenir of Zevon's five rousing nights at the Roxy. The record is a galvanizing celebration; it is at once an explosion, a triumph, a comeback, a rescue. Zevon avoided a coward's death, and appeared to be focused on making up for a decade of self-inflicted disorder. He compared being onstage at the Roxy in front of a supportive, hometown crowd to "rescuing the little boy who'd fallen through the ice . . . while the whole world is watching" (Nelson 1981, 70). In Fricke's view, Zevon performed as if "drunk on resurrection and gratitude" (6). During Zevon's touching introduction to the solo piano rendition of "Hasten Down the Wind"—one of the four additional tracks on the reissued album, and its closing song—the self-aware, redeemed antihero tells the audience, "Speaking as one who has abused privilege for a long time, I tell you, it's great to be alive."

6

LOOKING FOR THE NEXT BEST THING

With two albums released in 1980, the new decade was off to a productive and promising start for Warren Zevon. However, there were looming shifts within the struggling music industry that would impact the course of Zevon's recording arc during the remainder of the decade. Interestingly, Zevon's trusty lead guitarist David Landau whispered suspicions during the Roxy performances that became *Stand in the Fire*. Landau indicated that he "was aware that the live record was to fulfill a contractual obligation," and at the same time "had a sense that Warren's success was on a downswing" (C. Zevon, 173).

"VIDEO KILLED THE RADIO STAR"

On August 1, 1981, midway between *Stand in the Fire* in 1980 and Zevon's next record, *The Envoy* in 1982, the declaration—"Ladies and gentleman, rock and roll"—announced the arrival of the cable music television network, MTV. The debut was brimming with "giant leap" allusions to music's "new frontier." The opening sequence featured NASA space shuttle footage, from countdown to liftoff; the iconic image of astronaut Neil Armstrong's "one small step" onto the moon's surface during the Apollo mission in 1969, with the stars and stripes on the American flag replaced by the MTV logo. The foretelling music video, the Buggles' "Video Killed the Radio Star," followed, and MTV officially launched.

While a cable network devoted exclusively to music videos was groundbreaking, the music video aesthetic itself had been present in film and television for years. Director Richard Lester laid the foundation by visualizing music narratives in the Beatles' 1964 film, *A Hard Day's Night*. The form continued to be present in 39 episodes of the Beatles' Saturday morning cartoon series, which aired for three seasons on ABC (1965–1969), and in the Monkees' madcap musical adventures on NBC (1966–1968).

MTV and its marketing synergy revitalized, if not saved, the music business. Rock music, its culture, and the record industry entered the 1980s in a state of disarray and recession. In a "state of the music industry" address published in *Rolling Stone*'s 1980 year-end issue, critic Dave Marsh suggested that the music industry may have been the biggest star the 1970s created. Neil Young affirmed Marsh's notion during his 1979 "Rust Never Sleeps Tour," appearing on stage dwarfed by oversized amps, instruments, and mike stands, a statement by Young that "the music business was getting so huge performers could feel like little kids" (Crowe, 62). The disproportionality was glaring, with distortions other than those represented in Young's stage props. For example, Fleetwood Mac's *Tusk* sold two million copies in 1979, yet was not considered a hit because their album *Rumours* from two years earlier sold six times that many units.

Numerous factors contributed to the industry's financially stressed circumstances. Production costs escalated, while record sales steadily declined within the shifting demographic of the music marketplace. Widespread home taping also syphoned sales. As evidence, in 1979, platinum album awards (1 million units sold) were down to 42 from 112 in 1978, while gold albums (500,000 units sold) declined to 112 from 193 the previous year. In addition, an undeclared war with radio over programming and promotion further hindered profitability.

There were ramifications for artists and their music. In Marsh's assessment, "suddenly, records were judged not on the artistry—or even whether they're hits—but on their chance of putting the machinery back into gear. Almost nowhere, and from no one, does anyone presently feel a sense of reaching" (2). Record companies were less inclined than ever to invest in marginally commercial acts, or push hard to break in new artists. Tour support for mid-level acts was reduced as audiences with less disposable income were more selective about the concerts they attended. Marsh believed the problem could be summed up in one word—marketing.

By the decade's cusp, rock culture had splintered, its foundation fragmented from community to corporation, with an entrepreneurial emphasis over artistry. Emerging genres such as reggae, disco, new wave, and punk did not prove to be a sustaining "third coming" that would resuscitate the music industry's economy. Nor was there a "next" Elvis or Beatles or Dylan, until MTV in 1981, which became music's "next big thing" for the industry, audience, and artists alike. MTV represented a cross-industry convergence between music, film, and television. The music video/clip format supplemented, if not supplanted, radio singles as the exposure vehicle for artists and their albums. Music video was the new jukebox and Top 40. The cable music network, its VJs (video versions of radio disc jockeys, or "DJs"), visual style, and montage editing attracted a younger audience and fostered an instant sensation, a videogenic environment that gave rise to artists such as Prince, Cyndi Lauper, Culture Club, the Eurythmics, Duran Duran, and parodist "Weird Al" Yankovic, and further elevated superstars Madonna, Michael Jackson, and Bruce Springsteen to megastar status.

DESPERADO DECRESCENDO

In the midst of MTV's onset and the burgeoning music video movement, Zevon hit the road for a solo tour, with meager record label support. His lone traveling companion and crew consisted of road manager George Gruel, who "had a two-track tape of three songs under my arm and we did every European version of *American Bandstand*" (C. Zevon, 174). Gruel documented his years of adventures on the road alongside Zevon, eventually compiling over 150 rare photographs and commentary into an aide-de-camp memoir, *Lawyers Guns & Photos*, published in 2013.

During that time a new album began to take shape, with the material informed by the international scene, along with the Hollywood circle of Zevon's girlfriend, actress Kim Lankford. According to Gruel, "We were in Belgium, and he's [Zevon] upstairs in the casino thinking he's James Bond, with his zillion dollar suits on. It was a movie, basically.

Back in L.A., Warren's out on the LAPD target range shooting guns, still in his own movie" (174).

Zevon's fifth Asylum album, *The Envoy*, released in July 1982, marked a turning point in Zevon's recording chronology. Previous producers Waddy Wachtel and Greg Ladanyi joined Zevon to fashion a sound that frequently utilized the synthesizer. Like *Bad Luck Streak in Dancing School*, *The Envoy*'s title, album cover images and opening/title song were thematic. While the album is dedicated to Lankford, the album title and song "The Envoy" were inspired by veteran U.S. diplomat and special envoy to the Middle East, Philip Habib, and his high-profile shuttle mediation during Israel's Lebanon infiltration in 1982. Zevon viewed Habib as "just this kind of workmanlike, self-disciplined version of a James Bond–style agent" (Wild, 4).

Zevon's secret agent fixation is evident in Jimmy Wachtel's cover photos and design. Set in an airport hangar, Zevon stands in the foreground, posed as an international man of intrigue, dressed in suit and tie, with a trench coat draped over his arm and newspaper in hand. He is surrounded by an entourage of well-dressed, sunglasses-wearing, agent types and a pilot. Some are talking into hand-held devices, others hold briefcases, and another exits a limo. Their elongated shadows stretch across the concrete floor as a private jet awaits boarding in the background. Among the participants in the photo were Lankford's *Knot's Landing* costars Ted Shackelford and James Houghton. The rear cover features a tour montage of foreign newspaper articles and reviews about Zevon, black-and-white photos, air mail envelopes and stamps, guitar picks, foreign coins and currency, a crumpled cigarette pack, a micro-cassette recorder with tapes—one labeled "Symphonies Requiem Canticles"—and the album song list printed neatly in a pocket-sized ring-bound notebook.

Most of Zevon's familiar songwriting traits, themes, and moods circulate throughout *The Envoy*'s nine songs. The more maturing perspective that began to surface in *Bad Luck Streak in Dancing School* continues to evolve into acceptance rather than futile internal struggles. Zevon told *Rolling Stone*'s Mikal Gilmore that he thought of *The Envoy* as "Excitable Boy Grows Up" (49). The change is evident in the first cut, the "The Envoy," as Zevon's approach to foreign affairs involves a mediator rather than his customary mercenary or the CIA. The peacemaker tribute depicts a skilled delegate being routinely transported around the world's volatile hot spots, from the Middle East to Central America, to deal with various crises and threats to world peace. Within a portentous arrangement, Zevon nimbly frames the geopolitical conflicts in a quatrain: "Nuclear arms in the Middle East/Israel's attacking the Iraqis/The Syrians are mad at the Lebanese/and Baghdad does whatever she please." The song's international discord can also be read as a metaphor for Zevon's individual disorder. Zevon was drawn to Habib for qualities that were as personal as they were political, saying that he liked the envoy "because he has a will, he's a problem-solving kind of guy and because I need his kind of control" (Gilmore, 49). In the liner notes of his 1996 anthology, Zevon proudly mentions that Habib sent him a note of appreciation for the song on State Department stationery.

"The Overdraft," cowritten with friend and novelist Thomas McGuane, marks the beginning of numerous literary songwriting collaborations that became commonplace on Zevon's subsequent records. The Montana-based McGuane, whose own tales of debauchery in the 1970s earned him the title "Captain Berserko," is the author *The Sporting Club* (1968), *The Bushwhacked Piano* (1971), *Ninety-Two in the Shade* (1973), and *Panama* (1978), among other works. He also wrote the screenplays for the cattle rustler comedy *Rancho Deluxe* (1975), featuring Jeff Bridges and Sam Waterston, and *The Missouri Breaks* (1976), starring Jack Nicholson and Marlon Brando.

McGuane's and Zevon's paths crossed in Los Angeles when McGuane was working in the movie business during the day and Zevon was recording *The Envoy* at night. McGuane admitted that he and Zevon did not have the greatest comfort level, which he largely attributed to Zevon's intensity. He characterized Zevon as "prickly, complicated . . . not the kind of lost child you give a hug to." McGuane was concurrently enamored with Zevon's enigmatic character, with his life in rock and roll and his mind in high culture—art, serious literature, classical music. "It was an anomalous combination of traits, which was one of the things that was so interesting about him," said McGuane. "I was sitting around saying, 'Well, which one are we, Warren? Which will we be today?' That was always a mystery to me" (C. Zevon, 176). Their collaboration on "The Overdraft" reflects what McGuane referred to as Zevon's style, "everything dialed up to ten" (C. Zevon, 175). The song is a hard-driving, "just up against it, can't let go, don't take no for an answer" rollick, heightened by Lindsey Buckingham's fevered background vocal.

Zevon's outlook remains unruly and wry in places. The reckless recovery anthem that leads off the album's side two, "Ain't That Pretty at All," profiles the painful pursuits of someone who has seen, heard, and done everything but remains unimpressed and discontent. Here, Zevon converts the head-on-the-railroad-tracks penance of "Poor Poor Pitiful Me" into a sadistic sequel of anhedonia and nihilistic extremes that includes spending a short vacation getting a root canal, and wanting to return to the Louvre Museum in Paris to "get a good running start and hurl myself against the wall." His rationale for the merciless self-abuse is "'cause I'd rather feel bad than not feel anything at all."

"The Hula Hula Boys" is a droll cuckold calamity set in Hawaii. The adulterous escapades are frequent: "I saw her leave the luau with the one who parked the cars," swaying arm in arm with "the fat one from the swimming pool" and coming home from seeing the Polynesian band "with her hair all wet and clothes filled with sand." Amidst "the ukuleles playing down by the sea" there is hurt and humiliation: "I didn't have to come to Maui to be treated like a jerk/how do you think I feel when I see the bell boys smirk?" Zevon conceals cleverness in the chorus by utilizing the traditional Hawaiian verse—"ha `ina `ia mai ana ka pua-na"—an idiom meaning "disclose (or get to) the essential point" or essentially, "sing the chorus." Zevon's son Jordan, who was 13 at the time, was the only one who could pronounce the language, so Wachtel and Zevon enlisted him to sing the background parts. Excerpts from "The Hula Hula Boys" surfaced the following year in Hunter S. Thompson's *The Curse of the Lono* (1983), his gonzo memoir of the 1980 Honolulu Marathon and other island adventures. Thirty years later, in January 2013, in a season two episode of the HBO series *Enlightened*, Zevon's song provides a pitch-perfect and ironic soundtrack moment during the closing scene with actor Luke Wilson's character Levi at a Hawaiian drug and alcohol rehab center.

There are two brooding strands on *The Envoy* in which Zevon confronts mortality, pharmaceutical fate, and likely, his own fears. The autobiographical "Charlie's Medicine" is a requiem for a young, starstruck dope dealer who "used to sell me pills." Charlie, who worked at a pharmacy on Hollywood Boulevard where Zevon got his legitimate prescriptions, was gunned down by another drug dealer in the street in front of the apartment where he lived with his mother. Zevon's rumination is chilling. After revealing the details of the demise—"Some respectable doctor from Beverly Hills shot him in the heart"—Zevon cuts to an empty emotional core: "Charlie didn't feel a thing/Neither of them did. Poor kid." Despite regretting his association—"I gave Charlie all my money/What the hell was I thinking of?"—and recognizing the inevitability—"Charlie had to take his medicine" and "got his prescription filled"—Zevon nonetheless expresses sympathy while (literally) attending Charlie's funeral—"I came to say goodbye/I'm sorry Charlie died/I came to finish paying my bill."

With "Jesus Mentioned," Zevon joined the significant cross-section of songwriters who recorded songs of homage and critique about the life, death, and myth of Elvis Presley. The eclectic discography spans popular artists such as Billy Joel and U2 and avant-gardeans the Residents and Laurie Anderson, to alternative acts and fringe dwellers such as Mr. Bonus, Syd Straw, Death Ride '69, Pink Lincolns, Wall of Voodoo, and Dead Milkmen. Zevon weaves sacred and secular adoration into an austere acoustic dirge, his solemn vocal accompanied only by Wachtel on guitar. The somber meditation turns a ghoulish notion into an act of devotion as Zevon heads to Memphis (where he wrote the song) and Graceland thinking about the King, "remembering him sing." Zevon's visit is not Paul Simon's "Graceland" (1986), a place where "poor boys and pilgrims, we all shall be received"; nor is it Elvis Hitler's "Disgraceland" (1988). Zevon's eerie reverence is without redemption; there are shadows in the spirituality. Zevon blurs grave robbing with resurrection when he asks, "Can't you just imagine digging up the King? Begging him to sing about those heavenly mansions Jesus mentioned?" His delivery shivers slightly over Wachtel's meticulous, downbeat chords as he repeats a Jesus miracle allusion three times—"He went walking on the water"—before completing the verse, deeply intoning a demystifying—"with his pills."

Zevon's view may be morbid, but he isn't detached. The unassuming brilliance of his contemplation lies in his ability to hauntingly tap into the cultural consciousness and collective curiosity, envisioning the "what if" possibility and whispering suspicion during the Graceland tour when the guide states that visitation to the upstairs and kitchen are prohibited. Or the allure of the bathroom where Elvis died. The song's title alone evokes Elvis's final days and final moments when he reportedly had been reading *The Face of Jesus*, about the Shroud of Turin. Zevon clearly recognizes Elvis's religiosity, the Christ comparisons, and the grief and denial of the Presley-terian true believers. Many did not have to "imagine digging up the King" because they had refused to bury Elvis or repeatedly resurrected him following his death on August 16, 1977. "Elvis is alive" became a sustaining cultural phenomenon structured around a flourishing network of fanatics, a belief system, conspiracy theories such as witness protection, and widespread Elvis sightings and suspicions across the country in the aftermath of his "alleged" death. The social and religious movement was in large part stirred by author Gail Brewer-Giorgio's works, notably the novel *Orion* (1978), the story of a popular Southern singer who faked his death to escape fame; and *The Most Incredible Elvis Presley Story Ever Told*, retitled as *Is Elvis Alive?* (1988) and packaged with *The Elvis Tapes*, an audiocassette of voice verification, further proof that his death was a hoax. The decade-long spectacle was perhaps best summarized by the Mojo Nixon and Skid Roper novelty hit, "Elvis is Everywhere" (1987).

In the vast "songs about Elvis" canon, Zevon's "Jesus Mentioned" is an unsung narrative, aligning with Bruce Springsteen's "Johnny Bye Bye" (1985), the B-side of "I'm on Fire" that was adapted from Chuck Berry's "Bye Bye Johnny" into a vignette of Elvis's funeral; and Steve Forbert's diary-like recollection of the day Elvis died, "House of Cards," written in 1977, recorded a few years later, but not available until his *Young Guitar Days* (2001). Zevon would revisit Elvis as a subject with "Porcelain Monkey," fittingly on his album *Life'll Kill Ya* (2000).

The Envoy's noir shadows are balanced by a trio of sweetly optimistic songs of surrender and perseverance. In the wistful "Looking for the Next Best Thing," cowritten with LeRoy Marinell and Kenny Edwards, Zevon rationalizes appreciating the best, but settling for less. Career allusions and disillusion are an undercurrent, as Zevon states he "worked hard but not for the money and did his best to please, until he realized it was all a tease." To support his "next best thing" premise, Zevon looks to fellow romantic adventurers Don Quixote and his windmills, Ponce de Leon's cruise, and notes that it took Sinbad seven voyages "to see that it was all a ruse." Zevon's interesting phrasing characterizes the isolation and scrutiny of his journey—"All alone on the road to perfection/At the inspection booth they tried to discourage me." In

relinquishing, he settles somewhere in between compromise and conformity, stating that "believing what you want will never change it," and
"you'll have to come around eventually." The lilting harmonies by Graham Nash and J. D. Souther in the chorus alleviate dismay and tint the
song with an acquiescent, rather than bitter, tone.

The buoyant "Let Nothing Come Between You" sounds like an update of the Dixie Cups' 1964 "Chapel of Love." Zevon is smitten; he's
got the license, the ring, the blood test, and everything; he's putting on
a boutonniere—"her favorite flower"—and walking to the altar and
gonna take the vow. He also incorporates the phrase "she's good around
the eyes" that originated from a Jackson Browne observation of a woman Zevon was engaged to, presumably Kim Lankford. A girl group–style
"de de de de de, de de de de, ooh" prefixes Zevon's bold advice for
the young and old to "get together and let nothing come between you."

The resolute closing, "Never Too Late for Love," is an inspirational
piano tune that addresses the weariness of heartache. Zevon is both
empathetic and mildly scolding—"you say you're tired, how I hate to
hear you use that word," punctuated with "everybody hurts," a phrase
that foretells not only the title, but the tenor of R.E.M.'s hit single from
Automatic for the People (1992). The concluding verse's encouragement to "live for today, and don't stop believing in tomorrow" is a
sentiment that approaches motivational speaker cliché, but may be Zevon at his most sincere and sympathetic.

Within the changing environment of the early 1980s music market,
The Envoy's sales were meager, charting at number 93. Despite the
modest commercial reception, Zevon maintained his critical cachet. Reviewers recognized his shifting musical persona on the album without
disparaging or ardently embracing the record. Most conceded that Zevon was relatively restrained and his tone more tentative; the album a
decrescendo for the desperado who "steps back from the edge" and
reveals a view that was about moderation more than it was menacing
(DeCurtis and Henke, 802). Though the songs, as usual, were well
crafted, the minimal rather than ceaseless chaos was striking in its departure from the Zevon norm. The album's lower key, lighter songs
were arguably the most enduring of the set. Perhaps the harshest critique of *The Envoy* may have come in distant hindsight. In his review
essay on Zevon's Asylum catalog reissues in 2007, Phil Sutcliffe offered
a blunt appraisal of Zevon at the five-album mark of his career. Writing

in the U.K. music publication *Mojo*, Sutcliffe found *The Envoy* overall to be "pallid by Zevon's bloody standards," with Zevon plodding through the conventional post-Eagles, Cali-country rock moves. More specifically, he noted that the ferocious wit had gone missing, and that Zevon sounded uncertain, "maybe about to realize how lost he'd become." Sutcliffe's summation was severe, stating that *The Envoy* stood as a "diminuendo outro to a talent on the wane" (124).

"AIN'T THAT PRETTY AT ALL"

> *"everything is in flux"*
> —*Heraclitus* (the inscription on the inside cover of Warren Zevon's
>   1983 diary)

The quote from "the Weeping Philosopher," Heraclitus, that prefaces Zevon's journal could not be a more fitting characterization of his life in *The Envoy* aftermath. Zevon's 1983 tour title—Live at Least—was a public pronouncement of its instability. With his "star dimming in Los Angeles," the period became "one of Warren's darkest and drunkest," according to Crystal Zevon (185). The flux was both personal and professional. Zevon's relationship with Lankford ended; he completely detached from Crystal, son Jordan, and daughter Ariel; and he had accumulated significant debt. Creatively, Zevon was at a standstill. His productivity withered; there were no songs being written or plans to record a new album. Asylum, with hopes of recouping some of the money it advanced Zevon for *The Envoy*, sent him on a cross-country solo tour that seemed liked it was penance as much as it was payback. He and Gruel traveled by car. During a break from the tour, Zevon relocated from Los Angeles to Philadelphia, were he moved in with Anita Gevinson, a popular radio disc jockey to whom he was briefly engaged. Gevinson self-published a desperately shallow groupie memoir, *You Turn Me On, I'm a Radio: My Wild Rock 'N' Roll Life*, in 2012. The move to the East Coast further amplified Zevon's aimless state. In Crystal's view, by moving to Philadelphia Zevon "removed himself from the mainstream of his own existence, he was oblivious to what was going on with his own career back in Los Angeles" (186). In late May 1983, while in Philadelphia, Zevon read in *Rolling Stone*'s "Random Notes" column that he had been dropped by his record label, which was in the process of reconfiguring its name, logo, and roster. Zevon was "freaked and enraged" (186), particularly at finding out the way he did. "They had it in this little box as if it was an obituary," he recalled (Milward, 187). The Asylum years were over.

Zevon's record label fate was not an isolated case, rather typical of the times, and a precursor of further fallout. In July 1984, Warner Brothers dropped Van Morrison and 30 other artists, among them Bonnie Raitt, T-Bone Burnett, and Arlo Guthrie. Releasing artists of Morrison's and Raitt's stature was unprecedented. The company line from Warner president Lenny Waronker was that the difficult decisions were based on economics, and designed "to establish a manageable roster" so they "could pay attention to each record they put out." He insisted Warner was committed to being "an artist-oriented label" (Connelly, July 1984, 41).

In the most unusual case of artist/record company discord, Geffen Records filed a $3 million lawsuit in June 1984 against Neil Young, claiming he produced two "non-commercial" records for the label—the techno *Trans* (1982) and retro rockabilly *Everybody's Rockin'* (1983). Geffen argued that the records were uncharacteristic of Young's earlier work; they expected "Neil Young records."

The music video revolution had effectively masked some serious issues for artists. Joe Jackson was at the forefront of the backlash when he declared he would not do a video for his 1984 album *Body and Soul.* In a two-page statement entitled "Video is Killing Music," Jackson declared that "desperation and greed are blowing the importance of video way out of proportion." Among the grievances Jackson cited were video's devaluation of music and musicians, unreasonable pressures to make videos, and the exorbitant production costs (Connelly, August 1984, 32).

Critic Jon Pareles attributed the divisive music industry atmosphere to "rock Reaganomics," as "the richest part of the record business pulls rapidly away from the rest of it" (1985,137). Within that hierarchy, the chart toppers with marketing support generate huge profits, with nothing trickling down to the "also rans"—the mid-level artists, particularly those whose songs were not in MTV's video rotation, such as Zevon; new and unexposed acts; and independent labels that scrape by and try to survive in the music marketplace.

RECORD LABEL LIMBO

Zevon's five-year exile between *The Envoy* and his next studio album was marked by disorder and a revolving-door routine at rehab facilities from Minnesota to Los Angeles. Zevon's aide-de-camp George Gruel, echoing Crystal's grim outlook for her ex-husband during the period, feared that Zevon's lifestyle had finally caught up with him and that his "spark was gone" (C. Zevon, 194). Amidst the bedlam, there was always a compassionate soul—Crystal, Jackson Browne, Jorge Calderón, Paul Nelson—who steadfastly believed in Zevon and gallantly swooped in to redirect him from the depths, if only temporarily. This time, it was Andrew Slater. The 25-year-old publicist for Irving Azoff's prominent Frontline Management, who eventually became the CEO of Capitol Records, inherited Zevon as a client. Slater literally stood up for Zevon when his fellow Frontliners were ready to terminate the agency's association with the troubled and labelless artist. A former reporter/music writer for the *Atlanta Journal Constitution*, *USA Today*, and *Rolling Stone*, Slater defended Zevon as "the best artist we have . . . the best writer here." "He was so smart and funny and sarcastic and endearing when he wanted to be that I just fell in love with the guy," said Slater. "I got completely swept up in Warren's world" (C. Zevon, 192, 194).

Slater's mission was to get "the great outlaw of the L.A. music scene" back in the record business. Beyond his biggest challenge of dealing with Zevon's persistent alcohol and pill consumption, Slater's strategy was to get Zevon out of Philadelphia and on the road touring, with Duncan Aldrich as his new, long-term road manager and producer. Slater also secured money to record some demos to circulate to record labels. He contacted his college friend, Peter Buck, lead guitarist for the up-and-coming band R.E.M., and enlisted the group to back Zevon on the demo sessions in Atlanta early in 1984. R.E.M. was part of the emerging music scene in Athens, Georgia, that included the B-52s, Pylon, and Love Tractor. R.E.M.'s debut EP, *Chronic Town* (1982), followed by the album *Murmur* (1983), created an underground buzz. Their intricate sound blended post-garage, post-punk, jangle-pop influences underneath Michael Stipe's idiosyncratic, moody, and mumbling vocals and cryptic lyrics. R.E.M. became the most popular group in the college/alternative rock genre during the 1980s. As the band transcended its cult and college status, achieving mainstream success and critical acclaim, the group maintained its artistic integrity while producing an impressive body of work over three decades before breaking up in September 2011.

Slater shopped the demos from the Zevon/R.E.M. sessions to various labels. No one was interested. He conceded that "they sounded like an indie rock band fronting the great songwriter, and not so great singer at the time" (C. Zevon, 191). Zevon and R.E.M. members Buck, Bill Berry, Mike Mills, and only occasionally Stipe, along with Bryan Cook from the Athens band Time Toy, played several gigs together in Athens at small venues, including the 40 Watt Club. In between the bicoastals—New York City's CBGB's and the Whiskey a Go Go in Los Angeles—the 40 Watt Club was an integral locale for the punk and new wave movements. Calling themselves the hindu love gods—frequently, though not exclusively, a lowercase preference that was dually a Zevon lyme and cybelle/e.e. cummings redux, and clever counter to R.E.M.'s capitalization—the group performed mostly covers, along with a few Zevon songs and some of his works in progress. That summer, the outfit certified its side project status by recording two songs for a seven-inch single. The A-side party tune "Gonna Have a Good Time Tonight" was a cover of "Good Times" by the Easybeats, an Australian band best known for their 1966 hit, "Friday on My Mind." The B-side composition by Berry, "Narrator," was quirky surf-riff homage to the famous French undersea explorer Jacques Cousteau. The single, a hip collectible packaged in a picture sleeve, was released as a 45 rpm on R.E.M.'s I.R.S. label in 1986.

As impromptu as the hindu love gods live gigs, studio sessions, and single might have appeared, the musical partnership evolved into subsequent Zevon recording projects, and was among several things that began to fall into place for Zevon in 1986. The year marked a turning point for Zevon individually and as an artist. The most momentous change was his commitment to sobriety, followed by his signing a record deal. Slater was fully aware that Zevon's drinking was undermining his exhaustive master plan to get Zevon's career back on track. By mid-decade, he had taken Zevon to rehab on three separate occasions. The third time was a breakthrough, one that was lasting. Beginning in March 1986, Zevon remained sober for the next 17 years.

In October, *A Quiet Normal Life: The Best of Warren Zevon* officially completed Zevon's Asylum catalog. Zevon, who appears cozily clad in a gray turtleneck on the cover, adapted the album's wishful, ironic title from a Wallace Stevens poem. The obligatory collection was a relatively thin set compared to the four more extensively curated compilations that followed—a two-disc, 44-song anthology (1996), the 22-song *Genius* (2002), and the posthumous *Love Songs* (2006) and *Preludes* (2007). Sequenced by Zevon, ten of *A Quiet Normal Life*'s fourteen songs are from his self-titled debut and *Excitable Boy*, with only "Play It All Night Long" from *Bad Luck Streak in Dancing School* and the remaining three songs from *The Envoy*. Zevon was appalled to find out that Asylum edited "Lawyers, Guns and Money" on the compilation, cutting 30 seconds to avoid the resounding closing verse that contained "the shit has hit the fan." Zevon channeled his frustration with the record company meddling into the song "The Factory" on his next album.

The release of the "Best of" collection, though contractual, was also calculated to coincide with "Werewolves of London's" inclusion on the film soundtrack of Martin Scorsese's *The Color of Money* that premiered the same month. Scorsese's pool-hall sequel to *The Hustler* (1961) featured an Academy Award–winning performance by Paul Newman and an original score by Robbie Robertson. Zevon's hit song was placed in a pivotal scene involving Tom Cruise. While songs written by Zevon previously appeared in the films *Midnight Cowboy* (1969) and *FM* (1978), which used Ronstadt's version of "Poor Poor Pitiful Me," *The Color of Money* marked the first time a Zevon original was used in a soundtrack. Zevon's catalog continued to be featured regularly in film and television series soundtracks, with "Werewolves of London" not surprisingly being the most frequent.

"RECONSIDER ME:" THE VIRGIN RECORDINGS

The song haunted me for years. I was so moved by "Reconsider Me" that I was obsessed about getting Warren a deal—based on that song. The song struck a chord in me that has not been rung too many times since.

—manager Andy Slater (C. Zevon)

It was very exciting being the first American on Virgin and having Paula Abdul videos and Herb Ritts [photo] sessions. The down side of it was, I think that Jeff and Jordan [Virgin Records executives] woke

up one morning, looked around and said, "Who's this guy again? Did
he come with you?" And the other one said, "Isn't he like Jackson
Browne, with novelty hits?"

—Warren Zevon (Roeser)

Slater was resolute about landing Zevon a record deal. He approached
his friend, Jeff Ayeroff, who was part an executive team that was in the
process of launching Virgin Records America, a division of entrepreneur Richard Branson's worldwide Virgin music enterprise established in
1972. Slater convinced Ayeroff to sign Zevon as one of the new label's
first artists. His pitch was largely based on Zevon's Scorsese soundtrack
presence and a demo of "Reconsider Me," one of Zevon's emblematic
desperate and sincere second-chance pleas that he wrote on Ritten-
house Square in Philadelphia. Slater no doubt recognized that the "Reconsider Me" premise could extend beyond a broken relationship, ap-
plying to Zevon's standing with record companies, critics, and fans. The
song was a fitting campaign slogan for a labelless artist hoping for a
record deal, not to mention a potential title for a comeback album.
When the demo initially failed to entice record labels into signing Zevon, Slater's next strategy was to find somebody to cover "Reconsider
Me." He played a cassette for Jimmy Iovine, producer for Stevie Nicks,
insisting it was a good song for her to cut. Iovine agreed, and Nicks
recorded "Reconsider Me" in 1987, as did Chrissie Hynde of the Pretenders. Both Nicks's warm, husky voice, and Hynde's soulful, tight
wavering delivery convey the song's lovely vulnerability. Both versions
became obscurities that were eventually released on box sets—Nicks's
Enchanted (1997) and the Pretenders' *Pirate Radio* (2006). Their covers of "Reconsider Me," along with Grace Weber's less edgy rendition
in 2011, continued to advance the interpretive rapport between female
vocalists and the Zevon songbook initiated by Ronstadt in the 1970s
with Zevon's Asylum debut.

Zevon's recording hiatus ended in 1987 with the release of what was
indisputably a "comeback" album, *Sentimental Hygiene*, his first record
in five years. The unusual title phrase, according to Zevonian psycho-
semantics, means "feelings so clean you can eat off of them." The
steady, tuneful ten-song set provides a solid midsection to the Zevon
discography. As coproducers, Zevon, Slater, and Niko Bolas assembled
an impressive supporting lineup that gave the album a different sonic
contour than Zevon's previous works. The R.E.M. alliance continued

before the group's commercial breakthrough, with Buck, Mills, and Berry completing Zevon's quartet as a forceful, rhythmic backing band, and Stipe contributing harmony. Among the old reliables present are Jorge Calderón; Mellow Mafians Waddy Wachtel, David Lindley, and Leland Sklar; with Don Henley and Jennifer Warnes filling in vocal intervals for ranges Zevon couldn't reach on the album's tender songs. There are also prominent cameos by Bob Dylan, who delivers a spry harmonica thread on "The Factory," and Neil Young providing a jagged lead guitar on the title track. Brian Setzer, Tom Petty Heartbreaker Mike Campbell, and Red Hot Chili Pepper bassist Flea also contribute. Funk innovator George Clinton arranges "Leave My Monkey Alone" into a dance track, bedding a mildly menacing touch to Zevon's continued global view, this time set in an old colonial home "under the Southern Cross" during the Mau-Mau uprising in 1952 Kenya.

In addition to his geopolitical-historical perspective, Zevon's writing on the album is sharp, sarcastic, and self-referential, with the usual few flourishes of tenderness and heartache. The lead title track ruminates on a dying decade, Baby Boomer nostalgia, and lost freedoms during the AIDS era. Zevon searches for relief from the world weariness of monotony and routine—"get up in the morning and go to work and do my job—whatever," and coming home every night "exhausted from trying to get along," surrounded by "everybody joining up for the right to be wrong." He proposes a "mini-surrender"; the sentimental hygiene that he needs is so hard to find. The song's accompanying music video, a rarity in the Zevon body of work, was in the regular rotation on VH1 (Video Hits One), the music video cable network that launched in 1985, building upon MTV's success but targeting an older demographic. Shot in black and white, matching well-known photographer Herb Ritts's album cover and sleeve photos of Zevon, the production is standard music video style with a nonliteral narrative and indie film imagery—a mysterious dark-haired woman, beach scenes, an electrical outlet, boots on a radiator, and a cat among the shots. Zevon is frequent, doing his best to embrace the video's cinematic noir intentions, particularly with the line "Sometimes I drive my car up and down the boulevard." However, Zevon's wind-in-his-hair lip sync, another music video convention, is awkward, and undermines the verse's shadowy Scorsesian nature that inherently conjures images of a City of Angels version of Travis Bickle wanting to clean up the streets of New York in *Taxi Driver* (1976). The video concludes awkwardly, with Zevon, wearing a long overcoat, wading in ankle-deep waves beneath a pier.

The album's central thread scrutinizes the travails of fame, primarily through a mocking critique of celebrity, media coverage, and the music industry, framed by Zevon's own experiences. According to *Rolling Stone* writer and Zevon girlfriend, Merle Ginsberg, "Warren made fun of celebrity, but he loved being famous. It was the only way he felt validated." Songwriting collaborator LeRoy Marinell added that there was a "real star-fucker aspect of Warren," one that was "not pretty" and "hurtful" (C. Zevon, 258).

Zevon bundles his personal history of alcohol and substance rehabilitations and interventions, and the Paul Nelson *Rolling Stone* cover story, into the blatantly self-referential "Detox Mansion." The term originated from a Calderón jibe directed at Zevon, "I see you're drinking Coca-Cola, I guess you don't want to go back to Detox Mansion." According to Zevon, the song's first version sounded like Johnny Cash's "I Walk the Line." Though institutional traces remain in irreverent descriptions such as "last breath farm" and the padded wall confinement slang, "outside the rubber room," "Detox Mansion" conjures a Magic Kingdom for the pampered famous more than it does a prison. Zevon mingles self-deprecating humor with ridicule of trendy, highly publicized celebrity rehabs ("I'm dying to tell my story for all my friends to read") that he was at the forefront of, and of the sanctimony of sobriety proselytes. The troubled star in the narrative leaves his home in Music City (presumably a generic connotation rather than specifically Nashville and country artists) in the back of a limousine headed for the mansion. Up on Rehab Mountain there is a resort-like atmosphere, with glamour in the chores—"rakin' leaves with Liza (Minnelli)/me and Liz (Taylor) clean up the yard"—and activities that include therapy, lectures, and golf in the afternoon. Zevon's Rehab Mountain manifesto resonates recovery doctrine short of a 12-steps or Serenity Prayer paraphrase: "it's tough to be somebody and not to fall part . . . we gonna learn these things by heart."

"Trouble Waiting to Happen" is (un)inspired by Zevon reading in the rock press that he had been dropped by his record label. The uptempo song, cowritten with J. D. Souther, who was in Philadelphia with Zevon at the time, is a living-at-home-alone, luckless narrative ("This just ain't gonna be my day. . . . Things just ain't gonna go my way") with a portentous beginning—"woke up this morning and I fell out of bed." "Just when I thought it was safe to be bored," the day becomes more confounding when the "mail man brought me the *Rolling Stone*." Zevon is amused at the sensationalism, reading about "things I didn't know I'd done," wryly observing that "It sounded like a lot of fun" before a self-scolding shrug, "I guess I've been bad or something." The closing stanza rhymes its way through the gloominess: "My day was over by a quarter to ten/I climbed right back into bed again/I'd write this down if I had a pen/I might get better but I don't know when/So I'm gonna wait right here 'til then."

The hapless state shifts to a cosmic context in the comparably droll and pulsating companion song, "Bad Karma." Unobtrusive sitar strands provide an "agreeable gag" for Zevon's self-described "mild reincarnation spoof" (1996). "Was it something I did in another life?" asks Zevon in the opening line, wondering why "nothing comes out right" no matter how hard he tries. Though Zevon doesn't see his fate as his fault, he woefully says he "ought to hang my picture in the All-Time Losers' Hall of Fame." His destiny is "uphill all the way"; perhaps the result of a "wrong turn on the astral plane," but he keeps thinking his luck is going to change. Someday.

Zevon directs disdain at the music business in the jaunty "Even a Dog Can Shake Hands," a songwriting collaboration with Buck, Mills, and Berry. The proverbial L.A. star laments "everybody's trying to be a friend of mine" and "wanting their twenty percent 'cause he knew you back when." Zevon is just "trying to survive up on Mulholland Drive," and trying not to lose his head, end up dead, or worse, "be living in the Valley." The Asylum aftermath lingers into flagrant acrimony toward the "worms and gnomes having lunch at Le Dôme, all living off the fat of the land." He concludes, "You'll make the scene 'til they pick your bones clean," and "they don't leave much for the fans." In 1999, the song proved to be a relevant opening theme song for *Action* (Fox), an irreverent situation comedy about Hollywood culture, starring Jay Mohr as a producer trying to recover from his latest box office failure.

"The Factory" also contains music industry subtext as Zevon's expression of frustration, anger, and powerlessness when the record company edited "Lawyers, Guns and Money" on his Asylum "Best of" collection. According to Zevon, that's what the feelings in "The Factory" are about: "the guy who's trapped in his job and can't change the job and can't walk away from his job" (Tannenbaum, 25). The up-tempo tune aligns along the axis of Bruce Springsteen and John Mellencamp working-class-hero songs. Zevon's "we get by the best we can do" struggle is set in "Mechanicsburg" in '63—but "don't know much about Kennedy/ I was too busy working in the factory." Blue collar conventions abound: family values—Daddy worked for Pontiac 'til he got hurt, now he's on disability, "and I got his old job at the factory"—a good medical plan, union man, up early in the morning, six days a week, factory whistle blows, and a chugging "Yes sir, no sir" chorus chant of conformity. In the cleverly structured final nine verses, Zevon delivers an enumeration of labor in an assembly line cadence, each line punctuated with "at/in the factory," the final four in the sequence being: "Kickin' asbestos . . . Breathin' that plastic . . . Punchin' out Chryslers . . . Makin' polyvinyl chloride."

"Boom Boom Mancini" embodies another of Zevon's savvy sportsfigure subject selections. Just as his baseball ditty "Bill Lee" is an antihero homage, Zevon's intriguing, machismo boxing bio is a cold appraisal of the sport that is far from a feel-good Rocky Balboa sequel. "Boom Boom Mancini" ricochets to Dylan's eight-minute protest ballad "Hurricane" (1975) about imprisoned boxer Rubin Carter. Zevon's ringside seat offers a three-dimensional perspective; he writes as the son of a boxer, as a boxing fan, and as a cultural observer fascinated with fate. Zevon also leans on the boxing metaphor for his own inner fights, with lines such as "If you can't take the punches it don't mean a thing." Accompanied by a tough arrangement, the opening hook urges "hurry home early, hurry on home" for a Mancini-Bobby Chacon fight on HBO. Zevon backtracks from that January 1984 Mancini title defense that was stopped cautiously and controversially in the third round with Chacon battered and bleeding. Zevon efficiently plots the Youngstown, Ohio, lightweight's arc, from contender through a beating by Alexis Arguello, to a first-round defeat of Arturo Frias for the World Boxing Association crown in Las Vegas in May 1982 at the age of 21.

A tragic plot twist ensued on November 13, when the 21-year-old Mancini defended his title against South Korean challenger Duk Koo Kim at Caesar's Palace in Las Vegas, with the bout televised on CBS. Mancini won the fight, which lasted 14 rounds. However, Kim suffered brain injuries that led to his death four days later. The ripple of grief was widespread and devastating. The following week, the ring misfortune was a *Sports Illustrated* cover story. The World Boxing Council soon took steps to shorten title bouts to a maximum 12 rounds. Several months after the fight, Kim's mother committed suicide by pesticide, and the bout's referee, Richard Green, killed himself in July 1983. Mancini was predictably traumatized by the incident, and particularly haunted by the misperception that he "killed" Duk Koo Kim. Mancini was never the same. He lost his title two years later and retired from boxing in 1985 at age 24, though he returned to the ring in 1989 and fought for the final time in 1992.

Zevon is in Mancini's corner. He empathizes, while also taking a few straightforward swings of his own. He jabs at those who asked about the responsibility for the fatal fight and "made hypocrite judgments after the fact," and ultimately attributes the tragedy to the nature of the sport: "But the name of the game is be hit and hit back." During the July 3, 2013, edition of the legendary free-form radio show *Idiot's Delight*, originating on WFUV public radio in New York and airing on Sirius/XM satellite radio, host Vin Scelsa, framing Zevon's intellectual superiority as a songwriter within "Boom Boom Mancini," was particularly captivated by the breadth of Zevon's knowledge and his inclusion of the song's secondary characters Arguello and Frias. On Sun Kil Moon's album *Ghosts of the Great Highway* (2003), Mark Kozelek also documents the fatal Mancini-Kim fight in a 14:32 narrative, "Duk Koo Kim."

Sentimental Hygiene's two love songs are painfully pretty. "Reconsider Me" pleads the habitual "that was then, this is now" and a likely false promise never to make you sad or cry, "'cause I swear that I've changed since then," a phrase that exacts a transformative vow made previously in "Bad Luck Streak in Dancing School." The less hopeful "The Heartache" is a treatise on "the trouble with relationships," colored in "blue feeling to the maximum." Zevon is straightforward— "Look what happens when you love someone and they don't love you"—yet avoids sulking by adroitly wrapping risk, sorrow, loneliness, sadness, ending too soon, rain, and darkness in a characteristic lovely melody that averts the aching.

LIVING IN THE SHADOWS: "NOIR PROPHET," NOR PROFIT

Though an undeniable comeback album, *Sentimental Hygiene* did not promptly revitalize Zevon's career. Critics welcomed his return, as the album was well received, from the rock press to the *Village Voice* and *New York Times.* On the charts, the album stalled at number 63, a respectable but somewhat disappointing plateau considering Virgin's generous promotional, music video, and American and European tour support that accompanied the record. Virgin invested over $1 million in the recording and its marketing, while Zevon and company spent twice their budget. Sales suggested Zevon's fan base might be showing signs of dwindling, a likely result of the changing music environment and his extended absence from recording more than the quality of the material on the album. On the road, Zevon described his audiences as "politely enthusiastic," but lacking the excitable boisterousness of his yesteryear crowds. In places where Zevon ticket sales were weak, his concert hall bookings were downgraded to clubs. Zevon's girlfriend at the time, Merle Ginsberg, noticed that in the wake of the career distress, traces of resentment toward the successes of his California colleagues such as Browne, Henley, and Frey began to surface in Zevon. In addition, Zevon's obsessive-compulsive behaviors and habits, which may have been disguised by his alcohol and drug excesses, began to assert themselves, with bad luck and the color gray among his most notable fixations. Jimmy Wachtel offered an amusing glimpse of Zevon's OCD, observing that "he had like forty pair of gray socks all balled up in this drawer, and I thought it was one of the greatest art pieces I'd ever seen" (C. Zevon, 224–25). The socks matched Zevon's ever-accumulating collection of Calvin Klein gray t-shirts that he purchased but never wore, keeping all of them in their original packaging. Nor would Zevon smoke cigarettes from a carton or pack with an "objectionable warning" on it, meaning "the C-word." According to tour manager Stuart Ross, who frequently had to acquire Silk Cuts for Zevon, warning labels mentioning heart disease, emphysema, or any other condition linked to smoking cigarettes were fine, as long the packaging didn't have the word "cancer" on it.

The uncompromising Zevon applied any corporate patronage he had remaining from Virgin toward an ambitious project based on another of his shorter-term fascinations—the science fiction subgenre, cyberpunk. *Transverse City*, released in 1989, is Zevon's compelling, misanthropic vision of a futuristic dystopia, "where life is cheap and death is free." The "trans" prefix in the apt title is polysemous—"*trans*ition, *trans*portation, *trans*formation, *trans*gression, *trans*figure." While the cover's colorful collage of mall images that create a halo effect around Zevon's figure is incongruent with the contents inside, the image of a bespectacled skull with a cigarette dangling from its mouth imprinted on the inner circle label of the album provides fitting reinforcement of the album's grim demeanor. The skull image, "Old Velvet Nose," quietly introduced himself as the logo or brand that would mark every subsequent Zevon album and product.

Transverse City is strongly influenced by the speculative fiction of "noir prophet" William Gibson, Thomas Pynchon's sprawling technological parable, *Gravity's Rainbow* (1973), and periodicals such as *New Cyber Punk*. Zevon's only concept album is at once grand, grim, and glossy, as he digs deep into the heart of the last days of the Reagan era and, more broadly, perestroika, a movement resulting in economic and political reform of the Soviet Union during the 1980s under Mikhail Gorbachev. The ten-song portrayal of a culture in collapse is a lurking novella, with a dark, dreamlike mood similar to the Los Angeles noir on *Warren Zevon*, fortified with unforgiving themes, vivid imagery, rich language, and multilayered production.

The complex and, at times, dense textures in the arrangements incorporate Zevon's classical Stravinsky influences within the album's prevalent electronic and synthesized sound. Zevon, who lobbied for greater control as a producer alongside Slater and Aldrich on the album, in large part because he was sober, continues to surround himself with impressive backing. Contributors include the familiar session standbys Calderón, Wachtel, Lindley, Bob Glaub, and J. D. Souther on harmony; Neil Young again; and revered newcomers Mark Isham on flugelhorn, jazz and fusion pianist Chick Corea, jazz bassist John Patatucci, Pink Floyd's David Gilmour, Little Feat drummer Richie Hayward, Jefferson Airplane and Hot Tuna veterans Jack Casady and Jorma Kaukonen, Grateful Dead head Jerry Garcia, and Heartbreakers Mike Campbell, Howie Epstein, and Bentmont Tench.

The lead song, "Transverse City," evokes Ridley Scott's film *Blade Runner* (1982), as Zevon depicts a "place we can't remember, for a time we won't forget," a subterranean refuge of "dancing quanta" where "everything exists at once," and above it where "every weekend lasts for months." Among the image-laden noir landscape are condensation silos, an all-night trauma stand, castles made of laser light, a shopping sector in the vortex of the night, shiny Mylar towers, and ravaged tenements. Zevon assembles a striking lyric litany into an imposing flow of desolation row, with each line beginning with "Here's the": "hum of desperation, test tube mating call, latest carbon cycle, clergy of the mall, witness and the victim, relatives' remains, well-known double helix, poisoned waves of grain, song of shear and torsion, bloodbath magazine, harvest of contusions, the narcoleptic dream."

The transition to the milieu of "Run Straight Down" is seamless. The focus in the companion song is ecological, beginning with a haunting vocal line listing industrial carcinogens contaminating the environment, an inventory Zevon acquired from the Sierra Club. Zevon walks wearily through a wasted city by its ruined river, his mood and observation engulfed by entropy. The atmosphere reverberates "Sentimental Hygiene"; he's fatalistic and culpable, asserting that "we've been living in the shadows all our lives," blinded by conformity, "standing in line and don't look back, look left or right, hiding our eyes and wondering who will survive." He appears resigned to a place where soon "there's not a creature stirring 'cept the robots at the dynamo." As for thinking about "then and now," he'd rather sit back and "see it on the news at eleven."

Beyond the opening pair of songs, the culture critique is less onerous. "Long Arm of the Law," written by Zevon along with "Splendid Isolation" in the back of his tour bus, is a post-Orwellian life-of-crime-during-hard-times account of a fugitive whose first words ever heard were "Nobody move, nobody gets hurt." In "Gridlock," an edgier update of Guy Clark's "L.A. Freeway" that was a hit for Jerry Jeff Walker in 1972, Zevon is outnumbered—"one of me and two million of them"—and "going nowhere, stuck on the edge of the urban sprawl." Insatiability is the central premise of the consumer anthem, "Down in the Mall," where "You buy everything you want and then you want more."

In "Networking," Zevon offers a sly, mechanized point of view of the proliferating computer and information age, just ahead of the Internet's mass adoption and impact in the early 1990s. He sees the techno-evolution as a "way to live that's right for us," analogous with the ancients—"like Mayans in Manhattan and Los Angeles." While initially blurring networking's usages to include the entertainment-industry lifestyle— "scaling up, breaking down, and doing lunch all over town"— Zevon diffuses computer language lightly throughout, declaring that he's "user friendly," using "every bit of byte" on "a long, hard road and a full, hard drive." Virtual is vital, "a sector there where I feel alive." The myth of "technology as savior" circulates with measures of incisive wit tinting technology's social and spiritual aspects. The interactive line, "I will upload you, you can download me," reads like a vow. And a nightly prayer revises "Now I lay me down to sleep" into "Let the data guide me through every day/And every pulse and every code—Deliver me from bypass mode."

Zevon expands his view to a global scale in "Turbulence," a somewhat demystifying observation of perestroika, the "glasnost" policy of openness, and Soviet reform initiated by Gorbachev. The chorus chant—"Turmoil back in Moscow brought this turbulence down on me"—with Souther's matching harmony, and an occasional "Hah!" and "Huh!" from Zevon—saturates the song. A soldier petitions comrades Shevardnadze (the Soviet minister of foreign affairs) and Gorbachev— "what's a poor boy like me to do?" and "Can I go back to Vladivostok, man?"—from "fightin' the mujahideen down in Afghanistan." The worldly Zevon provides a cultured, authentic touch by inserting verses delivered in Russian that loosely translate: "Village is lost in the red desert; On all sides, silence of an enemy; And we want to see our mothers."

The album contains one of Zevon's most enduring, tuneful hits, "Splendid Isolation," an homage and critique of the virtues of seclusion. The song highlights some of Zevon's most spirited harmonica playing (along with "I Was in the House When the House Burned Down" in 2000), and features vocal backing by Young, who requested to sing harmony on the song rather than play lead guitar (which he does on "Gridlock"). Zevon further demonstrates his breadth of world awareness by employing the phrase "splendid isolation," which originated with Lord Goschen as a flattering characterization of the general course of foreign policy pursued by Great Britain during the second half of the nineteenth century. The country's refusal of long-term alliances and its minimal involvement in European affairs were notable practices under the Conservative Party premierships of Benjamin Disraeli and Lord

Salisbury. Zevon's anti-fame application is more about personal prefer-ence than political policy. He's "putting tin foil up on the windows" in self-sentenced solitary confinement, with a lengthy list of "don'ts" that resemble commandments: "don't need no one; don't want to see their faces, hear them scream or wake up with no one beside me; don't come by without calling first; don't want to take up with nobody new; don't want nothing to do with you." As solitude-seeking endorsements, Zevon invokes reclusive archetypes Georgia O'Keeffe "all alone in the desert" and "Michael Jackson in Disneyland," where the blissful self-seclusion reveals its narcissistic side. The King of Pop "don't want to share it with nobody else" either, instructing "lock the gates Goofy, take my hand and lead me to the World of Self." The reference is timely; Jackson purchased the Neverland Ranch in California in 1988.

Romance cannot lighten the mood or redeem the dystopian dread of *Transverse City*. Each side of the album closes with one of Zevon's standard songs about the devastation of lost love. "They Moved the Moon" is an eerie lament that leads with oppressive disillusion, "I was counting on you to stand by me." From there, the universe—stars, sky, and moon—were moved and changed around "when I looked down" and "looked away," Zevon's way of saying, "Everything that I depended on has been rearranged." In "Nobody's in Love This Year," Zevon oddly mixes a stanza of fiscal terms— "invested, yield to maturity, rate of attrition, steadily on the rise"—with heartbreak, vulnerability, hurt, and the fear of being the one left behind. The rueful meditation on the fate of romanticism in a time and place where solace is a scarce commodity provides a proper finale to the apocalyptic album.

Following in *Sentimental Hygiene*'s promotional path, a black-and-white music video of "Run Straight Down" accompanied *Transverse City*'s release. The video features Zevon and David Gilmour playing guitars on separate industrial platform interiors intercut within a clut-tered montage of shadow and light. The machine noir visual aesthetic is derivative of Fritz Lang's utopian/dystopian film *Metropolis* (1927) and Charlie Chaplin's *Modern Times* (1936). A large crane hook hovers above right of Gilmour on guitar, silhouettes of giant fan blades spin, workers in contamination suits are in motion, as chemical names, for-mulas, and laboratory-like wavelengths strobe the screen.

While *Transverse City* may be Zevon's most ambitious record, it is also among his least accessible. As expected, the album did not do well commercially, with its appeal largely confined to Zevon core devotees and perhaps a pocket of curious sci-fi aficionados. Typical of most concept albums, Zevon's divergent work attracted an array of critical responses, described in reviews with the terms overwrought, art rock, epic scale, elaborate, absorbing, prophetic, dark, and an unmitigated downer.

Transverse City may be the most conveniently dismissed or overlooked album in the Zevon catalog, though "Splendid Isolation" perseveres as an appealing melodic memento that links listeners to the record. Though the album does not merit "messy conceptual" repute, *Transverse City* is an irrefutable acquired taste, one that is well worth revisiting if for nothing else, Zevon's vision and writing. While "auteur" may not be pertinent, the album represents an artist's willingness to explore new directions inspired by individual cultural awareness, tastes, and curiosities, in this case, Zevon's interest in science fiction and cyberpunk. Zevon's swerve into the genre with *Transverse City* is nowhere near as extreme or perplexing a stylistic transformation as Neil Young's conceptual computer-age project, the similarly titled techno *Trans* (1982) from earlier in the decade, which filtered his wailing vocals through a vocoder on multiple songs. Just as Young's subsequent live, unplugged rendition of *Trans*'s "Transformer Man" provides a pleasant sample of the album that might have been, Zevon's stripped-down demo of "Networking," the lone bonus track on the *Transverse City* reissue in 2003, holds similar intrigue and alternate allure for Zevon purists. The acoustic and harmonica version, in which Zevon intermittently drifts into a Dylan delivery, conjures a substitute metropolis, one that could be relocated perhaps somewhere in the vicinity of Springsteen's sparse *Nebraska*.

For Zevon, the decade that began auspiciously with two albums in 1980, followed by a lengthy recording exile and noteworthy comeback, waned at the era's end with the audacious *Transverse City* steering Virgin into replicating Asylum as one of Zevon's former record labels.

7

INTRUDER IN THE DIRT

And if I have any self-mythologizing idea of myself, it's that I'm this sort of homeless, Graham Greene kind of character. Which is not so far from the truth.

—Warren Zevon (Roeser)

At the decade's cusp, with *Transverse City*'s Millennium Paranoia Tour, Warren Zevon continued to embrace the rockupational "road goes on forever" mythology. Zevon found relief, consistency, and musical autonomy on the road, not to mention fewer repercussions for his excessive and eccentric behavior. To him, touring was "a good thing" as "it put me in touch with the reality of what I was doing, and who was listening, and what it was like to go out and play, earn a living that way"(Cromelin, n.p.). Zevon had a routine circuit, usually in the frequency pattern of a couple of months, a couple of times a year, booking clubs in tiny-town U.S.A. and occasional concerts in bigger cities such as Chicago, New York, and Boston. Increasingly, as Zevon mellowed into his "quiet period," his solo tours outnumbered those with a band.

In late 1989 Zevon was cast in the unusual position of opening for Richard Marx. It was an odd pairing, if not humiliating record-label penance for Zevon. The headliner Marx was a huge pop star with teen appeal, nudging the quip that other Marxes— namely Groucho and Karl—were much better matches for Zevon than Richard. In 1987, Marx became the first male artist to reach the Top 3 with four singles from a debut album. His follow-up, *Repeat Offender* (1989), released the same year as Zevon's *Transverse City*, was equally huge, pushing

Prince out of the number-one spot on the *Billboard* album chart. Zevon followers were embarrassed for their antihero, calling his subordinate opening act relegation shameless, disappointing, and pretty hilarious, among other things. By most accounts, the older segment of the audience attended the shows just to see Zevon perform and left after his solo piano opening act, leaving behind a predominantly teen audience.

The Marx mismatch seemed to foretell a peculiar period for Zevon during the 1990s, one that was more idiosyncratic than usual and marked by striking music miscellanea. Zevon's individual recordings were concentrated in the first half of the decade, when he maintained a biannual album pace that included a riveting, live international acoustic set in between two studio albums that were as invisible as any Zevon solo works. His multifarious peripheral projects spanned the entire decade, quietly yielding worthwhile rarities and imprints in the Zevon body of work that not only underscored Zevon's noir tones, humor, and intelligence, but more significantly, revealed his versatility as a writer, musician, performer, and entertainer. The array of activity included a small-scale indie super group, literary collaborations, film and television theme songs, scores and soundtracks, a rare tribute record contribution, writing liner notes, substituting as a late-night talk show bandleader, several quirky comedy cameos in television series, and a performance at a gubernatorial inauguration. The diverse output could not deter another five-year record label disconnect for Zevon during the second half of the decade.

TAKE A GIANT STEP

Unlike his extended post-Asylum drift, Zevon did not remain without a record contract for long following his parting with Virgin after *Transverse City*. Zevon signed with Giant Records, a subsidiary of the reactivated Reprise Records that had been dormant from 1976 to 1987, and was part of the mighty Warner Music Group. The once-renowned Reprise was formed in 1960 by Frank Sinatra to better accommodate creative control of his recordings and thus, the origin of Sinatra's "Chairman of the Board" sobriquet. Sinatra's fellow Rat Pack members Dean Martin and Sammy Davis, Jr., along with Bing Crosby and Rosemary Clooney, were among the label's early 1960s roster recruits.

Giant was a new label, launched in 1990 by Irving Azoff, who was part of the upper echelon of West Coast music industry figures along with Clive Davis, David Geffen, and others. Azoff moved to Los Angeles from Illinois in 1970 and promptly started representing artists, beginning with Dan Fogelberg and on to the Eagles, among others. Southern California music scene chronicler Barney Hoskyns (2006) wrote that singer-songwriter Randy Newman's song "Short People" was directed at Azoff, who had aggressively pursued Newman for his Front Line Management company.

Azoff, known in the music industry as the "Poison Dwarf," was urging Zevon to fire his manager, Andy Slater, and replace him with the prominent Peter Asher. The demand had deal-with-the-devil overtones, with the enticement of better promotion and marketing. At 44 and sober, in decent financial shape, and with a solid touring base, Zevon was nonetheless feeling like he was approaching a last-chance crossroads in his career. Zevon complied, or caved to the soul-selling overture, replacing his ardent loyalist Slater with Asher.

HINDU LOVE GODS: THE "SUB-ROSA" SESSIONS

During the waning days of recording *Sentimental Hygiene* in 1987 in L.A., Zevon and his R.E.M. instrumentalists, Bill Berry, Mike Mills, and Peter Buck, jammed their way through a number of covers and blues classics after hours in the studio. The helplessly literate Zevon referred to the all-night session as "sub rosa," a Latin word meaning "under the rose," to denote secrecy or confidentiality. In 1990, Giant decided to release a recording of the impromptu session as the self-titled *hindu love gods* album. The record company move seemed a bit transparent and opportunistic, even to Zevon. His precipitous transition to a new record label and an equally efficient initial record release, albeit as the substitute front for hindu love gods' Michael Stipe, did not diminish Zevon's suspicions about the music business and his place within. In his skewed view, the fledgling Giant was "overexcited" at the prospect of capitalizing on R.E.M.'s gold, platinum, and critical cachet and side-project marketability. The label's motivation may have also been driven by the music market's renewed interest in, and the inherent novelty appeal of, the "super group" in the wake of the Traveling

Wilburys. Perhaps music's most legendary collective of artists, the troupe featured Bob Dylan, Roy Orbison, George Harrison, Tom Petty, and Jeff Lynne of Electric Light Orchestra, assembled to record two albums between 1988 and 1990.

The hindu love gods' I.R.S. 1986 single, "Gonna Have a Good Time Tonight"/"Narrator," was not a promotional prelude, nor was it included on the album. Besides being on a different record label, the pair of songs had little in common with the collection of covers assembled for the long play. The album loosely qualifies as a predominant, though not exclusively, blues record, with Zevon revisiting influential roots by way of indie rock, trying to make an album that sounded like his blues hero, John Hammond. The casually spirited ten-song set displays slight strands of compatibility with Zevon's *Stand in the Fire*, with a spontaneous studio sound that projects as a suppositional sequel to the Roxy chronicles ten years after, or had the live set been expanded into a double album of outtakes and extras. The immediacy in hindu love gods' production emanates a good-natured, rehearsal ambiance that is true to its nocturnal knock-around origins. Though sporadically clumsy and allowably negligent of syncopations from the originals, the group's roots affection in their renditions is overriding.

The quartet picks up where Zevon left off on *Stand in the Fire*'s "Bo Diddley's a Gunslinger/Bo Diddley," with Chicago, Mississippi Delta, and New Orleans blues standards their predominant interpretive mode, and Zevon's growling the vocals. Included are Robert Johnson's "Walkin' Blues" and "Travelin' Riverside Blues"; Willie Dixon's "Wang Dang Doodle"; Tommy McClennan's bawdy "Crosscut Saw," usually associated with Albert King; a soul-shuffling, jailbird-beat "Junko Pardner"; and a seven-minute take on Muddy Waters's "Mannish Boy," which Zevon frequently performed live early in his career. The album's final three songs interrupt the continuity, while expanding the musical heritage beyond deep blues to include alternative, country, and folk. The sequence shift includes "Battleship Chains," a Terry Anderson tune the Georgia Satellites recorded on their 1986 debut; Johnny Horton's "I'm a One Woman Man," also a country hit for George Jones in 1989; and a Western riding rendition of Woody Guthrie's "Vigilante Man," a particularly fitting outlaw song for Zevon.

The album's highlight and most accessible four minutes is a vigorous version of Prince and the Revolution's chart-topping "Raspberry Beret."

In relative close proximity to the 1985 original, the hindu love gods' badass single reached number 28 on the Modern Rock chart, and was considered Zevon-enough to be included on his subsequent "best of" compilations distributed by Rhino in 1996 and 2002. The album itself made it into the Top 200 at number 168, a foreseeable spot considering the hindu love gods were merely an affable side project with alternative appeal rather than a star-studded super group.

MR. LYRICS' SECRET DREAM

My lack of a vast knowledge of episodic TV music may have been what appealed to [the producers]. I wouldn't know a Rockford [Files] tension cue if it was floating in my coffee cup.
—Warren Zevon (Fretts)

Mr. Lyrics had a secret dream to just compose and not have that responsibility of the lyrics that people expected of him.
—Debbie Gold, music supervisor (C. Zevon)

Throughout the 1990s, Zevon's songwriting status was further validated, and his musical arrangement skills as a composer were presented in an impressive accumulation of thirteen music credits spread across five films and six television series in a wide range of genres. Zevon's versatility, musical mood, and variation were equally notable, and not limited to merely licensing his existing songs. The range included early-era and new songs from the Zevon catalog, cover versions, series theme songs, scores, and originals composed exclusively for a variety of scenes and episodes. "Things to Do in Denver When You're Dead" doubled as part of the soundtrack and the film title for a neo-noir crime thriller in 1995.

Pop and rock musicians and songwriters redirecting their focus to film and television music was not uncommon. Interestingly, some of the most notable crossovers had New Wave backgrounds: Stewart Copeland (Police), Hans Zimmer (Buggles), Danny Elfman (Oingo Boingo), Mark Mothersbaugh (Devo). Other prominent and prolific figures were guitar virtuoso Ry Cooder and Randy Newman, whose satirical songwriting and piano composing closely aligned with Zevon. The thought of Zevon emulating Newman by doing Disney productions, whether lyrics and/or scores, was wildly intriguing and amusing, although highly improbable that such a partnership would have ever materialized.

The score and soundtrack work was important for Zevon, not only as an exposure vehicle, but artistically for scene-specific songwriting and arrangements, and as an outlet to explore and integrate his classical proficiencies. His decade-long soundtrack stream began in 1990 with the Australian film *Heaven Tonight. Excitable Boy*'s unsung "Johnny Strikes Up the Band" provides a fitting theme for the story of a father (John Waters) who fronts an aging band that performs 1960s music and is jealous of his son's (Guy Pearce) success with a techno-pop band.

The same year, jazz/New Age score composer Mark Isham, who was introduced to Zevon by manager Duncan Aldrich and had appeared on *Transverse City*, recruited Zevon to contribute to the Alan Rudolph detective film, *Love at Large*. Rudolph and Isham were not only interested in Zevon the songwriter—according to Zevon, he'd "use anything I wrote"—but for an uncommon interpretation of the Great American Songbook. With his timid rendition of "You Don't Know What Love Is," Zevon joined a celebrated lineage of vocalists and instrumentalists— among them Ella Fitzgerald, Billie Holiday, Dinah Washington, Miles Davis, Chet Baker, and John Coltrane, who recorded the Don Raye/ Gene DePaul jazz standard. Accompanied by Isham on trumpet and electronics, Zevon tiptoes through a languid, late-night lounge-like version that demonstrates that he is clearly more comfortable rendering his own romantic melancholies.

The songwriting solicitation for *Love at Large* was more memorable, yielding one of Zevon's sentimental staples that would be included as the concluding cut on his album *Mr. Bad Example* (1991) the following year. Rudolph prodded Zevon by mentioning that Neil Young wrote a song in one night for Isham's previous film project. Zevon replied skeptically, "Oh yeah, did it have a bridge?" (Zevon 1996, n.p.) Zevon came through with one of his lovely songs of longing and quiet despair. The smooth, shadowy mid-tempo "Searching for a Heart" could be a companion piece to "Reconsider Me." Amidst the "darkness in the morning" emerges the gentle objection that "certain individuals aren't sticking to the plan." The lesson is that love "requires a little standing in line, waiting, pacing the floor, watching the door." Staying inconspicuous and out of sight, the hopeless romantic delivers a treatise worthy of a noir Valentine greeting: "They say love conquers all/you can't start it like a car, you can't stop it with a gun." In 2011, Rebecca Pidgeon's delicate version further augments the inventory of requisite female variations of Zevon's tender ballads.

Director Lawrence Kasden also employed "Searching for a Heart" the following year in *Grand Canyon*. The film, billed as "the *Big Chill* of the '90s" (also directed by Kasden), explores random events and their effect on race and class in a Los Angeles community. The recurrence of "Searching for a Heart" is somewhat surprising, as directors and music supervisors usually try to avoid repeating a song that was used in another film, particularly within such close proximity. Though neither film was a huge box office success, the song placement provided further exposure for *Mr. Bad Example*, which was released two months before *Grand Canyon*'s December 1991 premiere. Zevon's "Lawyers, Guns and Money" is also in a scene in the film, playing on the radio as a character gets lost after hours in a seedy part of downtown L.A.

Zevon's involvement in television may have been incongruent with his high-culture literature and film affinities, yet the experience was creatively challenging. The tasks were also highly compatible with his composer qualities, as he was hired to score, arrange, and write lyrics for several television series theme songs. Zevon's small-screen initiation began with scoring for *Drug Wars: The Camarena Story*, Michael Mann's 1990 miniseries for NBC based on Elaine Shannon's 1988 book, *Desperados*. Music supervisor Debbie Gold, who recruited Zevon to compose for the Mann miniseries, said "it was a dream for Zevon not to have to write lyrics," adding that "he was a like a genius when it comes to music but he's also a little tricky to work with" (C. Zevon, 243–44). The compelling drug war chronicle was brimming with Zevonian intrigue, desperation, and noir atmosphere, centered around undercover DEA agent Enrique Camarena, who exposed a massive marijuana operation in northern Mexico that led to his death and a comprehensive investigation of corruption within the Mexican government. Working with Mann on a project was significant. His mid-1980s "MTV Cops" series, *Miami Vice* (NBC, 1984–1990), redefined the form and the role of music in television drama, bringing soundtrack to the forefront as a thread and a tool of storytelling. The initial *Miami Vice* soundtrack (1985, MCA), featuring score music by Jan Hammer and hit songs by Phil Collins ("In the Air Tonight") and solo Eagle Glenn Frey ("Smuggler's Blues"), among others, stayed at the top of the charts for 12 weeks, establishing the television soundtrack album as a viable cultural artifact.

The "Music by Warren Zevon" credit next appears in a 1992 episode—"King of the Road," featuring Brad Pitt—on the HBO horror anthology series *Tales from the Crypt*, based on the EC Comics series dating from the 1940s through the mid-1950s. Zevon faced "the impossible challenge" of replacing songs by Bruce Springsteen and AC/DC, among others, that producer Tom Holland had used as the series' temporary score. The music Zevon fashioned had a *Miami Vice* vibe with a *Born to Run* undercurrent that was more literal than nuanced, which was fitting for the melodramatic production. Zevon's compositions hit the high dramatic, romantic, character, and emotional cues. In the tire-screeching opening drag-racing scene, the straightaway rocker in the vein of "The Overdraft" repeats "bad road, wretched road," establishing the setting for the fast-and-furious conflict that triangulates between a lawman father, his daughter, and a hoodlum.

Zevon's writing continued to distinguish itself in any context. The episode's centerpiece song, "Roll With the Punches," which Zevon refers to as his "faux Bruce tune," leads with a boxing metaphor employing a clever duality of love at first sight/love at first fight: "Johnny never knew what hit him when he first met Julia." (The episode's actual characters, Billy and Karen, lacked alliterative lyric punch.) The phrasing is stock Zevon, at once rebellious ("used to be so wild and free") and fatalistic ("time treats everybody like a fool," "sun is sinking low"), with Springsteen accents ("Johnny has a '57 Chevy with four on the floor and a 429," "run it out to the end of the line") and a "two lanes will take us anywhere," "Thunder Road" romantic ending ("Honey, we ain't never goin' home").

Zevon was hired as music director of the short-lived remake of *Route 66* (NBC, 1993), a summer replacement series that lasted four episodes. Zevon's self-described "grunge-classical" instrumentals were a stark contrast to the jazzy Nelson Riddle Orchestra arrangements of the 1960–1964 original series. The low-self-esteem title theme, "If You Won't Leave Me I'll Find Somebody Who Will," is ironic and racing with urgency. Just as the song gets rolling, with son Jordan singing harmony on the catchy chorus couplet—"I'm a refugee from the mansion on the hill" followed by the rhyming title—the fun abruptly ends at 43 seconds. No fade out, or suggestion of a bridge; no second verse or progress toward a three-minute narrative. Only a Zevon smirk. A practical joke. A segment, not a song. While the concise length reflects the norm for opening television titles and themes, Zevon apparently never completed the song, which is disappointing considering how the initial hurried, hooky appeal begs for a continuance to conclusion. "If You Don't Leave Me I'll Find Somebody Who Will" remained in its sample state on Zevon's 1996 anthology, with its sudden finality even more striking within the context of the compilation. Nor has a finished version surfaced in any of Zevon's posthumous releases and reissues.

Zevon's theme music shifted from the retro *Route 66* to a futuristic setting in William Shatner's *TekWar* (USA/Sci Fi Channel, 1994–1996). The science fiction series, based on the *TekWar* novels ghost-written by Ron Goulart from outlines by Shatner, is a Zevonian setting that echoes *Transverse City* with detective noir shades. Set in the year 2045, the story follows ex-cop Jake Cardigan, who lost his badge after being framed for dealing the illicit narcotic substance *tek* and murdering his fellow officers during a bust. When his sentence in cryo-detainment is reduced, he becomes a private investigator trying to clear his name while working for the security firm Cosmos and pursuing the Tek Lords. Zevon's pulsating ending theme for the series, "Real or Not," featuring harmonies from legendary 1970s back-up vocalist Rosemary Butler, reflects the surroundings and Cardigan's nightmarish circumstances: "walking in the wasteland with a ghost in the machine," a "simulated sunset" and "pessimistic sky, filled with miracles and half of them are lies." He concludes, "These are strange times and I don't want to live this way." According to Zevon, the concise 1:45 minute track revealed his secret fondness for English techno records.

SO YOU WANT TO BE A SITCOM STAR

> *Well, that's the problem. I think they're eventually going to run out of parts where they need an actor to play Warren Zevon. I think I can go on from here to play a thirteenth-century Scottish hero.*
> —Warren Zevon, *Jon Stewart Show*, 1995

Zevon's television credits were not limited to music. He was also part of an unusual undercurrent of Baby Boom–era pop and rock star cameos in television comedies during the 1990s. Among the unlikely troupe of singer-songwriters who appeared as themselves in sitcom episodes were Yoko Ono (*Mad About You*, NBC), Joe Walsh (*The Drew Carey Show*, ABC), the Pretenders' Chrissie Hynde (*Friends*, NBC), and perhaps the most improbable, Bob Dylan in an episode titled "Play Lady Play" (*Dharma and Greg*, ABC). The trend initiated around 1987 in an episode of the unconventional *It's Garry Shandling's Show* (Fox), when "neighbor" Tom Petty, as himself, shows up at Garry's door returning the hedge clippers he borrowed. Petty, who also voiced "Lucky" on the animated *King of the Hill* (Fox), was cast as a semi-regular who frequently dropped by Shandling's condo, whether Christmas caroling or singing with the neighborhood quartet. In his most memorable visit, Petty serenades expectant mother Jackie with an acoustic living room rendition of his "The Waiting," after negotiating with Garry to trim his hedges while Petty was touring. Petty's droll presence marked the understated beginning of an undercurrent of pop/rock sitcom cameos that continued in television during the next 20-plus years.

Two of the most prominent showcases for the guest appearances were *The Simpsons* (Fox), which has routinely animated rockers since the series' inception in 1989, just as Nickelodeon network's offbeat *The Adventures of Pete and Pete* (1993–1995) cast alternative artists in roles, among them Luscious Jackson, R.E.M.'s Michael Stipe, Kate Pierson of the B-52s, Juliana Hatfield of the Blake Babies, as well as Iggy Pop, Debbie Harry, Marshall Crenshaw, and others.

For Zevon, acting was more than a whim and welcome diversion from the demands of writing. He always considered himself an entertainer in the broadest sense of the word, and fancied the notion that he possessed some talent for acting, should the opportunity arise. In the early 1980s, when he was dating actress Kim Lankford, Zevon auditioned for minor villain roles on the *Knot's Landing* television series that Lankford was cast in. Zevon was one of the few musical artists who managed multiple guest appearances, including episodes of two comedy series on the cable network HBO—the show biz satire *The Larry Sanders Show* (starring Shandling) in 1993 and *Dream On* in 1995—and in *Suddenly Susan* (NBC, 1999) at the end of the decade.

Both HBO comedies perpetuated the running gag of "Werewolves of London" as Zevon's hit song torment. On *The Larry Sanders Show*, Zevon is backstage negotiating with the late-night show's producer Artie (Rip Torn) on which song he'll perform. Artie expects "Werewolves of London," as it is host Larry's favorite, much to Zevon's chagrin. "Listen, I don't want to be a prick, but every single show I do, I play 'Werewolves of London' and it's driving me fucking crazy." Artie, at once compromising and clueless, asks Zevon about doing something from his first album, maybe the "French . . . French Connection." "'The French Inhaler?'" Zevon curtly corrects. "Is that under four minutes?" asks Artie. "I'll play it fast," snaps Zevon. As the two part, Artie mutters, "Fucking musicians!" Following Zevon's performance, host Sanders veers from the show's strict schedule, invoking the talk-show cliché— "Do we have time for another?"—requesting, of course, "Werewolves of London." Artie approves. An annoyed Zevon obliges. Waiting in the wings as the next guest, actor John Ritter is also disgruntled, sensing his scheduled appearance is being victimized by Zevon's "Werewolves." As Zevon plays off camera, ensuing backstage commotion reflects the song's mayhem. A drunk, shirtless fan staggers toward the set, slurring and howling, "Gotta go say hi to Warren. Ahh-wooo," and is wrestled to the ground by Artie. Bumped guest Ritter stomps in, flanked by his publicist, as Artie rises from the floor: "Arthur, this is the last time I'm ever doing this show." The episode duplicates the eerie irony of the May 22, 1978, issue of *People* magazine, both juxtaposing Zevon and Ritter, who died four days apart in September 2003. The line, "Werewolves of London, again," seems fitting.

In *Dream On* the lead character, Martin, recognizes Zevon, in ponytail and tux, while at the food table of a music awards ceremony. Starstruck, he clumsily insults Zevon by confusing "Poor Poor Pitiful Me" with "Mohammed's Radio," dismissing them as basically the same song, same chords. Zevon gets in his face, and delivers a teeth-clenched "Get away from me before I call security, you little fuck! You're probably the idiot who yells 'Werewolves of London' at every concert." Zevon, with ire more authentic than affected, then thumps Martin's tuxedo tie— "Cocksucker!"—and walks away.

RIDING THAT (TRIBUTE) TRAIN

Tribute records saturated the 1990s music marketplace, transcending trend into full-fledged phenomenon. The seemingly endless and varied tributes to aural objects of affection extended beyond artists and bands to include genres, individual songs and albums, record labels, causes, commemorations, and even bands that weren't "real," such as the Rutles, the superb Beatles parody group. Zevon became an aberrant participant, teaming with multi-instrumentalist pal David Lindley and backed by Jorge Calderón, Faces keyboardist Ian McLagen, and drummer Stan Lynch, for a rendition of "Casey Jones" on the Grateful Dead tribute record, *Deadicated* (Arista, 1991), with proceeds going to the Rainforest Action Network. Much like Zevon's rapport with Calderón, his enduring musical partnership with Lindley, though understated, is significant. Lindley, who states in the compilation's liner notes, "It's always fun to work with Warren," has recorded more Zevon songs than any single artist. Though he was one of a few figures from the Los Angeles music circle who presumably chose not to contribute commentary for Crystal Zevon's oral history, Lindley routinely shares insightful Zevon anecdotes with affection, admiration, and humor during the solo string spectacle of his exquisite live shows.

Zevon, who opened for the legendary San Francisco jam-band pioneers a few times in the early 1980s, pays homage: "You haven't lived 'til you've swung with the Dead. Jerry (Garcia) is a bona fide genius." Zevon's appearance on the compilation is an exclusive, as it stands as his only guest spot on another album during his entire career, either as a musician or singer. The absenteeism is conspicuous, not only within the context of the tribute profusion during the era, but more so considering the all-star casts of colleagues that routinely contributed to Zevon's records, and the assumed opportunities for him to return the favor. Convenient conjecture suggests Zevon's excesses over the years, artistic conceit, his jagged record-label status, and the prevailing perception of him as a songwriter first and foremost with pianist, guitarist, and singer secondary, were factors in his lack of guest credits on other records. Zevon seemed dismissive about his nonparticipation and uninvited status, shrugging, "Nobody's asked. I guess I'm perceived as somebody who plays his own songs and that's it" (Lim, 1).

MR. BAD EXAMPLE: "RENEGADE ALL MY DAYS"

The core of Zevon's productivity during the period lies in his three records between 1991 and 1995. A survey of the captivating, often droll titles of each studio album's ten songs alone foretell some of Zevon's most misanthropic four-minute outlooks. The acerbic tone that is established from *Mr. Bad Example*'s (1991) lead lines of the bitter kiss-off, "Finishing Touches"—"I'm getting tired of you, you're getting tired of me"—winds through to the serene boat-rocking subtext of the closing song and title track of *Mutineer* (1995) four years later, which avows, "Ain't no room on board for the insincere." In between, the naturally noir-ish Zevon juxtaposes what are some of his nastiest narratives and creepiest character sketches with love's futility. The "Excitable Boy" of the late 1970s grew up to be "Mr. Bad Example," then matured, mellowing into the "Mutineer."

Wachtel returns to produce *Mr. Bad Example*, alongside standby sessionists Calderón, Bob Glaub, drummers Jim Keltner and Jeff Porcaro, and Lindley contributing his eclectic touches of fiddle, lap steel, saz, and the Turkish cumbus; Zevon's son Jordan is among those singing harmony. The chiaroscuro profiles of a cigarette-dragging Zevon on the cover and booklet (and the trademark smoking, bespectacled skull on the back bottom corner) present a proper shadowy palette that plays out in the songs.

The record begins with "Finishing Touches," the "final act of our little tragedy" and what Zevon described as a "hate song." The "no use hangin' around" fait accompli displays a similar malicious tone as "The French Inhaler" from 15 years earlier. The narrator, "sick and tired, my cock is sore," dictates, "You can screw everybody I've ever known, but I still won't talk to you on the phone." Zevon had always shown a willingness to draw from or disguise personal wounds in his songwriting. Following his "cowboy days," Zevon transferred his addictive behaviors from alcohol and drugs to a gluttonous sexual appetite. His proclivities are well documented in Crystal Zevon's 2007 oral history. During the late 1980s and much of the 1990s, Zevon moved rapidly through relationships, from the rock-and-roll duty of one-night stands, to shooting stars such as fellow songwriter Karla Bonoff and Eleanor Mondale, daughter of Jimmy Carter's vice president Walter Mondale, to more serious romances and girlfriends that approached long-term possibilities, among them Annette Aguilar-Ramos (the subject of one of Zevon's final songs) and actress Julia Mueller.

In "Suzie Lightning," Zevon offers a "composite of women who'd recently made me unhappy (and vice versa)." Zevon pirated the title from a stripper's name in the credits of a British horror B-film, *I Don't Want to Be Born* (1975), retitled in the United States as *Sharon's Baby*. In contrast, the song itself was inspired by a Bartók postcard that bassist Bob Glaub sent Zevon from Budapest. The failed relationship in "Suzie Lightning," who strangely "only sleeps on planes," is more fleeting ("lights up the sky then she's gone") than ferocious. She "takes no prisoners" and is "tired of going nowhere," unable to see that he is "burning up, burning down, burning out," leaving him to conclude, "I need a girl from earth."

The series of character sketches continues to unfold with a darkness at the end of the cul-de-sac in the morose "Model Citizen." Simmering in the suburbia settings from the early morning to the cool of the evening is the law-abiding, tax-paying (when he can), Good Samaritan, "don't bring the milk in/Leave it on the porch," and "don't read the paper or mow the lawn no more." "Driving to the market at the break of dawn to watch 'em unload the produce, then ride right back home" is among Zevon's most mundane and lurking lyrical observations. The comic quatrains of the family-man portrait invite cringes of irresistible amusement, from "tormenting the mail man, terrorizing the maid, try to teach 'em some manners," to a card game double entendre— "wife's playing canasta with everyone in town," to a darkly ingenious discipline method —"the Craftsman lathe down in the basement to show to the children when they misbehave." While Zevon's seething profile falls short of bodies in the crawlspace or buried in the backyard, or *Breaking Bad*'s Walter White cooking meth, when the model citizen feels the pressure and needs a break, he will "load up the Winnebago, drive it in the lake." Each verse is punctuated with a hypnotic chant-like "model citizen." The chorus rises slightly to a summary, as if an exhale seeking relief: "It's the white man's burden, and it weighs a ton." The song's most curious compliment may have come from esteemed baseball writer and musician Peter Gammons, who recorded a version of "Model Citizen" for his album, *Never Slow Down, Never Grow Old* (2006), a benefit for Foundation to Be Named Later, part of the Hot Stove, Cool Concert series based in Boston.

The similarly loathsome, though lighter, "Mr. Bad Example," is a lyric-laden, worldly whirling polka, cowritten with Calderón. The rollicking, rhyming stream of comic couplets that echoes the cynical cadence of Billy Joel's "The Entertainer" was composed after Zevon and

Calderón had consumed so much Turkish coffee they were "seeing Kirlian auras." The "intruder in the dirt"—a substitution for the Faulknerian "dust"— is "very well acquainted with the seven deadly sins," and "likes to have a good time and don't care who gets hurt." The debauchery begins with an altar boy pocketing bills from the children's fund cash box at church. From there, the plot sickens to "laying tackless stripping and housewives by the score" while working part-time at his father's carpet store, on to law school and counselling all his clients to plead insanity, then to hair replacement swindling the bald, to global schemes in Adelaide, Monte Carlo, and Sri Lanka, hiring aboriginals to work in opal mines along the way. Bridging the bad-boy behavior, "Angel Dressed in Black" is a contemporary "Carmelita," its narrator "sitting on the sofa suckin' a bowl of crack," worried and waiting for his Queen of Downtown to return.

In Zevon's first down-home divergence into country since "Bed of Coals" in 1980, "Heartache Spoken Here" provides one of the album's gems. Zevon proves a welcome outsider rather than a trespasser in the genre. His posture is not as parodist. The delivery is unaffected, with Dwight Yoakam accenting Zevon's vocal with twang textures over a neatly crafted arrangement driven by Porcaro's backbeat, with Dan Dugmore's weeping, velvety strands of pedal steel and Wachtel's nimble guitar enhancing the authenticity. Zevon carefully sifts the country songwriting vocabulary for phrases befitting a heartbreak-and-tears tune. From the "when I was young" opening to the casually comforting "So come on down, we'll talk about it" to metaphors for disappointing love affairs—"watching stars burn out one by one," "a house of cards," "a castle made of sand." He even inserts a requisite "little darlin'" in two verses, adding to the charm of one of the buried treasures in the Zevon songbook. The following year, Yoakam countrified Zevon's "Carmelita" with accordionist Flaco Jiménez on *Partners* (1992).

The innocence in a sky filled with stars in "Heartache Spoken Here" darkens into an ominous atmosphere in "Quite Ugly One Morning," the title a Dylan Thomas paraphrase. There, the sky "looks funny"; more specifically and bizarrely, it looks "kinda chewed-on like." The song lives down to its "early" to "ugly" turn-phrase title, with unsettling abruptness ("We all said goodnight/It came without a warning/Just a flash of light"), dawn-to-sundown weariness ("a hollow triumph when you make it to the bottom of another day"), funny feelings inside ("when you feel like laughing and everybody tells you ought to be cry-ing"), and fatalism ("there'll be nothing left but the sound of drums"). In 1996, Scottish crime writer Christopher Brookmyre borrowed the song title for the name of his debut novel, which was later adapted into a television movie in 2003.

The pessimism hovers, along with the persisting sky motif in the lead line of "Renegade"— "some prayers never reach the sky," just as "some wounds never heal" and "some wars never end." The song is a declara-tion of defiance: "don't want to grow old gracefully" or "go 'til it's too late," and "rather break than bend." The narrator envisions being "the old man in the road somewhere kneeling down in the dust by the side of the Interstate." A self-referential "rebel all my days" chorus is wrapped in regional verses that wave a tattered Confederate flag. The Southern accent is not as deep and dark as in Zevon's "Play It All Night Long." Hope and skepticism coincide. The undying decree—"They still say someday the South will rise"—elicits the renegade response—"Man, I want to see that deal." Yet, he "ain't seen no reconstruction . . . just the scorched earth all around and the high school band played 'Dixieland.'"

The album's shortest song at just under three minutes, "Things to Do in Denver When You're Dead," is more surreal than sinister as suggested by its title. Zevon, who spent considerable time in Colorado, often with Hunter S. Thompson, cowrote the tune with Wachtel and Marinell again. The trio are protagonists in the narrative, as if a drunken ramble or relating a dream; "I'm afraid to be alone, I got some weird ideas in my head," sets a *Twilight Zone* tone. As is common in Zevon arrangements, a bouncy melody disguises the darker shades and peril. The offbeat chorus conjures a seedy side—"you won't need a cab to find a priest" and "a place to stay where they never change the sheets"—balanced by a fitting Chamber of Commerce slogan for the Mile-High City—"You just roll around Denver all day." Interestingly, the line "And home is just a place to hang your head" was an inadver-tent echo of Elvis Costello's "Home is Anywhere You Hang Your Head" from *Blood and Chocolate* (1986). "Things to Do in Denver When You're Dead" was appropriated, without compensation or acknowledg-ment, for the title of a 1995 crime lord film featuring Andy Garcia, Christopher Walken, and Steve Busccmi as a hit man known as "Mr. Shhh," with the song, also uncredited, playing over the closing credits.

The song is a somewhat questionable inclusion on both Zevon "best of" anthologies in 1996 and 2002.

The smooth conclusion, "Searching for a Heart," is a reminder of Zevon's signature redemptive romantic notes and emotional songwriting depth amidst the album's predominantly trenchant milieu. The song contained undeniable mainstream appeal, with Zevon "out-Eagling the Eagles," in the view of *Mojo* critic Luke Torn (2014, 47). (Don Henley delivers a solo-Eagle version of "Searching for a Heart" on the Zevon tribute, *Enjoy Every Sandwich* [2004].) In addition to being featured in two film soundtracks, the song also reached the late-night landscape of network television, with Zevon performances on David Letterman's *Late Night* (NBC) and the syndicated *Arsenio Hall Show*, where then-presidential candidate Bill Clinton famously played a saxophone rendition of "Heartbreak Hotel" on the 1992 campaign trail. Despite the exposure, "Searching for a Heart" did not make a notable difference for the album commercially. Though well crafted, *Mr. Bad Example* simply did not connect. Some reviews thought Zevon took a leap backward, as the record was more rancorous than usual, with vitriol overwhelming nuance. The album was easily shunted aside by the emerging sounds of the early-1990s music marketplace, particularly hip-hop and grunge, led by Nirvana's *Nevermind* (1991), which included the Gen-X anthems "Smells Like Teen Spirit" and "Come as You Are." *Mr. Bad Example* became Zevon's first record taken out of circulation due to dismal sales.

UNPLUGGED: "MY MISS SAIGON"

The standing joke I've made in the States is the last time I did a live album it was an election year [Stand in the Fire, 1980], so it's perhaps that lust for personal advancement in the air that I smell.
—Warren Zevon (Reid)

After being on the road to support *Mr. Bad Example*, backed by the Canadian band, the Odds, and with sets frequently including covers of Van Morrison's "Into the Mystic" and Leonard Cohen's "First We Take Manhattan," Zevon embarked on a solo world tour in the spring of 1992. He was accompanied by engineer/producer sidekick Duncan Aldrich, who recorded every performance live-to-DAT (digital audio tape). "The show has developed into something longer than I originally intended and now it's a whole evening thing, the full two hours," Zevon told a reporter in New Zealand. "I refer to it as my *Miss Saigon*" (Reid, n.p.). Together Zevon and Aldrich culled songs from the recordings of nearly 100 acclaimed live shows from North American cities to England, Germany, New Zealand, and Australia into an audio chronicle of the acclaimed four-month tour. The resulting *Learning to Flinch* (1993)—its title is a phrase from the Robert Lowell poem, "Eye and Tooth," rather than the suspected twist on "Learning to Fly" in reference to the Pink Floyd and Emerson, Lake and Palmer late-1980s tunes, and Tom Petty's popular 1991 song from *Into the Great Wide Open*—is Zevon strictly solo, playing piano and sparkling-crisp 12- and 6-string guitars, with no instrumental or vocal backing, and no audience repartee.

Learning to Flinch is essentially *Warren Zevon: Unplugged*, his version of the MTV live music series that premiered in 1989 and rapidly ascended from trend to phenomenon to franchise. *MTV: Unplugged* featured popular artists performing acoustic versions of their electric repertoires in a casual, intimate setting before a live audience. The initial episodes were hosted by Jules Shear, whose songs "If She Knew What She Wants" and "All Through the Night" were 1980s hits for the Bangles and Cyndi Lauper. Among the many artists who performed on the one-hour episodes were Bob Dylan, Neil Young, R.E.M., 10,000 Maniacs, and Tony Bennett, who was never plugged in to begin with. Nirvana's casual counter-grunge, platinum performance was particularly memorable, as it marked Kurt Cobain's last television appearance, and a cool set list that featured covers of songs by David Bowie, Leadbelly, the Meat Puppets, and Vaseline. In other memorable moments, Bruce Springsteen violated the show's performance code in 1992 by plugging in the amps and going electric with E-Street substitutes, following his opening acoustic rendition of "Red Headed Woman."

MTV maximized the marketability, releasing about one-third of the sessions as live records, with occasional accompanying videos of the show. The recontextualized songs, lesser-known material, and frequent intriguing interpretations, such as 10,000 Maniacs' version of Springsteen/Patti Smith's "Because the Night," enhanced the appeal. Eric Clapton's *Unplugged* (1992)—highlighted by a striking laid-back rendition of "Layla" and the heart-wrenching hit single, "Tears in Heaven," about the death of his young son—reached number one on the charts and earned six Grammys.

MTV: Unplugged was a major mark on television's live music time-line. The familiar format was rooted in Public Broadcasting Service's earlier concert series, *Soundstage* (1974), and the iconic *Austin City Limits*, Bill Arhos's home-brewed concert concept that evolved from grant to pilot to premiere in 1976, with Willie Nelson performing. *Austin City Limits* introduced much of America to "progressive country" and "redneck rock," a regional mix of rock and counterculture-colored lyrics by country singer-songwriters and "cosmic cowboys," a marked contrast to the traditional, mainstream country sounds of Nashville. In the late 1980s, the unsung late-night music series, *Sunday Night/Michelob presents Night Music* (1988, NBC; 1989–1990, syndication), featured hosts Jools Holland and David Sanborn exploring and orchestrating mix-matched musicians performing together. MTV's successful un-plugged format prompted the mid-1990s *Live from the House of Blues* (1995, TBS), and VH1 variants: the short-lived, collaborative *Duets* (1995), which paired artists performing each other's songs, and *Storytellers* (1996), which evolved out of Ray Davies's solo Storyteller Tour in 1996. The musical memoir performance concept featured artists illuminating the origins of their best-known songs with stories and anecdotes. The following year, *Sessions at West 54th* (1997), taped at the Sony Music Studios in New York City, enlisted hosts from Santa Monica's famed KCRW, Talking Head David Byrne, and singer-songwriter John Hiatt in its three seasons. Into the 2000s, *Crossroads* (CMT, 2003) paired country artists with musicians from other genres, song-swapping and dueting, while the cable Sundance Channel series *Spectacle: Elvis Costello with . . .* (2008) integrated talk-show conventions into music mutuality and experimentation. With *Austin City Limits* enduring to the present, public broadcasting remained at the forefront of music performance, adding National Public Radio/NPR.org's delightful *Tiny Desk Concert* series to the live lineage in 2008, inaugurated by a Laura Gibson performance.

Zevon's compelling unplugged presence on *Learning to Flinch* holds its own with best live sets that emerged from the era's varied presentations. The carefully curated, 17-song, 75-minute set is a riveting, un-adorned acoustic complement to Zevon's rocking Roxy shows from 1980 on the live *Stand in the Fire*. The opening 45 seconds of steely acoustic guitar and harmonica emit a Neil Young vibe, leading into the "Splendid Isolation" vocal. The stripped-down sounds, many in different keys than their originals, inherently provide a fresh context. The London performance of "Werewolves of London" is more regal than restrained, with Zevon's delivery a more deliberate annunciation, and the usual playful lyric substitutions intentionally absent in honor of the song's namesake location. While "Lawyers, Guns and Money" maintains its bravado without a band, and most of the piano songs such as "Hasten Down the Wind" and "Excitable Boy" remain within the spirit of the originals, other translations that go from piano- and electric-based to resolute acoustic guitar renditions, such as "Searching for a Heart" and "Jungle Work," provide worthy and curious contrasts. There are also the extended versions that mark most live albums, with misguided attempted-epic intentions. "Roland the Headless Thompson Gunner," with a 90-second chorale prelude, is unnecessarily long at over 11 minutes. However, the excess is smartly sequenced as the set's midpoint, and plays like a mercenary intermezzo between two sides of an album. The prolonged preludes, bridges, and finales on the album's songs provide some of the purest showcases on record of Zevon's musical virtuosity and dexterity on guitar and piano, and his inventiveness as an arranger. In the engaging extravagance of "Poor Poor Pitiful Me" at 9:30 minutes during a performance in Adelaide, Australia, the mindful tourist Zevon seamlessly integrates the country's best-known bush ballad and unofficial national anthem, "Waltzing Matilda," musically, and the Civil War–era "Rose of Alabama" lyrically.

While the collated set features Zevon's best-known works, *Learning to Flinch* is not exclusively a "greatest hits live." Zevon previews three new songs—"Worrier King," "Piano Fighter," and "The Indifference of Heaven," with the latter pair re-recorded and included on his next studio album, *Mutineer*. "Worrier King" finds Zevon again cleverly tinkering with vowels, substituting "Worrier" for the more common "Warrior." The song's anxiety-ridden character resides in the same writing neighborhood as "Model Citizen." He's "hiding from the mailman. And I hate to hear the telephone ring," and is "up all night wondering what November's gonna bring." The angst is amplified by a bluesy six-string slide, Zevon's homage to John Hammond.

"Piano Fighter" is as explicitly biographical as any Zevon song, from a Chickering piano Ma and Papa bought that he "practiced hard and played with grim determination, Jim" (a name Zevon likes to punctuate lines with), to sessions, bands, "a thousand casuals and one night stands," playing *Clair de lune* (Debussy's most famous movement) in a quiet saloon, strung out, painted in the corner of a limousine, cutting a single that made it to the charts—then summarizing, "I took my money and played the part." In addition to the "fighter" referencing his father, the boxer, the characterizations are noteworthy—holy roller, real low rider, thin ice walker, freelance writer—as are the emotional pleas— "hold me tight . . . tighter, then let me go."

"The Indifference of Heaven," according to Zevon, is "the first of many depressing songs about the departure of my flaxen-tressed fiancée," actress Julia Mueller, who managed a songwriting credit on *Mr. Bad Example*'s "Angel Dressed in Black." Zevon acknowledges the song's literary debt to English novelist Martin Amis, a kindred-spirit satirist whose narratives of "the new unpleasantness" explore sordid, debauched undertows, futility, and embattled masculinity in characters who are middle-aged antiheroes and passionate iconoclasts. Zevon's gray-sky, gentle-rain rumination intermingles embittered existentialism with bloody hands in the till at the 7-11 to contemporary music couples. He is acutely aware of the yin and yang—"Time marches on, time stands still; past and present, all life folds back into the sea." The "same olds"—sun, moon, story, tune—are wearisome, as are the optimistic "They say" aphorisms: "Someday soon my sins will be forgiven," "Everything's all right," "Better days are near," "These are the good times." The tone turns to self-awareness that teeters on peer antipathy—"But they don't live around here, Billy (Joel) and Christie (Brinkley) don't; Bruce (Springsteen) and Patti (Scialfa) don't"—before descending to the familiar woeful finality of love lost. Zevon's girl left town, the town burned down, "nothing left but the sound of the front door closing forever." Curiously, "vast" is part of the divine chorus phrase —"we contemplate eternity beneath the vast indifference of heaven"—though it is not a part of the song's title. However, Lindley expands the title to "Beneath the Vast Indifference of Heaven" with his version on *Big Twang* (2007), which also includes two more covers from Zevon's subsequent *Mutineer* album, "Seminole Bingo" and "Monkey Wash Donkey Rinse."

Learning to Flinch was also available in an attractive deluxe edition, featuring Zevon's trademark "Old Velvet Nose" embossed on a silver plate centered on the compact disc's gray velvet cover. Inside, a booklet contains lyrics, photos, and souvenir images, the most notable a signed wallet card: "Mr. Zevon has gone with the Great Beaver." The package, undoubtedly designed with Zevon aficionados and the popularity of *MTV: Unplugged* in mind, was a mildly surprising extra considering *Mr. Bad Example*'s weak reception and Giant's relative newness as a record label.

JIMMY BUFFET'S EVIL TWIN: "I'M YOUR MUTINEER"

I intended the song ["Mutineer"] as a gesture of appreciation and affection to my fans, none of whom bought the record.
                                                            —Warren Zevon (1996)

The solo touring sensibility carried over to Zevon's predominantly autonomous approach to his next album, *Mutineer* (1995). Rather than resorting to his signature use of stellar sessionists, Zevon wanted to lean on his own strengths and his own sound. He retreated, producing and recording at his home studio and handling most of the instrumentation, with only intermittent accents from Calderón, Lindley on cittern and fiddle, former Joni Mitchell bassist and producer Larry Klein, keyboardist Bruce Hornsby playing accordion, and renowned background vocalist Rosemary Butler, who routinely recorded and toured with Jackson Browne, James Taylor, Bonnie Raitt, and many other artists in the 1970s and 1980s.

Throughout *Mutineer*'s ten songs, Zevon further advances his literary influences and alliances, partnering with Florida journalist and novelist Carl Hiaasen on two Sunshine State–centered narratives, while dedicating the album to gonzo journalist Dr. Hunter S. Thompson. In Hiaasen's novel *Native Tongue* (1991), published around the time Zevon recorded *Mr. Bad Example*, one character's means of coping was to retreat to his home, lock himself in, and play a Zevon album full blast. The two met at a Hiaasen book signing, a frequent Zevon activity. Their bond was instantaneous and lasting.

According to Hiaasen, when visiting Florida, Zevon's dual demeanor was embodied in his rugged individual "Hemingway mode" and his being drawn like a magnet to hokey tourist traps. The album's title originated from a tourist joint called the Mutineer at the end of the long causeway leading to and from the Keys. Similarly, "Seminole Bingo" derived from a Florida tourist brochure Zevon randomly grabbed from a rack of pamphlets. Not only was Zevon fascinated with the Native American bingo operation, he was immediately attracted to the cadence of the phrase, declaring to Hiaasen he would like to write a song with that title. Months later, Hiaasen and Zevon "started hammering out the lyrics long distance" to "Seminole Bingo" (C. Zevon, 286). The sense of place is cinematic in the witty, white-collar adventure of junk bond kings on the run with a suitcase full of money from a Luxembourg bank. With the Securities and Exchange Commission far behind, the wily Wall Streeters buy a double-wide on the Tamiami Trail down in the swamps with the gators and flamingoes outside the reservation, "a long way from Lichtenstein."

Surly paranoia and desperate aggression persist on their other co-write, "Rottweiler Blues." The language is ominous: a Glock on the bedside table, machine gun leaning by the bedroom door, a Kevlar bulletproof vest in the closet, shadows at the window, peepholes. The machismo cast includes Guardian Angels, slackers, bangers, and skin-heads on the golf course, of all places, "hunting for their balls." The menacing canine sentry is the "one hundred pounds of unfriendly per-suasion sleeping on the Florida porch," dreaming of intruders and the promise of burglar blood, "yearning to chew on a gangster tattoo and to hear the proverbial sickening thud." The refrain warns: "Don't knock on my door if you don't know my Rottweiler's name," because he'll be "mauling with intent to maim."

Nestled in a two-minute midsection of *Mutineer* is another interest-ing cover selection by Zevon. He pays tribute to one of Asylum's first artists, Judee Sill, with a splendid rendition of "Jesus Was a Cross Mak-er," which was also recorded in the early 1970s by the Hollies and Cass Elliot (solo from the Mamas and Papas) in the immediate aftermath of Sill's original. The reverent tone is enhanced by Butler's hymn-like harmonies. Zevon shared a classical music kinship with Sill, as she was influenced by Bach's metric form and suites. Lyrically, "He wages war with the devil, with a pistol by his side" and "Blinding me His song remains reminding me he's a bandit and a heartbreaker" are lines with a romantic desperado reading that translate well with, and to, Zevon, though they are alleged to be about fellow songwriter J. D. Souther.

Interestingly, Linda Ronstadt's secular interpretation, recorded in 1989 and available on her box set in 1999, was retitled "Bandit and a Heartbreaker." Rachel Yamagata is among artists who have recorded versions of the song as part of a wider rediscovery of Sill's work. Yamagata's version, along with the Hollies' 1972 cover, appeared on the rare two-volume soundtrack that accompanies Cameron Crowe's *Elizabethtown* (2005).

Zevon leans on unusual and recognizable sources for analogies in a series of songs with familiar failed-relationship and risks-of-romance themes. "Something Bad Happened To a Clown" is a queasy connection to the Kinks' 1967 toast to a circus demise, "Death of a Clown." There is a laughterless, three-ring noir atmosphere—"Sunny skies are seldom seen in the land of few and far between," where "everybody wears a frown." Surrounded by a freak-show vibe of dirge-like electronic keyboard and circus percussion sounds, the imagery is a clowning achievement—squirting rose, red nose on the ground, painted smile, and honking horn. The circus saga is a missing-person mystery—"He's been gone for quite a while"—with comic crime inferences within a deteriorating relationship—"She doesn't think he's funny anymore"—and a brilliantly bizarre procession tracing "footsteps in the sawdust leading to the edge of town."

"Similar to Rain" casts a soft shadow over a fairy tale—"Once upon a time these stories always start"—with the handsome prince and the princess, "a beautiful kid," who said "she'd never leave him but she did." The delicately delivered cautionary account parallels nature's elements with love's hazards—falling in thin ice, wet and cold, fall over, gray skies, storm clouds, "sadness in the air feels like rain."

The distant phrase—"she's so many women"—from "Hasten Down the Wind" reverberates in "Poisonous Lookalike," the title snatched from botanical dialogue Zevon heard on the radio while in Rhode Island. This woman is denounced as "Little Miss Gun-to-a-Knife Fight." She is an imposter, acting strange, treating him like a criminal, and telling him he has to change. Just when he was getting used to her, she changed her tune, leaving the casualty confused and harboring evil-twin suspicions: "You're not my girl . . . what have you done with her?" The studio versions of "Piano Fighter" and "The Indifference of Heaven," though presented with more textured arrangements, lack the verve of their live predecessors. "Piano Fighter" contains accordion washes with banks of keyboards building from the noodling, tinkling toy piano sound that replicates Zevon's childhood Chickering cited in the biographical narrative. "The Indifference of Heaven" is anchored by melodic strumming highlighted by handsomely layered harmonies from manager Asher, conjuring his Peter and Gordon days and sweetly softening the void of "nothing left" that the lyrics lament.

The macabre "Monkey Wash Donkey Rinse" is a waltzing invitation of inevitability to the "party in the center of the earth"—"Hell is only half full/Room for you and me." There is more to Zevon's apocalyptic Dance of Shiva and Debutantes Ball than the common religious icon representation of the monkey as the devil and numerous vices. Lindley, who contributes fiddle, provides broader context in a monologue during his live performances of the song. He recounts that when Zevon invited him to play on the song, Lindley was intrigued by the strange title and asked what the song was about, to which Zevon dead-ended, "You don't want to know." Which only made Lindley more curious. Zevon explained to Lindley that while he was in Marrakesh, in a courtyard square where musicians gather and play sometimes for hours nonstop, they brought in a donkey and his "very, very good friend," a monkey, who was happily riding the donkey's back. The satisfied monkey climbed down and gave the donkey a fast and vigorous massage, which in turn made the donkey very happy. And because he was very happy, the donkey reacted in a certain way. As Lindley explains, "So, the monkey washes, and the donkey rinses, to which Warren said, 'I realized humanity is dead.'"

Mutineer concludes with the tranquil synth and nautical sounds title song, another read-between-the-lines or connect-the-dots of a self-referential relationship song, with romance and record-label relevance. The desperado motif shifts to a pirate persona, as suggested in Zevon's seaside "selfie" (long before self-directed photo ops were labeled such)—a close-up pose on the album cover with Zevon, wearing a bandana and mirrored Ray-Bans—"looking a bit like Jimmy Buffet's evil twin" (Dretzka, n.p.)—and the song's very first line, "Yo ho ho and a bottle of rum." Zevon as mutineer is not a man overboard, nor a swashbuckling, excitable boy. The wake of turbulence may be subsiding into sailing off into the sunset, with happiness on the horizon, accompanied by "my witness," to a safe place where lightning and thunder "could never find us here." He acknowledges being "born to rock the boat," but the defiance is now anchored in perseverance and promise that "some may sink but we will float." The unassuming song sustained, surfacing in some surprising places. Among the most notable was as a regular part of Bob Dylan's set list during live shows in 2002. In 2015, Americana artists Jason Isbell of the Drive-By Truckers, and his wife, violinist Amanda Shires, released a two-song, nautical-themed cover EP, *Sea Songs*, that oddly paired a sparsely elegant "Mutineer" with a version of Swedish indie pop electronica artist Lykke Li's "I Will Follow Rivers."

Mutineer, and to a slightly lesser degree *Mr. Bad Example*, perpetuated the artistic air and vision that was evident in Zevon's ambitious approach to *Transverse City*. While the intellect, humor, heartache, and themes in his songwriting were constants, it was Zevon's unwavering commitment to his own creative and musical instincts that pushed against the sound and style expectations and allegiance of his audience. Critics generally found the prevailing bleak, introspective tone of *Mutineer* to be uncharacteristically self-indulgent, lackluster, and pretentious, frequently citing Zevon's disjointed, poorly focused homemade production for its lack of punch and melody and its reliance on synthesizers that ultimately undermined some strong material.

"SOME MAY SINK BUT WE WILL FLOAT"

> *My career is about as promising as a Civil War leg.*
> —Warren Zevon, to Hunter S. Thompson, December 8, 1998

Zevon, the mutineer, did not sink despite his ninth album suffering the worst sales of any record during his career. He found himself facing a familiar fate as he was once again without a record label. And, like his previous interval between Asylum and Virgin, he remained unsigned for five years. Zevon was also minus a manager as Asher took a position as senior vice president of Sony Music Entertainment. Asher's abandoning ascension further reinforced Zevon's industry skepticism, and the perception that he was treated "more like a charity case than an artist of merit" (C. Zevon, 276). From the 1990 hindu love gods' release forward, Zevon never completely trusted Giant's interest in championing him as a songwriter. Even with his management change to Asher, the anticipated better budgets and promotion were pledges unfulfilled, leaving little chance that his three records for the label would be marketable beyond the most faithful followers of his fan base.

Nevertheless, Zevon stayed afloat, and "scrambled for higher ground" (C. Zevon, 351). Beyond playing his regular circuit of venues, there was an unusual array of Zevon activity dotting the second half of the decade, keeping his name, music, and presence in circulation. In 1996, Rhino issued what remains the most comprehensive Zevon compilation, *I'll Sleep When I'm Dead (An Anthology)*. The two-disc, 44-song collection not only spans the Asylum, Virgin, and Giant essentials, but contains Zevon's film and television soundtrack and theme song rarities. Also included is the obscure "Frozen Notes," in Zevon's droll view, "written during the Mesozoic era" and left out of the initial *Excitable Boy* sequence in 1978. Re-recorded many years later with a string quartet arrangement, the song was added as an extra track on the expanded reissue of *Excitable Boy* (2007). Another highlight that distinguishes the anthology's package is the accompanying booklet featuring Zevon's concise humorous and insightful notes on each song.

The same year, Canadian country artist Terri Clark's version of Zevon's "Poor Poor Pitiful Me," the lead single from her album, *Just the Same* (1996), topped Canada's RPM (Records Promotion Music) country charts, and reached number five in the United States.

In late August 1997, Zevon had a two-week stint sitting in as David Letterman's *Late Show* bandleader while Paul Shaffer was away shooting *Blues Brothers 2000* (1998). Zevon was in his entertainer element, musically and comically, not missing a beat when bantering with host Letterman.

The hindu love gods was not the only band Zevon affiliated with in the 1990s. He frequently gigged with a merry band of bards, the Rock Bottom Remainders, many of whom were both amateur musicians and popular book, magazine, and newspaper authors. The self-mocking name derived from the publishing term "remaindered book," referring to languishing unsold copies that publishers dump at discounted prices. "We play music as well as Metallica writes novels," humorist Dave Barry playfully proclaimed. Formed in 1992 by "writer's catalyst" Kathy Kamen Goldmark, the band debuted at the American Booksellers Association in Anaheim, California, with one of its notable bookings at the opening of the Rock and Roll Hall of Fame in Cleveland in 1995. Among those in the original lineup were Barry, Roy Blount, Jr., *Simp-*

sons creator Matt Groening, Stephen King, music critics Dave Marsh and Greil Marcus, and Amy Tan, with Carl Hiaasen, Mitch Albom, and Scott Turow among others who joined the shifting company of literary luminaries. Al Kooper was the Remainders' first rock-star-in-residence music director. Hailed by critics as having "one of the world's highest ratios of noise to talent," the band's performances raised millions for charities.

In 1998, the Remainders reconfigured as the Wrockers—a hybrid of "writer" plus "rocker"—and released the cleverly titled *Stranger Than Fiction*, a two-disc, 32-song "freedom of screech" charity compilation of mostly covers on Don't Quit Your Day Job Records. Maya Angelou, Norman Mailer, Molly Ivins, Ben Fong-Torres, *Chicago Tribune* syndicated columnist Bob Greene, and film critic Leonard Maltin were among the notable roster additions. Zevon was one of the house band's special guests, along with Jimmy LaFave, Jerry Jeff Walker, and Doobie Brother Jeff "Skunk" Baxter. Zevon backs Barry with guitar on "Tupperware Blues," plays keyboards on King's nod to his novella *The Body* with "Stand By Me," and offers his deepest Ike Turner vocal on "Proud Mary," performed with Tananarive Due.

While Zevon's musical contributions blend in with the compilation's cluttered novelty, again it is his writing—though *not* songwriting in this instance—that manages to come cleverly to the forefront and mark the project. Amidst the project's diverse and esteemed literary assembly, it is Zevon who provides the liner notes for *Stranger Than Fiction*. What is Zevon's most unusual and obscure career credit is also revealing and reaffirming. Zevon clearly embraces the opportunity to be on the same page with writers he considered to be his peers and heroes as much as his fellow songwriters and musicians. He channels his inner Dorothy Parker into a Wrocker celebrity roast, crafting a strand of riffs that coalesce into a taut, rhythmic review that sparkles and smirks with endearing intellect, wit, and phrasing.

Framing the Wrockers as "some of the most distinguished men and women of American letters, obstreperously practicing a common avocation," Zevon offers historical context for their hobby: "Hitler did watercolors. However, as far as we know, he didn't paint in public . . . " And midway, he prompts that "Sylvia Plath collected bees: a nice quiet pursuit, although it didn't seem to cheer her up." He suggests the Wrockers' music skill levels range from the "amusingly inept to the downright

catastrophic," while addressing "the inappropriateness of their participation" in music. He views Stephen King in biblical terms, "probably
the most popular author since Luke" with no worlds left to conquer,
analogous to "The Sultan of Brunei plays polo." Zevon wonders with
reverence, "Why is Norman Mailer willing to jeopardize his well-earned
place alongside Proust, Dreiser, and Mann in the front rank of twenti-
eth century novelists for a bizarre and unsavory flirtation with the
blues?" He further submits that rock musicians only receive felony con-
victions, not Pulitzer Prizes; thus, "Dave Barry had better stash that
plaque in a bowling ball bag and hide it in the garage." Zevon comes full
circle back to Hitler to conclude, "After all, it wasn't really the watercolors we disesteemed the Führer for." Beneath the warmly ostentatious
tone that threads the surface of Zevon's concise liner note passage lies
an undercurrent, a declaration by Zevon that he is a writer beyond
lyrics; he is critic, poet, satirist and, if he quit his day job, a novelist.

Though obviously well informed and socially aware, Zevon was never as outwardly a political presence or socially conscious songwriter as
fellow artists such as Browne, Henley, and Springsteen. Beyond his
campaigning for the Democratic congressman from Tennessee, Steve
Cohen, Zevon's political positions vacillated, with his thinking characterized by Billy Bob Thornton as "moderate radical." Zevon's most vis-
ible political moment took place on January 16, 1999, when he performed at the inaugural ball of Minnesota governor-elect Jesse Ventura,
the Reform Party candidate and former professional wrestler nick-
named "The Body." Following Zevon's acoustic "Lawyers, Guns and
Money," Ventura joined Zevon onstage for a version of "Werewolves of
London." Zevon's versatility was again on display, this time as the con-
genial entertainer. As a one-man bandleader/master of ceremonies with
a slight Elton John persona, he guides Ventura through the verses from
his keyboard, with frequent "Minnesota" and "Minneapolis" substitutions, and clever political/wrestling repartee directed at Ventura's oppo-
nents— "Who pinned Norm Coleman to the mat?" and "Who put a
flying head scissors on Skip Humphrey?" (son of former vice president
Hubert Humphrey). When Ventura—outfitted in a Jimi Hendrix t-
shirt, fringe jacket, bandana, earrings, and feather boa—delivers the
line, "I'd like to meet his tailor," Zevon jests, "I think you have." Following the rendition, Zevon has the distinction of officially introducing the
governor. In a subtle homage to Ventura's service in the navy, Zevon

nimbly leans on "Roland the Headless Thompson Gunner," employing the phrase "Talkin' about the man." In turn, Ventura acknowledges Zevon as he exits stage right, clumsily mispronouncing his name as "Warren zuh-VON."

Zevon's musical presence in film, television, and music soundtracks continued to the decade's end and beyond. Inevitably, "Werewolves of London" persisted, playing in an episode of the science-fiction comedy series *Mystery Science Theater 3000* (*MST3K*) in 1997. Patty Larkin covered "Tenderness on the Block" in *Sliding Doors* (1998), a British-American drama with a parallel universe story line, starring Gwyneth Paltrow. Larkin's version, an echo of Shawn Colvin's interpretation from 1992, only appears in the film and is not included on the sound-track, nor is it available on any of Larkin's records. Though Zevon and the producers were unable to reach an agreement on an original com-position for intro and outro music for the television series *Action* (Fox, 1999), the sneering invective from *Sentimental Hygiene*, "Even a Dog Can Shake Hands," cowritten with the Stipe-less R.E.M. trio, was a fitting fallback that was incorporated as the theme song for the hostile Hollywood comedy.

In March and May of 1999, Zevon's television acting roles culminat-ed with appearances in two episodes of *Suddenly Susan* (NBC), the prime-time situation comedy starring Brooke Shields and Kathy Griffin. The episodes feature another odd pop pairing, with Rick Springfield cast as Zevon's friend, Zach Hayward. Springfield, who had an acting stint on the popular daytime soap opera *General Hospital*, had several Top Ten songs, including "Jessie's Girl," a Grammy-winning number one hit in 1981. The double-date story line is constructed around scenes in Susan's apartment and a small club where Zevon is performing. Be-fore the show, Susan, Zach, and Vicky wager tequila on the opening song, which Vicky insists is never "Werewolves of London." She rightly predicts "Mr. Bad Example." Zevon, outfitted in his customary gray throughout the episode, is a natural. He displays comfortable presence and excellent comic timing, including smirks and raised eyebrows when delivering his lines, whether reluctantly admitting that Isaac is his favor-ite Hanson, or revealing that "a certain rock star isn't wearing any underwear." Most of his lines are standard rock star cliché, such as stereotypical line lobbing of "extra room key" and "California king bed" flirtations. The career references and self-effacing "Excitable Boy" punch lines play the best. When Griffin naively asks if "that was really Neil Young playing on 'Sentimental Hygiene,'" Zevon replies, "To be honest, I don't remember. I was a little medicated during the 1980s. I'm not even sure if I was on that album."

Zevon also had the opportunity to bring his desperado persona to the big screen when he was cast as Mr. Babcock in the existential Western, *South of Heaven, West of Hell* (2000), written and directed by Dwight Yoakam. Zevon has no speaking lines in his brief scenes. Dressed in formal gray, including a derby hat, Zevon sits politely as the silent sidekick (who also did not have a sense of smell) in between ethereal traveler Brigadier Smalls (fellow OCDer Billy Bob Thornton in long blonde tresses) and frontier lawman Valentine Casey (Yoakam) conversing in a saloon dining room. The cast also included Bridget Fonda, Peter Fonda, Paul Reubens (Pee Wee Herman), and Bud Cort (*Harold and Maude*).

HIGHER GROUND: HISTORY REPEATS

> *The failures that marked the mid-'90s were swept aside as Warren scrambled for higher ground at the close of the millennium, but the ravages of hard times remained. He had never taken success for granted, however. Where he once nurtured hope that the notice he received in the 1970s would set a standard for years to come, he now looked at recognition with a kind of suspicious scorn. . . . By this time, he had no illusions of grandeur, he was just grateful that someone let him record [his songs].*
>
> —Crystal Zevon

During his record-label lull of the latter 1990s, Zevon was diligently writing what were soon to be recognized as some of the best songs of his career. No matter the circumstance, Zevon always maintained his songwriting self-esteem, telling *Los Angeles Times* reporter Richard Cromelin in 1992, "I suppose I was vain enough or optimistic enough to figure that when I wrote ten new songs, I'd get an opportunity to record them."

The stage was set for yet another Zevon comeback. Beyond the recurrence of Zevon's five-year record label lull, history repeated—with an Asylum aura. Just as Jackson Browne convinced David Geffen to sign

Zevon as an unknown songwriter to Asylum Records in 1975, the faithful friend once again stepped forward, unobtrusively circulating demos of Zevon's new songs. Among those Browne approached was Danny Goldberg, the founder, chairman, and CEO of the New York–based indie label, Artemis Records. Goldberg's credits included coproducer/codirector of the celebrated *No Nukes* (1980) rockumentary based on the September 1979 concert event at Madison Square Garden, featuring MUSE (Musicians United for Safe Energy), an all-star collective organized by Browne, Graham Nash, Bonnie Raitt, and John Hall. Goldberg's vision of Artemis resembled Geffen's artist-friendly approach with Asylum, with emphasis on creative integrity over corporate interests. Just as Zevon was a part of Giant Records' original roster when it launched in 1990, he became one of the first artists Goldberg signed to Artemis. The fledgling label, the fifth of Zevon's career, would be where he would record his momentous trilogy of final albums from 2000 to 2003.

8

THAT AMAZING GRACE SORT OF PASSED YOU BY

I have news for everyone, including myself—don't make long range plans, 'cause there is an inevitable adieu for everyone. I don't consider [death] a subject to be avoided.
　　　　　　　　　　　　　　　　　—Warren Zevon, 1981 (Alfonso)

Warren Zevon entered the new millennium with his early 50s focus on a familiar songwriting theme—mortality. He wryly ridiculed the term "middle age" because he didn't know anyone twice his age at 106 years old. On May 14, 2000, several months after the late-January release of *Life'll Kill Ya*, his tenth studio album, and first for the Artemis label, Zevon appeared as a musical guest on the long-running BBC TV music variety series *Later . . . with Jools Holland*, where he performed a deep track from the new album—the frank, foreboding, and funny "My Shit's Fucked Up." Within the studio's serpentine keyboard floor and backdrop design, the low lighting imparted a solemn, campfire atmosphere, with musicians and crew as background silhouettes awaiting a ghost story with the intimate audience. Following the nimble intro chords on his black acoustic guitar, Zevon, in his compulsory-color gray suit jacket, began: "Well I went to the doctor, I said 'I'm feeling kind of rough.'" The narrative unfolds with Zevon's characteristic unsettling amusement, as if having a conversation or telling a joke that unravels toward its forbidding punch line. The doctor says candidly, "I'll break it to you, son. Your shit's fucked up." "My shit's fucked up? Well, I don't see how," says/sings the puzzled patient. The doctor explains simply, "The shit that used to work—it won't work now."

Zevon is clearly comfortable in his well-established role as songwriting's Grim and Grin Reaper. His delivery is methodical, with a slight smirk or eyebrow raising to provide an occasional gestural accent for the clever rhyming couplets that follow the fateful finding. He counters the profane with bashful disappointment—"I had a dream, Ah, shucks, oh well/Now it's all fucked up, It's shot to hell"—followed by the pseudo-celebratory sing-alongy, "Yeah, yeah, my shit's fucked up," which is then punctuated by an admonition of inevitability that it has to happen to the best of us, the rest of us, rich or poor; and ultimately "It'll happen to you." The ugly reality settles in on the last stanza, with slight spiritual intimations—"That amazing grace sort of passed you by"—before descending into depression, waking up every day, crying, wanting to die but "you just can't quit." Zevon, the patient, concludes the cautionary tale by paraphrasing the doctor's diagnosis: "Let me break it on down, It's the fucked-up shit."

Shadowy and sparse musically and visually, the lurking live rendition of "My Shit's Fucked Up" is unequivocally one of Zevon's most captivating solo performances, electric or acoustic; one that would ironically accumulate significant emotional consequence. The song, the album, and Zevon's peripheral performance became prophetic, unknowingly setting a haunting tone for his next three years and records.

"AH, SHUCKS, OH, WELL": A MODEST MORTALITY MASTERPIECE

Zevon is one of the rare songwriters who could transform a routine visit to the doctor into three minutes of droll deterioration descending toward doom. In the vast doctor song discography, "My Shit's Fucked Up" is a glaring disparity from Huey "Piano" Smith and the Clowns' "Doctor told me son, you're living too fast" in the mid-1950s romp "Tuberculosis and the Sinus Blues"; Jackson Browne's world-weary "Doctor My Eyes" from 1972; or Robert Palmer singing "Doctor, doctor, give me the news" in 1978's "Bad Case of Loving You," on its way to becoming a Dr. Pepper soft drink commercial. Despite the sound on the surface of the song's dual vulgarity, not to mention additional profanity in the album's very first line, Zevon's songwriting was always about being authentic more than it was gratuitous, whether language, sexuality, or violence; every word had a purpose. The bluntness of the doctor's Zevonian bedside manner provides a real and refreshing diversion from clinical conversation and medicalspeak. (The song, positioned ninth in the album's sequencing, is omitted in the listing on the CD's back cover, though it is included on the booklet's back cover and its lyrics are printed inside.)

"My Shit's Fucked Up" is one of the dozen songs that make up *Life'll Kill Ya*. While the album may not qualify as conceptual, the majority of the songs are faithful to the matter-of-fact title, with sickness, aging, decay, and ultimately death a thematic thread. During an engaging, illuminating interview with KSGR Radio's Jody Denberg in Austin, Texas, in 2000 (which was eventually packaged as the bonus disc, "Primate Discourse," with the rarities/unreleased collection *Preludes* [2007]), Zevon said that the album isn't as much about aging as it is simply about the inevitability of "being dead, realizing you will be, and enjoying everything you possibly can every minute you're not [dead]." On the album cover, Zevon's tilted head, slight smile, and black-turtleneck pose exude a Burt Bacharach, easy-listening aura. However, marauding inside the record's booklet are images of a creepy skeletal marching mass and a faint, floating shadowy shroud of Zevon.

The duality, from deterioration to deliverance, is evenly arranged in the sequencing. The songs, which feature some of Zevon's sharpest opening verses, are wry and reflective, interspersed with fraught romance and religious allusions, from cross carrying to the Crusades. The prevailing tone is not excessive or weighty, as Zevon has always adroitly recognized the ironic underpinnings of the long, deliberate march toward fate and confronting our destinies.

Life'll Kill Ya's predominant production is simple, with sparse folk-rock instrumentation and scant vocal harmonies. Zevon liked records, and live shows, that "were really the person," citing Dylan's *John Wesley Harding* and Bruce Springsteen's *Nebraska* as models for his minimalist approach. On *Life'll Kill Ya* he avoided the do-it-yourself perils that undermined *Mutineer*'s production, conceding that it was difficult to not get self-indulgent when you have your own mini-recording studio. While Zevon recorded vocals and guitars for *Life'll Kill Ya*, the album was coproduced by Paul Q. Kolderie and Sean Slade, whose many credits include Hole and Radiohead, one of Zevon's favorite bands.

Though used sparingly on Zevon's records, harmonica is a more frequent and welcome accent on *Life'll Kill Ya*. The album launches with a lively harmonica preface that blows into the opening verse of "I Was in the House When the House Burned Down"—"I had the shit til it all got smoked." Zevon initially refused to edit "shit" for the radio single until Danny Goldberg told him that when he worked with Beat poet Allen Ginsberg, he gave Goldberg a clean version because Ginsberg wanted to be on radio. Zevon acknowledged that he was figuratively "in the house," and though he "didn't suffer third degree burns," he "got singed." The verses are almost exclusively first person, as if a string of confessions while teetering on the precipice of disaster—"I kept the promise till the vow got broke, saw the bride in her wedding gown, had to drink from the lovin' cup, stood on the banks till the river rose up, had the money till it all got spent, had to stay in the underground." He also "met the man with the thorny crown" and "helped Him carry his cross through town," establishing the album's thread of religiosity to redemption.

The title song is a restrained reprise of the brash "I'll Sleep When I'm Dead" from Zevon's Asylum debut. "Life'll Kill Ya"'s glimpse into the abyss of mortality is at once witty, unflinching, and accepting. In sneering shades of Randy Newman, a tinkling keyboard precedes a string of amusing affronts: "You've got an invalid haircut" that "hurts when you smile," and "better get out of town before your nickname expires," "need a permit to walk around downtown" and "a license to dance." Life and death are inevitably intertwined and "will find you, wherever you go." No one can hide, whether the "president . . . to the lowliest rock and roll star." Zevon leans on death vernacular—"The doctor is in and will see you now, he don't care who you are"—establishing the medical practitioner as a recurring grim-reaper figure who is also the messenger in "My Shit's Fucked Up."

Zevon flaunts his arcane pop acumen in the song, citing the titles of two 1977 sci-fi horror B-movies from the "rampaging nature" subgenre, *Kingdom of the Spiders* featuring William Shatner and giant tarantulas, and *Empire of the Ants*, loosely based on the 1905 H. G. Wells short story about the littleness and tenuousness of humanity. As part of a chorus couplet, Zevon blends sophistication with slang, pairing the Latin epithet for "rest in peace"—"*Requiescat in pace*"—with "That's all she wrote." Cause of death is also part of the clever contemplation— "some get the awful, awful diseases," the knife, the gun, or "get to die in their sleep at the age of hundred and one"—as are the afterlife possibilities—"Maybe you'll go to heaven"—with whispering speculation about maybe seeing Uncles Al and Lou—or be reincarnated, or worst case, pay the price if you were bad.

"Porcelain Monkey" is a more up-tempo "dead Elvis" reflection than its darker, dirge-like predecessor, "Jesus Mentioned" on *The Envoy* in 1982. Zevon's view of the King's demise has not changed much in 18 years. The lead line shrugs with predictability—"He was an accident waiting to happen, most accidents happen at home"—and he is wary of the isolation—"maybe he should have gone out more often or answered the phone." Zevon's account of the "rockabilly ride from the glitter to the gloom" is cluttered with familiar Elvis imagery: hip-shakin' shoutin' in gold lamé, shotgun-shack singing Pentecostal hymns, wrought-iron gates, velveteen, and Las Vegas, accentuated with Zevonian phrases such as "regal sobriquet." The song was inspired by Jorge Calderón's postcard of the TV Room at Graceland depicting a creepy white ceramic monkey with onyx eyes resting atop a glass coffee table. The figurine became Zevon's focal point rather than some of the more common Presley iconography such as prescription drugs or deep-fried peanut-butter-and-banana sandwiches. To him, the primate artifact was emblematic of Elvis's "little world, smaller than your hand" and his "throwing it all away." For Zevon, the King's exit catchphrase, "Elvis has left the building," translates into Elvis "eating fried chicken with his regicidal friends, that's how the story ends, with a porcelain monkey."

The album's midsection presents Zevon's usual unusual relationship dynamics, with a series of opening stanzas that are at once vivid, bizarre, and cartoonish, with Zevon's signature come-out-of-nowhere qualities. Much like his pessimistic divergence from the conventional doctor motif in "My Shit's Fucked Up," Zevon counters the popular "magic of love" theme with an amusing metaphor in "For My Next Trick I'll Need A Volunteer." Misery and mishap are center stage. "I can saw a woman in two, but you won't want to look in the box when I do," warns the clumsy magician, whose only trick is that he can make love disappear. Clearly, Zevon does not believe in the magic of the Lovin' Spoonful, nor is this an update of Glenn Miller's or Frank Sinatra's charming renditions of the 1940s Johnny Mercer/Harold Arlen tune, "That Old Black Magic." The spotlights have faded for the jinxed illusionist, and "it's lonely as hell, with no magic spell for a broken heart."

Zevon delivers "I'll Slow You Down"'s low self-esteem in a higher-pitched vocal supported by a melody that echoes *The Envoy*'s "Let Nothing Come Between You." The troubled relationship and wounded psyche are clear from the start, in another offbeat lead: "You know I hate it when you put your hand inside my head and switch all my priorities around." The feelings of inadequacy and the selfless insistence "go on without me" are accompanied by parting insults, from the adolescent "why don't you go pick on someone your own size," to the derisive "you think you're pretty tricky, but you're simply overbred." Zevon improbably, ingeniously draws from the popular game show *Wheel of Fortune*'s puzzle-solving catchphrase to complete a couplet: "You always say you know me, somehow I don't think you do, maybe you should buy another vowel."

Desperation and masochistic inclination urge the delicate and depraved acoustic "Mutineer" melody of "Hostage-O." Zevon attributed the song's odd title to his reading the works of writer, composer, and traveler Paul Bowles, best known for *The Sheltering Sky*. The opening, "I can see me bound and gagged dragged behind the clown mobile," dangles with the most peculiar Zevon lines, coupled with the condition, "You can treat me like a dog/If you make me feel what others feel." Unbearable loneliness contributes to a willingness to do anything, to pay any price "to see how far you'll go"—maim, sprain, strain, chain me to the floor, wear the creepy mask, make me lose control, and "stand in line for the sacrifice, for the shamefaced love of the ugly vice." The groveling plea "Let me be" is also a vow: "I will be your prisoner . . . your hostage-o."

The leering lovin' of "Dirty Little Religion" is a clever and comprehensive conversion of the spiritual into sexual, with the hypocrisy of scheming church and cult leaders as the subtext. The semi-biographical—"I like to think I've earned my reputation for rushing in where angels fear to tread"—precedes a litany of irreverent religion innuendo flows: meet the congregation, together in my tent, nailed to the floor, make a convert out of you, countdown to the Rapture, fundamentals of desire, can I get a witness and an amen from the choir?, I'll show you where I get my inspiration, and even a few "hallelujahs."

Steve Winwood's wistful "Back in the High Life Again" is one of the better known, not to mention fitting, songs that Zevon chose to cover during his recording career. At Artemis, Goldberg was hoping for some airplay with the version, and recruited Peter Asher to "commercialize" the song a bit. Asher, who admitted that "it was odd to be pursuing Warren with a non-Warren song" (C. Zevon, 374), tinkered with timing and added drums. The song's life-affirming outlook is congruent with *Life'll Kill Ya*'s theme, while its redeeming quality can be read as a salute to Zevon's sustained sobriety and another comeback, as evident in verses such as "It used to seem to me that my life ran on too fast."

The optimism dissolves into the quiet calamity of "My Shit's Fucked Up," followed by disillusion in that "Fistful of Rain," which opens— "You can dream the American Dream, but you sleep with the lights on and wake up with a scream"—and acquiesces into a slightly swaying, pub hoist "grab a hold" chorus. Zevon and Calderón wrote the song with Buddhist Gospel intent. As Zevon explained to Jody Denberg, "the harder you try to hold onto things the more they slip through your fingers sometimes; and the more they flow the more they stay with you."

Zevon consistently concluded his albums with memorable songs, whether epic, menacing, sentimental, or redeeming. *Life'll Kill Ya* follows suit, climaxing with a lovely, prayerful pairing of songs. Textured with harmonica and mandolin, "Ourselves to Know" is indebted to John O'Hara's novel of the same title, and to eighteenth-century poet Alexander Pope. The graceful holy ride begins in 1099 with the Crusades, from Constantinople to Jerusalem. The quest becomes contemporary and self-reflective, from the path of celebrity where "everyone got famous and rich," then "went off the rails ending in the ditch," to personal pilgrimage, with encouragement to "be loyal to the ones you leave with, even if you fail," and to "be chivalrous to strangers you meet along the road."

The solemn acoustic "Don't Let Us Get Sick" is a beautiful benediction that humbly petitions, "Don't let us get sick . . . old . . . stupid, all right?" and "Just make us be brave, make us play nice, and let us be together tonight." The poetic observation of "the moon smiling on the lake, causing the ripples in time" elicits contentedness—"I'm lucky to be here with someone I like, who maketh my spirit to shine." Though "maketh" may be patent Zevonian literary affectation, the uncommon

archaic usage usually reserved in contemporary texts for historical novels and Bible translations, it enhances the song's meditative nature. The
lyrical virtues and melody for "Don't Let Us Get Sick" are at once
emotional and spiritual, intimate and universal. Zevon's count your
blessings simplicity and sensitivity are among the qualities that make
the supplication a broadly appealing accompaniment for religious and
cultural rituals as well as dramatic narratives. The song has been widely
employed in television episodes, commonly in closing scenes, from Zevon's original in *The Good Wife* (CBS), to actress Madeleine Martin's
thrashing rendition on *Californication* (Showtime) and Jill Sobule's delicate version playing on Hanna's earplugs after she gets a call about her
grandmother's death on *Girls* (HBO). A range of artists in a variety of
genres have covered "Don't Let Us Get Sick," among them actor Tim
Robbins, the waltzing Americana group Franklin Ladies Aid Society,
country outfit Joe West and the Santa Fe Revue and, most notably,
Jackson Browne, whose version appears on the benefit compilation,
Sweet Relief: Pennies from Heaven III (2013).

   Life'll Kill Ya is a gem, a modest masterpiece. The record is Zevon's
sturdiest, sharpest, most cohesive set of songs, from start to finish, since
his self-titled Asylum debut in 1976. Critics endorsed the record with
some of Zevon's best reviews since early in his career. Despite the
critical acclaim, and tour and promotional support from Artemis as one
of the label's first releases, *Life'll Kill Ya* sold around 30,000 copies,
barely making it into the *Billboard* Top 200. Goldberg was among the
many who believed the album deserved a better reception in the marketplace, saying that *Life'll Kill Ya* "is an extraordinary record. I am still
frustrated that we didn't do better with it given how good it is" (C.
Zevon, 374). Browne agreed and, going even further, called the album
"one of the best records ever made, by anybody at any time" (Fricke
2003).

"STILL OUT HERE IN THE WIND AND RAIN"

The somber sensibility continued on Zevon's next record, *My Ride's
Here* (2002), with a slightly more subtle demise-driven title. The "ride"
is an allusion to a hearse; the album's cover image and inside booklet
contain shots of Zevon, in mirrored sunglasses, a passenger in the coffin

carrier's backseat, gazing out the window. Zevon frequently presented the album as a "meditation on death" during interviews and in the album's press kit.

Less unified, though harder rocking than *Life'll Kill Ya*, Zevon's self-produced ten-song cycle contains madcap, mordant, and novelty narratives as well as a few curious covers. The pastiche is marked by fiction and metaphor, an odd array of pop-culture references, unusual juxtapositions, and international accents, both musical and lyrical. Also notable are Zevon's numerous collaborations with writers—novelists, poets, and journalists—highlighted on a sticker in the CD cover. One of the strongest compositions, "Lord Byron's Luggage," is the only song on the album written by Zevon unaccompanied. Yearning gilds the melodic Irish musing on Zevon's kindred Romantic—"every dog has his day, still waiting for mine," and "out there in the wind and rain, look a little older, feel no pain, still looking for love." Zevon drolly rhymes into his own and the poet's notorious natures as well, being pronounced a rhyming "persona non grata" at the Henley Regatta, the renowned royal rowing event on the Thames River in Oxfordshire.

The mordant opening "Sacrificial Lambs," cowritten with music impresario Larry Klein, is faithful to Zevon's assertion to Goldberg that he was working on a "spiritual album," of course with trademark irony: "Those Coptic monks who knew how to keep it real, that Rosicrucian thing, that Zoroastrian deal who don't give a damn." Zevon's mantra is "eat my dust" (and I'll clean your clock)," while bemoaning everyone who wants something for free. References abound, among them leading Theosophicalist and occultist Madame Blavatsky, and Indian spiritualist philosopher Jiddu Krishnamutri. Another quatrain incongruently groups Smokey and the Bandit, Saddam Hussein, Russell Crowe, and Hafiz Assad together, "staying up late acting insane." In the end, the apocalyptic stage is set for "the man-made man." The kinks have been worked out with DNA; genetic engineering will be The End, not a plague or war. The scene and tone evoke *Transverse City*, while "You can be my sacrificial lamb" echoes the desperate submission of the willing prisoner in "Hostage-O."

Zevon teams with Carl Hiaasen again, loitering in psych-ward daftness in "Basket Case," a totally crazed rhyming romance involving "paranoid lovers lost in space." The ode to personality disorder is an extensive checklist: "a bipolar mama in leather and lace, face like an angel, a perfect waste, Dracula's daughter, Calamity Jane with water on the brain, manic depressive and schizoid, too, the friskiest psycho." She finally makes a madman out of him as he is dragged through the nuthouse gates in a straightjacket. In an ephemeral production touch, the fuzzy guitar veers into a brief Baroque choral interlude. As the album's first single, "Basket Case" was a convenient book tie-in soundtrack for Hiaasen's crime novel of the same name, centered around the death of the washed-up lead singer of Jimmy and the Slut Puppies, and published in January 2002, months before the May release of *My Ride's Here*.

Detroit sportswriter, best-selling author, and Rock Bottom Remainder Mitch Albom joins Zevon in expanding his sport song entries beyond the baseball and boxing bios of Bill Lee and Boom Boom Mancini. "Hit Somebody! (The Hockey Song)" is the story of Buddy, "born in Big Beaver by the borderline." The alliteration was at Zevon's insistence— "I love saying all those Bs." Buddy is a reluctant hockey "goon," the designated tough guy—"But what's a Canadian farm boy to do?"—who, after 20 years, achieves his career dream of "scoring one damn goal." When he finally gets his chance to put the "biscuit in the basket," he tragically gets coldcocked on the follow-through of his shot and "saw the heavenly light."

The rollicking gag runs into overtime at 5:27, with requisite hockey terminology, global representation on ice—Czech, Finn, Swede, Russian—and a nod to Montreal Canadien great Maurice "Rocket" Richard. *Late Show* bandleader Paul Shaffer guests on organ, while David Letterman sounds like a *Sesame Street* character shouting, "Hit somebody!" in the chorus. Mildly mirroring the Zevonian "Werewolves of London, again" novelty tune curse, "Hit Somebody!" with its Albom and Letterman marketing hooks, was released as a single and became a "little hit," particularly in Canada, where it received considerable airplay. In an ongoing effort by Artemis to cultivate latent interest in *Life'll Kill Ya*, "For My Next Trick I'll Need a Volunteer" was also included on that single. Director Kevin Smith, best known for his comedy *Clerks,* has been long rumored to be developing a film adaptation titled *Hit Somebody!*

Bracketing the humorous hockey saga in the album's middle-third sequence are a Hunter S. Thompson collaboration, "You're a Whole Different Person When You're Scared," and the brooding "Genius," cowritten with Klein. Each song exceeds five minutes. Zevon and Thompson craft a slightly sinister, paranoid, and melancholy narrative. A relationship that begins in a Turkish town ends there, when an expatriate returning to the United States leaves his lover behind because he didn't want her "hanging around in the Kingdom of Fear," where "dangerous creeps are everywhere." In the sneering opening for "Genius," Zevon is stirring a "a bitter pot of *je ne sais quoi*" with a monkey's paw after seeing his girl "coming out his barber's shop in that skimpy halter top." The monkey paw alludes to the "grant three wishes" supernatural short story published by W. W. Jacobs in 1902. The wounded Zevon asks his infidel if she lit candles, put on "Kind of Blue" and "used that Ivy League voodoo on him, too?" In his final acerbic dig, he concedes that she and the barber make a handsome pair, though he "never liked the way he cut your hair."

The betrayal stirs rumination on "everybody's place to stand" and the genius of their method for secrets, schemes, scams, and plans. Zevon cites Mata Hari, and how men were falling for her sight unseen. Then follows with one of his most unusual pop appositions, writing that "Albert Einstein was a ladies man . . . making out like Charlie Sheen." The acrimony turns obliquely personal in the "Songwriter's Neighborhood," specifically the "poet who lived next door when you were young and poor and grew up to be a backstabbing entrepreneur." In between, Zevon inserts a humorous grammar lesson: "Everybody's your best friend when you're doing well . . . I mean good." Zevon, undoubtedly aware of the "genius" whispers that had intermittently marked his career, concludes that he'd be a genius "if he could only get my record clean."

Zevon's classical proficiencies grace the song's scorn. Katy Salvidge, who almost singlehandedly provided the album's Irish sounds with fiddle and pennywhistle, was overwhelmed in the studio by Zevon's string orchestration on "Genius," saying, "It was the most unbelievable arrangement I've ever heard. It's probably my favorite string arrangement of all time. It was musically so advanced, and I could tell he [Zevon] wasn't a rock and roller" (C. Zevon, 383).

Later that same year, the song title was expediently, and perhaps suitably, adopted as the name of Zevon's third "Best of" collection. Released in October on Rhino Records, the 22-song *Genius* extends through *My Ride's Here*. There were no bonus tracks included, despite the label's adamant request for vault material. Despite having a thin, at best, archive, Zevon resisted on principle, reasoning that if a song "didn't come out on my records, it's not good enough to come out on any CD." The compilation's cover reflected the prevailing mortality mood of Zevon's new millennium recordings. Centered on a velvety black cloak is Zevon's signature skull, "Old Velvet Nose," with a Sherlock Holmes–style pipe in its mouth and an eye monocle with Zevon's image reflected within. The record's booklet features a gallery of "skull-istrations" of Old Velvet Nose photographed in a variety of costumes, props, and poses, each portraying a Zevon song included in the collection—pirate bandana and eye patch, bullet casings, Chinese menu, bondage gear, raspberry beret, a boxer's hooded robe.

Following his interpretation of the familiar Winwood tune on *Life'll Kill Ya*, Zevon returns to his norm of covering obscurities on *My Ride's Here*. He and his daughter Ariel share vocals *en français* on Serge Gainsbourg's trippy "Laissez-Moi Tranquille," roughly translated as "leave me alone" or "let me be." Zevon's attraction to Gainsbourg's work is no surprise. A multitalented cult figure, and one of the most prolific, provocative, and influential figures in French popular music, Gainsbourg is renowned for his vast wordplay and varied stylistic output. "I Have to Leave," a pedestrian parting tune written by Zevon's high school friend Dan McFarland, is a puzzling inclusion, unless the "leaving" is construed as death rather than a split. Obviously, sentimental breakup ballads were a forte of Zevon's songwriting. The rich musical arrangement that blends a 1960s California pop sound with Salvidge's pennywhistle salvages the song's worth.

Another wordsmith, Pulitzer Prize–winning poet Paul Muldoon, brings Irish heritage and his celebrated adroit language to two of the album's songs, the title track among them. Muldoon frequently referenced Zevon in his 1990s writings, and acknowledged the songwriter as one of his own literary influences. In September 2000, Muldoon wrote Zevon an unabashed fan letter. He didn't hear from Zevon for almost a year. When the mutual admirers met in New York City in 2001, just days after the September 11 terrorist attacks on the World Trade Center, Zevon "prevailed upon Muldoon to write some songs" (Kinsey, 34). One of the tunes they composed together, "Macgillicuddy Reeks," was in the style of a traditional folk tale. The title derives from a mountain range on Ireland's Iveragh Peninsula, which becomes the song's setting for heartbreak and romance. A fiddling Irish rhythm and geography that references Killarney Shore and Innisfallen lend merriment and authenticity to the poetic imagery—"a path that led through rhododendron days and fuchsia nights to the boatshed"—that includes an apt Zevon characterization, "a thorn trying to find a side." The starry-eyed account slyly sways toward parody: "she upset my applecart . . . was struck by Cupid's dart." With the love interest an analyst for a dot-com company, the mountain metaphor runs from the lovesick patient to a failed corporate merger, the valleys and peaks of an EKG chart to the NASDAQ's dips and starts.

Their collaboration that closes the album, "My Ride's Here," is an overlooked and understated Zevon treasure. The ingenious tale is a hearse-themed Western fever dream, with a faint though discernable "Thunder Road" melody. (Springsteen's slower tempo, live cover version of "My Ride's Here" is on the *Enjoy Every Sandwich* [2004] tribute.) The narrative is brimming with cultural cameos, several linking legends with hotels: at the Marriott with Jesus and John Wayne waiting for a chariot and train, Milton back at the Hilton, at the Westin with Charlton Heston and the Tablets of the Law, with Romantic "bravos" Shelley and Keats out in the street, and Lord Byron leaving for Greece. The song's couplets may provide the best confirmation of what Zevon told Albom when writing "Hit Somebody!" that "I can make anything rhyme. Are you kidding? Just get it close and I'll make it rhyme" (C. Zevon, 375). While a few rhymes may be "close," or utilize the slant rhyme device, such as "changeless/angels," most of the limericks flow with Seussical schemes—carrion/Marion, seraphim/Jim, pinto/San Jacinto, mazuma/ 3:10 to Yuma, bluebonnet/sonnet. In the end, Zevon tells Heston he'd like to stay, but his time has come, he is "bound for glory," his ride is here. Zevon and Muldoon continued to write together, working on *The Honey War*, a Broadway musical about a dispute over gaming rights to a Native American casino.

ON THE WAY TO THE MICHAEL JACKSON EXPO: NEVER A HAS-BEEN

Critical responses to *My Ride's Here* were divergent. What some considered a "pastiche of sorts" and an "eclectic, catchy opus" was to others a "little less focused" and a "misfire" that recalled second-tier Zevon works such as *Mutineer*. The positive takes on the album pointed to Zevon's signature irony, lingering hooks, subtle pleasures, and comparative glimpses of the enigmatic sweetness of Leonard Cohen. Countering the many who considered the record a letdown following *Life'll Kill Ya*, Robert Christgau (2002) deemed *My Ride's Here* an improvement over its honorable Artemis predecessor, in large part because Zevon did not dwell on his love life and the dysfunction that had accumulated over the decades. In the esteemed critic's view, Zevon's use of fiction and metaphor delivered the record from being therapeutic.

Other reviewers thought that Zevon's playfulness went too far on the album, with the humor heavy-handed, and indulgences such as "Laissez-Moi Tranquille" misdirected. Overlooking the sullen sophistication of "Genius," there were assertions that the record's few introspective moments missed their marks, whether due to the music lacking emotional strength or Zevon sounding distracted. There was also critic curiosity over the quantity, more so than the quality, of Zevon's writing collaborations. While there was little consensus on which songwriting partnership worked best, most critics attributed the album's pastiche quality to the multiple creative alliances.

Behind the scenes and outside the studio, tour support from Artemis for *My Ride's Here* became an issue. In an effort to be cost-conscious and efficient, Zevon had been increasingly writing and recording songs that he could play by himself, with minimal accompaniment. He was effectual performing solo on "little tours," referring to himself as a "heavy metal folk singer." Zevon decided he couldn't do any of the new album's songs live without a band backing him. Goldberg was willing to send him on the road with a band until manager and "shit handler" Brigette Barr (as she is labeled in the Zevon oral history) adamantly explained that subsidizing the tour did not make any sense economically for the small, relatively young, company.

Barr had a unique vantage point on Zevon's place not only as an artist on Artemis, but within the music industry in the early 2000s. She admitted it was difficult and "incredibly frustrating" to "get anything going" for Zevon, because other than his fans he had retained over the years, "truthfully there wasn't a market for him" (C. Zevon, 385). Though Zevon was known to obsess over fan comments about him on the Internet, he carried few illusions about the extent of his following, and maintained his typically droll outlook, saying "I don't think it's ever been a case of there being a big audience that stopped taking a ride with me so much as a big audience that accidentally stepped on a Mr. Toad's ride on the way to the funhouse, on the way to the Michael Jackson Expo" (Denberg, n.p.).

Zevon was in a constant state of push and pull with Artemis. The label tried to get him to do promotional things such as local press, radio stations, and programmer dinners, while Zevon, driven by his ego, absolutely refused. Barr explained that "it was a very difficult time for Warren because he was starting to have to face realities of where his career was at that point." For Barr, Goldberg, and the Artemis label, it became more "about trying to salvage something than really going out and promoting a record" (C. Zevon, 385). The folk festival circuit, with many well-paying bookings across Canada, proved to be an agreeable solution to Zevon's tour and promotion predicament. The casual weekend events, venues, and older core crowds were a natural fit for Zevon. And more significantly, in the words of his touring partner Matt Cartsonis, "He (Zevon) was never a has-been with these people" (C. Zevon, 386).

9

DIE ANOTHER DAY: A DESPERADO DETERIORATA

It's a good idea to be able to say goodbye to yourself.
—Warren Zevon (Fricke 2003)

The thematic continuity from *Life'll Kill Ya's* songs, written in the late 1990s, through *My Ride's Here* in 2001 is explicit, as if Zevon was coalescing a lifetime—in his case 55-years' worth—of dark visions into a recording arc of meditations on mortality. Zevon's songs and album titles suddenly turned chillingly prescient; the punch lines eerily personal and powerful. It was as if Zevon possessed a sixth sense. On August 28, 2002, at a time when Zevon ironically "had been working out more than Vin Diesel," he was diagnosed with mesothelioma, a rare, inoperable form of lung cancer. It was the same disease that killed one of his heroes, actor Steve McQueen. "I think I got a raw deal here, all I wanted was the Steve McQueen haircut," Zevon told Dwight Yoakam (Devenish, 13).

The medical prognosis was three months. Zevon did not flinch in the face of fate and his fleeting future. After all, he had continually confronted death with his lifestyle during his "cowboy days" and in his songwriting. Zevon envisioned his Last Stand. "It'll be a drag if I don't make it to the next James Bond movie" (*Die Another Day* in November 2002), he said. "And I want to wear sweaters, a scarf, the overcoat, the whole thing, like a Winona Ryder movie. And I can be this miserable, classic Walter Matthau invalid. Not that I haven't been that before"

(VH1.com). When Zevon returned to his cardiologist, he brought copies of *Life'll Kill Ya* and *My Ride's Here*, explaining, "This is why I'm not so shocked. Doc, just look at the titles and ask yourself why I have this eerie acceptance" (Gunderson, 12D).

EXIT STRATEGY: A BLACK SWAN SONG

Zevon's ride was late. The initial three-month prognosis prolonged past a year. Zevon was three-feet deep with six-feet-under expectations. He said he was "beginning to feel like a fraud" (Read). Not only would Zevon survive to see *Die Another Day* in the theater, but he was around for its video release on June 3, 2003. In a plot twist within the overarching irony, Bond's main villain in the movie, Gustav Graves, when asked how he manages his insomnia, utters one of Zevon's signature phrases, "I'll sleep when I'm dead."

Death's reprieve sustained long enough for Zevon to cultivate a unique variation of the rock-and-roll farewell tour. His exit strategy, for however long he had, was primarily devoted to writing and recording the final chapter of his "dirty life and times." In Zevon's own adaptation of *Die Another Day*, he continued to (de)compose what might be considered his own "Desperado Deteriorata," with Zevon singing a symbolic black swan song as the headliner, the guest of honor, in what was essentially his own living wake or funeral procession.

Zevon's unfolding dieography from diagnosis to death and beyond was a reconfigured rock ritual with an approximate three-act structure. His albums, *Life'll Kill Ya* and *My Ride's Here*, provided the prelude. The Core of the "Deteriorata," which began with Zevon's terminal diagnosis, was comprised of three significant happenings: Zevon's appearance on *The Late Show with David Letterman*, the setting for his last live public performance; the writing and recording of his twelfth and final studio record, *The Wind*; and the filming of the album's studio recording sessions for a companion documentary for VH1's *(Inside)Out*. The Posthumous Script advances from the 2004 Grammy Awards to the present with record reissues and citations across the cultural landscape.

CRYPTIC CONTEXT

Music epitaphs are embedded into rock's timeline, intermittently and varyingly, marking the larger-than-life-but-not-death mythology with morbid fascination and an appealing aura of romanticism and mysticism. Eerie coincidence haunted the single-car crash that killed rockabilly artist Eddie Cochran as his single "Three Steps to Heaven" was climbing the British charts in 1960. Similarly spooky, Lynyrd Skynyrd's *Street Survivors* (1991) was released three days before the plane crash that killed three of its members and ended the band. The album's cover pictured the group engulfed in flames, while record inserts included the itinerary for the never-completed tour and a mail-in offer for a merchandise item labeled "survival kit." Joy Division's *Closer* (1980) and Nirvana's *In Utero* (1994) were conveniently interpreted as musical suicide notes, as they preceded the self-inflicted deaths by hanging and shotgun of their fronts Ian Curtis and Kurt Cobain. On Queen's *Innuendo* (1991), "The Show Must Go On" chronicles the effort of flamboyant Freddie Mercury continuing to perform despite approaching the end of his life. In 1987, Mercury was diagnosed with AIDS, although he kept his illness a secret and denied countless media reports that he was seriously ill. Nine months after *Innuendo*'s February 1991 release, Mercury died from complications resulting from AIDS.

ENJOY EVERY *LATE SHOW* SANDWICH

A key juncture in Zevon's farewell procession took place on October 30, 2002, when David Letterman devoted his entire *Late Show* to Zevon. The date was fitting, beyond the underlying urgency of being two months into Zevon's three month prognosis. "I notice I have a particularly good gig around Halloween," said Zevon when asked about his sardonic songwriting (Brown, F8). The unprecedented solo scheduling on the show was not shameless celebrity exploitation. Zevon was well established as *Late Night*'s favorite son. Letterman estimated that Zevon had appeared on his show "a few dozen times" over a 20-year period, either as a musical guest, sitting in with the house band, or substituting for Shaffer as bandleader. Beyond his music, Zevon's wit was attuned with the show's comic stylings. As Zevon proclaimed during their interview, "Dave's the best friend my music ever had." In the dressing room following the show, Zevon presented Letterman with his electric guitar—"Gray Visitation"—which he always played when he was a *Late Night/Late Show* guest.

The show did not belabor the obvious or wallow in woeful spectacle. The first 30 minutes did not veer from the *Late Show* formula. Letterman's monologue, sketches, and the Top Ten List preceded Zevon's interview and performance. Letterman glorified his guest, promoting Zevon's recently released anthology, *Genius,* and marveling at the extensive Zevon song catalog, beginning with the requisite "Werewolves of London" mention. Letterman lingered in admiration of Zevon's "love conquers all" line in "Searching for a Heart"—"you can't start it like a car/you can't stop it with a gun." Adding levity to the litany, Letterman quipped that Zevon also wrote "White Christmas."

Shaffer and the band paid tribute by performing Zevon songs as instrumental interludes to the show's segments. As Zevon entered in delicate gait, the musicians matched Zevon's morbidity with a rendition of his "I'll Sleep When I'm Dead." Letterman cringed slightly, "I didn't know he (Paul) could play that." Zevon was dressed in a striped suit in his mandatory "lucky color" with an open collar that revealed a small gold cross and chain around his neck.

As a host, Letterman was in uncharted talk show territory. It was difficult to gauge whether his friendship with Zevon made the task easier or more difficult. Reflecting on the Zevon show years later in a post-retirement interview published June 12, 2015, in his hometown magazine, *Indianapolis Monthly*, Letterman acknowledged that he was "at a loss because I couldn't think of an entry point for a conversation with a dying man on a television show that's supposed to be silly," adding further that he "was really dissatisfied with my part of that conversation. I was ill-equipped to connect with a friend who was going through something like that."

Right before the break that preceded Zevon's entrance, Letterman wiped his brow, presumably in anxious anticipation of his guest. Their course of conversation was predictable considering the context, with exchanges about Zevon's diagnosis, his outlook, the consequences, life lessons learned, family, and the irony of his situation. The interaction echoed the widespread "death watch" coverage that filtered through primarily print media and Internet sources during the immediate aftermath of Zevon's terminal revelation. Letterman did not appear as ineffective as his hindsight self-critique suggested. He was gracious and reverential, avoiding past tense and looking for an occasional lighter note, which Zevon readily accommodated. Zevon was Zevon; he was courageously quotable and engaging. He responded to his despairing circumstance with usual profundity and droll aplomb (at least on the surface). When Letterman led with a comment about learning how his life had changed radically in a few months, Zevon replied, "You mean you heard about the flu?" Zevon explained that he "might have made a tactical error not going to a physician for 20 years. It was one of those phobias that didn't pan out." He mentioned his misguided reliance on his dentist, Dr. Stan (Golden), "If he can't fix it, I'm screwed." And how he only hired enabling crew members who told him his shortness of breath was just due to stress. Zevon's answers were laced with wry realism; he masterfully juxtaposed blunt with offhanded humor in the same sentence: "It's tough. You better get your dry cleaning done on special," and "I don't feel as bad as they say I am. . . . They don't discourage you from doing whatever you want." He was also exacting. When Letterman began to discuss the irony of his writing about death, and held up a copy of *My Ride's Here*, Zevon instantly interjected a "Hiyo!" echoing the sidekick style of Ed McMahon with Johnny Carson. His lines had become familiar, somewhat rehearsed and recycled; a morbid mantra of terminal talking points he had been delivering in the steady stream of dead-man-walking interviews and press releases in the short time frame since the August diagnosis. Yet the comments resonated more profoundly and emotionally when seeing Zevon discuss his condition live with Letterman.

The guest appearance carried greater gravity as it marked Zevon's final live performance. "Everybody who does this should think of themselves as an entertainer. I was reading a biography of Sammy Davis, Jr., and it said that even when he was diagnosed with cancer, he [still] went out there and danced 'Mr. Bojangles.' I thought, 'Okay, I'm gonna do it.' It's not the easiest thing in the world to say goodbye, so it was a little difficult," said Zevon in August (VH1.com).

The *Late Show* scene settled somewhere in between post-MTV *Unplugged* and VH1 *Storytellers-*, and the more contemporary YouTube, MySpace Music and "exclusive download" domain. Zevon avoided a greatest hits medley with his three-song set. At the end of the interview segment, there was a slightly awkward moment as Zevon, Letterman, and Shaffer were confused about the order of Zevon's songs to be played, despite a rehearsal earlier in the day. Following the commercial break, he led off with what he originally thought was going to be his closing number, "Mutineer." The staging framed the solemn piano "born to rock the boat" ballad in an atmosphere reminiscent of Zevon's foreshadowing performance of "My Shit's Fucked Up" on *Later . . . with Jools Holland* in 2000. Low lighting provided a formal recital hall meets Catholic Mass aura, with a standing trio of flute, horn, and clarinet accompaniment rising slightly in the background. Zevon's voice strained at times to reach high notes. Extreme close-up shots heightened the emotional impact. Zevon's punctual take to the camera on the phrase, "grab your coat, let's get out of here," was artfully affecting.

His second song, "Genius," was an equally intriguing choice. On the shallow surface, it may have appeared to be an opportunistic record-label ploy to promote the same-titled "Best of" compilation, released a few weeks earlier. The selection may have also been stirred by Zevon's self-awareness and underappreciated artist entitlement, as a bound-for-glory allusion to the "genius" label that had been frequently attached to Zevon in the "Songwriters' Neighborhood," a place he visits in the noir narrative. Zevon, with guitar, fronted a classical string quartet. While the brilliant "ladies man Albert Einstein making out like Charlie Sheen" lyric stands out, the song's concluding 30 seconds are the most revealing. Following the final line, "I'd be a genius," Zevon lowers his guitar, turns to face the string accompanists and strikes a cold conductor's pose, his arms weakly elevated and slightly swaying. The macabre maestro stance was not a charade but rather a classical climax for Zevon, at once a gesture of homage to his teenage encounters with Stravinsky and his own unfinished symphony. Following the moving orchestral performance, Letterman told Zevon, "I think the audition is going very well."

Zevon returned to the piano for the closing song, "Roland the Headless Thompson Gunner," with Shaffer and the band replacing the strings and horns. The selection from *Excitable Boy*, a Letterman request, punctuated the performance with a triumphant, recognizable souvenir of early-era Zevon.

Zevon's three-song medley was a unique self-elegy, an intimate, authentic, and solemn chorus. Each note, lyric, and close-up revealed glimpses of Zevon incarnate and his own antihero arc, from desperado to virtuoso. The sneering subtext asserted the antithesis of increasingly common disingenuous false farewell performances by bands breaking up, only to be reunited sooner rather than later, and pseudo-retiring entertainers who pervade entertainment culture, pulling a Celine Dion by reinventing themselves for the "16th minute" circuit, often in Las Vegas.

One of the most poignant moments of the night occurred earlier when Letterman asked Zevon what he had learned in his time living and dying. Zevon simply stated: "I know how much you're supposed to enjoy every sandwich." Letterman anointed the phrase, punctuating the unique farewell show with the expression as he shook Zevon's hand following his final live song. The expression proved pitch-perfect for the sound-bite era. "Enjoy every sandwich" was immediately transported to the Internet and tailored into 100-percent cotton, silkscreen, and memorabilia exploitation ready for opening bids on the eBay auction site. The phrase evolved into a slogan that was employed as a commemorative caption beneath Zevon's memorial photo on his website and enshrined as the title of a multi-artist tribute recording in 2004.

HASTEN DOWN *THE WIND*

> *What we wanted to capture on the album was these guys having fun playing with Warren, paying their respects. It was bittersweet, obviously, but it was a wonderful thing to see these legendary rock stars just being totally selfless, good friends to Warren.*
> —*The Wind* producer/engineer Noah Snyder (*Ice* interview)

Days after Zevon's diagnosis, Mitch Albom happened to be in Los Angeles and had arranged earlier to meet with Zevon. Having chronicled the dying process of his old professor in the best-selling *Tuesdays with Morrie* (1997), Albom was a primary resource for dealing with terminal illness. Albom recalls Zevon asking rhetorically, "So am I supposed to die with my boots on? Is that my fate? Is that how I'm supposed to approach this?" (C. Zevon, 393).

Ironically, Zevon felt that he was in the midst of the most creative period of his life. While he was determined to make as much music as he possibly could in the time he had left, he simultaneously wrestled with the practical, romantic, and spiritual aspects of his looming fate.

He met with Deepak Chopra and Catholic priests. He considered traveling to India and to Florida to fish with Hiaasen. Finally, Zevon decided that dying with his boots on was the way to go, and music the most appropriate way to say good-bye. He called ex-wife Crystal, declaring, "My job is music. It's all I leave the kids and the people I love so I'm going to stay in L.A. to make records." Longtime friend and collaborator Jorge Calderón was totally supportive, if not relieved. "Warren did the right thing. He went knee-deep into his music" (C. Zevon, 394–95).

Zevon contacted manager Brigette Barr, insisting they "go into showbiz mode," and gave her permission to "use his illness in any way she saw fit to further his career right now" (C. Zevon, 396). Danny Goldberg gave Zevon carte blanche at Artemis, explaining, "I never thought he would have the strength or focus to do a whole album, but I was happy for whatever he wanted to do. I knew it was going to be good and I knew it was going to be the last work. All the way through, I kept being amazed that he was still writing and that he was still doing it. Every time another song would come it was like a miracle" (396). The songs came quickly and easily for Zevon, something that never happened before in his career, as he told VH1.com: "inspiration always came painfully, brutally and rarely."

The subsequent writing and recording of *The Wind* was the climactic centerpiece, the Bartók, of Zevon's Deteriorata. Along with producer/engineer Noah Snyder, Calderón was the cornerstone of the project, appearing on each of the record's eleven songs and cowriting seven of them with Zevon. Beyond his role as coproducer, Calderón served as a spiritual guide and caretaker who kept the demanding, emotional session grounded and progressing toward completion. The inherently challenging and courageous musical mission grew more complicated as a steadily weakening Zevon became explicably depressed and returned to excessive drinking, often mixing liquid morphine cocktails. Calderón observed that "it got pretty bad. Just like the old days." Though empathetic, Calderón was uneasy about potential lethal mixtures, cautioning Zevon, "It would be a shame for something to happen before you could live out your life as long as you can" (403).

The recording of the album was a rite of passage that mingled the components and spirit of a smaller-scale studio version of the Band's *The Last Waltz* farewell concert spectacle at Winterland in 1976 with a traditional Irish wake and New Orleans jazz funeral. An inspiring parade of participants, many who had contributed to previous Zevon recordings, gathered to play and pay respects to their friend with requiem riffs. Among the all-star cast were Jackson Browne, Bruce Springsteen, Eagles Don Henley, Joe Walsh, and Timothy B. Schmidt, John Waite, Dwight Yoakam, Ry Cooder, David Lindley, drummer Jim Keltner, T-Bone Burnett, Emmylou Harris, Tom Petty, Mike Campbell, Billy Bob Thornton, Cuban percussionist Luis Conte, and Zevon's son Jordan. Due to the number of artists involved, eight different studios were utilized during the album's recording and mixing. Only Emmylou Harris's collaboration was done by remote. The personnel pairings were done on a song-by-song basis, and, according to Snyder, "ironed out before guests came in so it wouldn't be like pulling teeth" (*Ice*, 4).

The bulk of the songs were written and recorded between September 2002 and New Year's Eve while Zevon's strength and spirit were optimal. Though the process did not relieve any of Zevon's anxieties and fears, it did provide sustenance. "I think as long as I keep working it's keeping me alive," he said. "So I'm trying to expand the format as much as I can" (VH1.com). A six-week hiatus followed in the first months of 2003 as Zevon's condition steadily worsened. Though not well enough to return to a studio, Zevon was able to complete the record's final two songs at his home studio in April.

SHADOWS ARE FALLING: THE DAVENPORT OF DESPAIR

> *For somebody who had the amount of instability and difficulty that he [Zevon] had through a large period of his life, he finished in a blaze of glory. He was writing as well, or better, than he ever did when he died. That's hard to do, and that takes a real dedication to your craft—a seriousness of purpose.*
>
> —Bruce Springsteen (C. Zevon)

Yearning, intimacy, and preordained urgency are prevalent in *The Wind*. Context is everything. Inescapable metaphors and oblique allusions to Zevon's past, his present condition, and imminent future pervade the song titles and soul-baring lyrics. The album is bracketed by shadows, from the opening statement, "Some days I feel like my shadow's casting me," to the lead line in the final song, "Shadows are falling and I'm running out of breath." In the songs in between, phrases such as "rushes in like a fallen star," "die too hard," "shine the light on me," "couch of pain" "pale as a ghost" and the blatant "knockin' on heaven's door," among many others, convey deterioration, looming demise, and aching, without a trace of irony or sounding self-absorbed. On "Rub Me Raw," Zevon plainly declares "I don't want your pity or your fifty dollar words." His purpose more personal than philosophical, Zevon avoids the last-rite temptation to pursue an existential path seeking to deliver, in his words, "some bullshit insight I've had about living on the planet," beyond his "enjoy every sandwich" credo he offered Letterman on the *Late Show*.

True to Zevon's body of work, the album is a blend of rockers and tender ballads, with one down-and-dirty blues tune. Guitars—acoustic, electric, slide and lap steel—provide the predominant instrumental mode and several album highlights, as Zevon's piano and keyboard playing was reduced, in part due to his condition. Despite his weakness and the exceptional contributions from his peers, Zevon still commands the spotlight.

In the self-mythologizing summary that opens, "Dirty Life and Times," Zevon is self-accepting and unapologetic, saying he "couldn't go where he was told." Death lurking did not dull Zevon's sardonic sensibility, as evidenced in his desperate quest for love. Though he bemoans that "It's hard to find a girl with a heart of gold when you're living in a four-letter world," there is humorous hopefulness: "And if she won't love me then her sister will; she's from Say-one-thing-and-mean-another." In his winding down, Zevon delivers an extraordinarily forthright and desperately amusing lyric, "I'm looking for a woman with low self-esteem, to lay me out and ease my worried mind." Thornton who, along with Yoakam, provides vocals on the song, begged to sing that killer line, so they remixed the version specifically to accommodate his quirky pleading. Goldberg, upon hearing the song, was convinced that at some point, the "low self-esteem" lyric was going to be among the many lines Zevon is known for.

According to Zevon, the rowdy unraveling in "Disorder in the House" is an accurate description of his state of mind at the time. Zevon plays with the duality of "disorder" as chaos and a condition. This metaphorical house is not burning down, but rather in decay, with "the tub runneth over, plaster falling in pieces, doors off the hinges" and Zevon

"sprawled across the davenport of despair." The vivid vision of deterioration approaches apocalyptic, earth-opening proportions, with zombies on the lawn staggering around. Vocals and a screeching, careening
guitar from Springsteen amplify some of the politically tinged Bush-era
commentary—"reptile wisdom, flaw in the system, demons loose, big
guns spoken, we've fallen for the ruse, the less you know the better off
you'll be." Zevon involves celebrity, claiming the disorder is "a fate
worse than fame." The line is coupled with another of his signature
lyrics of strangely amusing wonderment—"Even the Lhasa Apso seems
to be ashamed." He also slips in rhyming recognition of his favorite
color and his youth—"gonna paint the whole town gray, whether a night
in Paris or a Fresno matinee." After assessing the disorder, Zevon declares, "All bets are off" and that he will "live with the losses." The
unruly anthem was eventually adopted as an opening theme for *Disorder*, a free-form, eclectic music show hosted by Meg Griffin on the
Sirius/XM Satellite Radio channel, The Loft. Zevon is also featured in
an ad for the satellite radio network's channel, The Spectrum, promoting its format/rotation, "From Ryan Adams to Warren Zevon."

Zevon precedes "Numb as a Statue" with an impromptu nod to his
longtime collaborator Lindley, whose signature slide laces the song with
the West Coast 1970s sound. "Let's do another bad one," instructs
Zevon, "'Cause I like it when the blood drains from Dave's face." Zevon
is "gonna beg, borrow or steal some feelings," presumably a reference
to his ghostly, medicated state. Aware that time is not on his side, he is
not asking to dig down deep, "just bring enough for the ritual, get here
before I fall asleep," which obviously can be interpreted literally or as
dying.

The brooding "Prison Grove" is a death-row lament that uses the
prison cell and the view looking down through the narrow space between the bars as metaphor for Zevon's inner space, his psyche, and life
sentence—"Iron will hard as a rock, hold me up for the fateful knock,
when they walk me down in mortal lock." Zevon's lyric conceit is on full
frontal in the grim-gallows setting of the closing quatrain, a rich and
unsettling intermingling of children's nursery rhyme and alliteration
with the bodily, spiritual, and emotional: "Knick Knack Paddy Wack,
They' say you'll hear your own bones crack, When they bend you back
to bible black, Then you'll find your love." The strands of string masters

from two eras—Cooder's sinuous slide and Lindley's saz—texture a wailing seven-person chorus that contributes to the portentous mood.

Early-era clock-counting classics such as Chuck Berry's "Reelin' and Rockin'" and Bill Haley's "Rock Around the Clock" rattle in the party tune "The Rest of the Night." The anthem to reckless abandon asks, "Why stop now? Why slow down? Why leave now?" with the rationale containing a life-is-short subtext, "We may never get this chance again." Petty's laid-back parallel vocals and Campbell's guitar lend a Heart-breaker sound to the revelry. Snyder calls the song "the comic relief of the album," explaining the source: when Zevon "had this idea that everyone would be waiting for this statement from his camp," Calderón suggested, "let's party for the rest of the night!" (*Ice*, 26).

Zevon revisits the blues for the first time since the hindu love gods' sessions in the raunch of "Rub Me Raw." Again, the terminal intimations are thinly veiled, as Zevon is "shaking all over . . . a shattering mass," but says he is "going to take it with class." In a reminder of his defiant nature, he concedes that he "should climb out quick" of the hole he fell in while walking pretty, "but I hate doing what I'm told." He also manages a parting shot at anonymous Internet messengers that he became obsessed with, disdainfully name-calling them "the green horned chicken hoppers," and advising, "get yourself a trade or go back to the chat room and fade in the shade." Walsh's searing guitar that propels the narrative resounds with his "Rocky Mountain Way" from 1973.

The longing for love and companionship persist until the very end with intensified urgency and emotional resonance. The two-word weariness in "Please Stay" may be the epitome of the desperate vulnerability that is fundamental in the Zevon's oeuvre. Hoping "to find the other side of goodbye," Zevon fearfully pleads, "Will you stay with me to the end? When there's nothing left/But you and me and the wind." Emmylou Harris sweetly graces Zevon's slight quiver with vocal support and presence. A rare saxophone bridge and fade out emerge as a sound encore from "Excitable Boy." "She's Too Good for Me" may be the one moment when Zevon's despair drifts toward poor poor pitiful me-ness and defeat, transparent in low self-esteem—"Trust me, I'm not good enough for her"—and selflessness—"I want her to be everything she couldn't be with me." The simple but affecting "El Amor De Mi Vida" ("love of my life") is a poetic correspondence to a lost love, "wishing it could have been us." The song was written for/to former girlfriend and "sober traveler" from the late 1980s and early 1990s, Annette Aguilar-Ramos, with whom Zevon had lost touch. The song's poignancy is enriched by Calderón alternating verses in Spanish. On piano, David Crosby's son, James Raymond, guides an arrangement that includes bongos and upright bass.

The album's definitive dirge, a cover of Bob Dylan's "Knockin' on Heaven's Door," was not planned. The fitting ballad, about a deputy sheriff dying from a bullet wound—"the long black cloud is comin' down"—originated on the soundtrack of the Sam Peckinpah Western, *Pat Garrett and Billy the Kid* (1973), starring Kris Kristofferson as Billy the Kid, James Coburn as Garrett, and Dylan as "Alias." The song cued the early career characterizations of Zevon as desperado, "the Sam Peckinpah of rock," a comparison largely based not only on Zevon's Western attraction, but his and the maverick filmmaker's shared affections for expressing graphic violence and for their lifestyle excesses. When Zevon said he wanted to record the archetypal "die with your boots on song," Thornton and Calderón both laughed, perhaps nervously. "I thought it was a little too much to do that song, but when I heard him sing it . . . I thought . . . if anyone will sing it, it's him," said Calderón (C. Zevon, 406). Recording the song was spontaneous, one of the spiritual high points of the sessions. They did not even have the lyrics. Fortunately, Calderón happened to have a copy of Dylan's *Greatest Hits* in his car. He brought in the disc, they transcribed the lyrics, and cut a version at Thornton's studio. The gathering of friends standing in a circle, singing choir-like into one mic, with Zevon's impatient cries "open up, open up, open up, please" as the chorus fades, was typical of the uplifting moments that marked *The Wind* sessions; at once moving, intense, soulful, and reverent, as described by Thornton and Calderón (C. Zevon, 407).

The album sequence crests gracefully into an exquisite farewell prayer, "Keep Me in Your Heart," marking the completion of the Zevon songbook. The quintessential "letting go" or parting song, featuring such heart-wrenching lines as "if I leave you it doesn't mean I love you any less," was Zevon's initial songwriting response to his diagnosis. Zevon's waning wishes are for his presence to persist in his absence, whether "when you wake up in the morning," or "sometimes when you're doing simple things around the house, maybe you'll think of me and smile." Within the context of Zevon's grim gravity, the vulnerability and sincerity in the verses swell with profound poignancy: the intimate connection in "You know I'm tied to you like the buttons on your blouse"; assurance that "When the Winter comes keep the fires lit, and I will be right next to you," an echo of Nick Drake's gorgeous "Northern Sky" from 1970, particularly the line "would you love me through the winter . . . 'til I'm dead"; and Zevon's palpable withering spirit, "These wheels keep turning but they're running out of steam." The lovely lyrics and melody, featuring a "Sha-la-la-la-la-la-la-li-li-lo, keep me in your heart for a while" chorus, are eased along by Calderón's lithe, comforting acoustic guitar and a harpsichord-sounding Cuban tres on the bridge and fadeout. Keltner's shuffling drum flourishes simulate the rhythm of "the train leaving nightly called when all is said and done," as "engine driver's headed north to Pleasant Station."

As Zevon's and *The Wind*'s final graceful reflection, "Keep Me in Your Heart" joins the closing songs on Zevon's two preceding records— "Don't Let Us Get Sick" on *Life'll Kill Ya* and the title track on *My Ride's Here*—to form their own compelling mortality triptych situated within Zevon's "Deteriorata" trilogy of albums.

STRANGER IN A STRANGE LAND

The Wind sessions were a unique ritual embodying collective delightful sorrow, passion, intimacy, and a range of emotions. "It's unbelievably sad and unbelievably brave," said Ry Cooder. "You get that kind of intense focus and every word and every note is heartfelt. . . . There's subtext all over the place. I went around in another mental atmosphere for quite some time after that" (Pareles 2003, 25).

Calderón compared the session's unrehearsed homage nature to the 1950s television show *This Is Your Life*. To him, recording *The Wind* was "like a drug—the creativity, the people that were coming to play, the beauty of this music. But there was also the other side of it for him [Zevon]: This is all happening because I'm dying" (Fricke 2003, 49). Goldberg agreed: "Then suddenly it was done. He [Zevon] was so happy and so sad, it was an amazing time to be around him. He was mostly enjoying all the attention. He was like a little kid . . . and this one was just a spiritual album for everyone" (C. Zevon, 413).

Browne suggested recording *The Wind* was analogous with "disincorporating" (Brown, F8), a concept presented in the opening chapter of Robert Heinlein's science fiction novel, *Stranger in a Strange Land*, when an artist dies in the middle of a project on Mars. The artist does not notice his own death because he is so involved in his work and there is life after physical death on the planet. His creation is completely unique, in that half of it was made when he was alive, and half when he is dead.

Zevon circumvented total "disincorporation," avoiding the necessity of posthumous post-production to complete a project-in-progress, unlike several other music passings within a five-year proximity to his own death. The Band's Rick Danko, Mama and Papa John Phillips, Beatle George Harrison, Latin Salsa Queen Celia Cruz, and legendary Johnny Cash and his wife June Carter Cash died between December 1999 and September 2003. Unlike Zevon, none of those artists were around to witness the release of their final albums.

The sessions for *Phillips 66* (2001) were completed days before Phillips died, and Carter Cash lived for two months after finishing *Wildwood Flowers* (2003). Producer Rick Rubin continued to curate Johnny Cash's *American Recordings*, an acclaimed series that began with *The Man Comes Around* (2002), followed by the noteworthy box set, *Unearthed* (2003), released two months after Cash's death, followed by the posthumous *American Recordings V: A Hundred Highways* (2006) and *VI: Ain't No Grave* (2010). On a much smaller scale, friends and family assembled Danko's last live shows and studio material from an abandoned solo project into *Days Like These* (2000).

Harrison's *Brainwashed* (2002) represented an unusually prolonged "disincorporation," due in large part to his lengthy battle with cancer. Tracks that eventually appeared on the album were recorded as early as 1988. Harrison continued to work on the album sporadically, focusing more intently on its completion after being attacked by an intruder in his home in 1999. The album was unfinished when Harrison died on November 29, 2011. However, he left guidelines for its completion with his son, Dhani, and old collaborator and Traveling Wilbury, Jeff Lynne, who had been working in close conjunction with Harrison on the project. After 14 years of "disincorporation," the album was released in 2002, almost a year after Harrison's death. Coincidentally, *Brainwashed* and *The Wind* were Harrison's and Zevon's 12th studio albums.

Zevon was the exception, hanging on long enough to catch a glimpse of the early sales of *The Wind* that eventually garnered a Grammy and gold. More significantly, he witnessed the birth of his first grandchildren on June 11, 2003, daughter Ariel's twin boys, Augustus Warren and Maximus Patrick Zevon-Powell.

On August 26, 2003, *The Wind* joined its pair of predecessors, *Life'll Kill Ya* and *My Ride's Here*, in completing a recording arc that had innately unfolded into Zevon's Deteriorata trilogy. Zevon's mortality triumvirate was analogous with other singer-songwriter album sequences, notably Dylan's "holy trinity"—*Slow Train Coming, Saved*, and *Shot of Love* between 1979 and 1981, and John Hiatt's succession of magnificent midlife "family albums," *Bring the Family, Slow Turning*, and *Stolen Moments* from 1987 to 1990. Perhaps more abstractly, Zevon's series of recordings also connects with George Harrison's post-Beatle baptism, *All Things Must Pass* (1970), a transcendent three-record set centered on spirituality. Beyond its existential theme and the Spectorian splendor of its production, Harrison's debut is notable as rock's first single-artist triple album, preceding the various artists' *Woodstock* soundtrack by six months, and as the first solo-Beatle record to top the charts.

FUNEREALITY SHOW: DEAD MAN WALKING

The most sacred, intimate parts of Zevon's procession, from *Letterman's Late Show* through *The Wind*, were chronicled in a stirring one-hour VH1 special, *(Inside)Out: Warren Zevon: Keep Me in Your Heart*, directed, produced, and photographed by Nick Read. Everyone involved seemed willing to concede the "death watch" opportunism inherent in the documentary project. The prevailing rationale was that it was a tribute and living funeral, and never too late for the underappreciated songwriter to get his due, fateful irony notwithstanding. Goldberg had approached VH1 earlier about featuring Zevon in their popular bio-series *Behind the Music*. "I did everything I could to convince them to do one on Warren, and they wouldn't do it, which is ironic given that they ended up having that big special [*(Inside)Out*] on him when he was dying," said Goldberg. "I always felt a little irritated that we couldn't have gotten that kind of exposure on *Life'll Kill Ya,* which I think is every bit as good as *The Wind*" (C. Zevon, 374).

The *(Inside)Out* premiere aired on the cable music network without commercial interruption on Sunday evening, August 24, 2003, two days before the release of *The Wind* and two weeks before Zevon's death. The documentary was a more dignified variation of the often scandalous, sensational *Behind the Music* episodes. The presentation blended reality show conventions of MTV's pioneering *Real World,* which launched in 1992 with *The Osbournes,* with prevailing rock-and-roll reverence and sensibility more aligned with Albom's best-selling *Tuesdays With Morrie.*

As director, Read's overarching approach is a video diary, with the recording sessions the unifying structural thread. The production deftly adapts traditional bio-documentary conventions into a life-affirming musical wake. Billy Bob Thornton leads with a litany—"the crazy bag of labels"—used to describe Zevon. He continues with voice-over narration of a career composite that is dotted with observations from Zevon's family and his music and literary entourage. From there, the approach shifts to a video diary, from the diagnosis in August 2002 through the recording of *The Wind'*s final song, "Keep Me in Your Heart," on April 12, 2003. Dates and brief Zevon notes appear on the screen in typewriter-style font, homage to Zevon's word machine, the Smith Corona. The entries are preface and transition. Most are inner reflections: "I have good days and bad days—weeks become months until . . ."

While the sessions are the focal point, the interior locales are not confining or claustrophobic. Intercutting concert footage, highlights from Zevon's *Late Show* appearance from arrival in New York City to rehearsal to the show itself and backstage departing, still photos, music memorabilia, and archival home movies shot by Jordan's mother, Tule Livingston, enhance the studio story and structure. The dramatic construction is more complementary than cluttered. On the soundtrack, carefully selected and placed lyric and instrumental samples of the Zevon songbook provide interludes, thematic accents, and emotional resonance to the visuals and narrative. Throughout, the prevailing tone is similar to the *Late Show* farewell, celebratory but with sweet sadness a subtext. Hugs and handshakes abound, heartache hovers and hides beneath occasional humor.

The portrayal captures Zevon's complexities, facets, and roles. He is thoughtful, engaging, and literate, quoting from Mickey Spillane, Steve McQueen in *Tom Horn*, Rilke, and Arthur Schopenhauer. He is a fan and friend when taking a picture of Springsteen in the studio. A prescription junkie, reaching into his bag of medications by flashlight, routinely popping pills and washing them down with diet Mountain Dew. A devoted father gently rubbing his pregnant daughter's stomach, and working on a piano arrangement next to son Jordan. A fashion-conscious stylist shopping for a suit for the visit with Letterman. And, of course, the Grin Reaper, emerging from a limo upon arriving in New York City proclaiming, "Dead man walking!"

The scenes are rife with poignant moments. Midway through a meeting with his oncologist, Zevon asks the cameras to leave as the discussion of his treatment and side effects becomes more personal. When the *New Yorker* calls his publicist for an interview, the uncompromising Zevon, staring out the limo window in a reprising image of the *My Ride's Here* cover, declines, uttering a brusque, almost resentful, "Too late." There are shots of Zevon cuffing cigarettes like Bogart outside the Cherokee Studios in defiant resignation, "What would you do if you had a month to live?" And the curious Zevon, confounded by Internet postings by fans who regard his refusal of chemotherapy treatment "heroic," ruefully rejects such a badge of honor, "I think it's a sin not to want to live." Hiaasen and others had cautioned Zevon for a few years not to get drawn into following Internet dispatches about him.

The recording of "Disorder in the House" two days in mid-December is a particularly riveting sequence. Zevon's diary entry signals a shift in tone from the preceding scene of lunch with humorist Dave Barry: "It's nearly Christmas and I still have two songs to complete. I hope I can stay well enough long enough." "Don't Let Us Get Sick," bedded under images of holiday lights and neon in L.A., magnifies the somber mood. December 17 marks the "start of a long and grueling day" recording the song which, according to Zevon, "accurately describes my state of mind." Zevon's state of mind becomes more of a focal point. Intercut with Jim Keltner drumming his tracks for the song, a series of shots of Zevon taking his medications follows as foreshadowing. Zevon explains that they "mask the symptoms" and that he "expected it to be worse." "Life's not over," he states. In contrast to Zevon's pill popping, Calderón is munching snacks behind the audio console, ready to record.

Zevon appears unsettled, a presumed result of the meds. He puts on his glasses and slouches in a studio seat, quoting from Schopenhauer about reading. When Noah Snyder's voice intones over the studio microphone, asking if he's ready to give it a shot, Zevon chuckles, "Yeah, why not. The rest of my short life has gone by while I wait for you to ask that question." Zevon continually misses cues. There is a cut to the audio room where Calderón adjusts his glasses and raises an eyebrow. He joins Zevon in the studio, counting, tapping on his knee, trying unsuccessfully to capture a useable take. Cast as an unflappable, nurturing parent or teacher, Calderón maintains a smile, "Maybe we should figure out what we need."

The scene shifts to Zevon and Calderón at the audio console, negotiating, with Snyder close by. A remarkable exchange follows. Calderón cautiously wonders about Zevon's energy level and its effect on the takes. Zevon interrupts, saying that he doesn't want to bring some "George C. Scott gloom" to the situation. Calderón continues, suggesting it might be better to return in the morning to record when Zevon is fresh. "I'm dying, Jorge, I don't have no 'fresh,'" replies Zevon. "'Fresh' is not in my vocabulary." Calderón displays saintly compassion within the circumstances. "I totally understand, but we're celebrating life everyday—yours, mine and everybody else's." Zevon may be medicated but he is not soothed: "You're taking this too seriously." Calderón disengages, turning his head away. Zevon is clearly feeling the end drawing closer. He slurs, "What do you think, boys, am I going out in a fiery hole a million miles long." Calderón leans back in his chair, snack in hand, looking straight. He calmly counters, "Where you go after this is way better. I have a special place for you though. Miles (Davis) will come visiting. Blow his horn; jam. There's no fiery hole there." Calderón's saintly presence is not a camera-conscious ploy. His genuine compassion and dedication are equally prominent throughout the Zevon oral history. Calderón, along with Browne, appeared to grasp Zevon's genius and demons more fully than anyone in the L.A. scene.

The studio atmosphere becomes slightly more upbeat the following day with the arrival of another heroic figure, Bruce Springsteen. The saving grace is reflected in Zevon's December 18 entry: "According to the doctors I should be long gone by now every day means the world to me. Especially when my old friend Bruce Springsteen is coming to the studio." Springsteen's 120-date tour had him in Indianapolis the night before. He was due home in New Jersey for Christmas. Instead, as Zevon proudly points out, "he chartered a plane to come see me." The absorbing sequence climaxes on an upbeat note. Following Springsteen's vocal track for the song, he rips a torrid, screeching guitar solo for "Disorder in the House" that literally blows the amp and rips the speakers. An awestruck Zevon bows, "You *are* him." Snyder felt as if they witnessed a "cosmic event . . . like Sir Galahad at the moment he finds the Grail. There was something magical about the energy that he brought. There was nothing left for the amp to do—it had achieved the highest state of amp-dom and went right up to God at that point" (C. Zevon, 412). "Warren just turned to me when he was done and said, out of the side of his mouth, 'Did anyone know Bruce Springsteen could play guitar like *that*?' It was very emotional. He was just a tornado of joy who blew through the studio and left. I don't think he was in town for more than 12 hours. It meant a lot to Warren at a very bad time." (Jones, 2014, 49–50).

The heart-wrenching closing scene of the documentary reveals Zevon's fierce resolve fading fast. Too fragile to record in the studio, he teeters on the couch next to Calderón in his home in front of two microphones. His baritone is weak and straining slightly, but rises to complete *The Wind*'s closing song, the hymn-like "Keep Me in Your Heart." The concluding scene is transcendent, arguably eclipsing the foreshadowing music video of Johnny Cash covering Trent Reznor of Nine Inch Nails' "Hurt" in 2002, and Kurt Cobain, in cardigan, as the most intimate unplugged performance in the music television era, at once a powerful, prayerful parting and shimmering lullaby.

DEADPAN: "PAINT THE WHOLE TOWN GRAY"

The shadowy packaging and design of *The Wind* CD and its companion *(Inside)Out* DVD complement the scope and spirit of the parting record and documentary. Both disc cases translate as burial vaults that contain the sacred audio and video artifacts of Zevon's Deteriorata. Muted tones and shades of gray, the primary palette for the color-compulsive Zevon, abound, from Zevon's clothing to backgrounds, letters, and graphics to the disc itself and a creased charcoal shroud that drapes the back cover.

The signature skull with sunglasses and dangling cigarette is stamped throughout. By the time Zevon posed for the parting portrait for *Rolling Stone* photographer Matthew Rolston, the "Old Velvet Nose" trademark as portrayed on both the CD and DVD covers had morphed into Zevon's own fading desperado guise, or vice versa—a companion piece to hang alongside the portrait of Uncle Warren in the Zevon family gallery. The long shot on the DVD cover depicts Zevon in a ghostly gunslinger stance. He is propped on the edge of a stool, shirt open three buttons down, sleeves rolled up. His right arm hangs, elbow bent, hand at the hip of his black leather pants, as if ready to draw his gun. The wristwatch on Zevon's opposite arm that rests on his inner thigh is a subtle but striking reminder of time. It ticks loudly, a count-down, the last stand. The close-up on the CD is calm yet confronting. There is no smirk, only a straight ahead stare, an aged version of the "complicated gaze" Ronstadt observed in the 1970s. The road map lines may not be etched in the cold candor of Zevon's face like the Keith Richards, Johnny Cash, Dylan, or Miles Davis close-ups, which rank among the most revealing in the rock and *Rolling Stone* Rushmore, but "the Look" is there. Point Blank. Point Noir. Point Gray. Deadpan.

Despite the gloom and imminent doom, the *(Inside)Out* documentary reveals a self-effacing Zevon assessing the photos at the shoot, telling "the last girlfriend," Kristen Steffl, that he looks like "a baboon from Newcastle trying to get a job in a toothpaste commercial."

BOUND FOR GLORY, GOLD, AND GRAMMY

> *I better die quick so they'll give me a Grammy nomination. It's a damn hard way to make a living, having to die to get 'em to know you're alive.*
>
> —Warren Zevon (C. Zevon)

> *If you're lucky, people like something you do early and something you do just before you drop dead. That's as many pats on the back as you should expect.*
>
> —Warren Zevon, 1993 (Fretts)

Zevon's comment about early- and late-career approval and expectation from an *Entertainment Weekly* interview ten years earlier circulated frequently during his Deteriorata. The luck-obsessed Zevon was lucky, as his chronology was bracketed by such praise. Early on, producer Peter Asher and Linda Ronstadt (un)covered his songwriting brilliance by baptizing "Carmelita," "Poor Poor Pitiful Me," "Hasten Down the Wind," and "Mohammed's Radio" into hits during the 1970s. Toward the end, Bob Dylan paid homage by covering Zevon songs during his fall 2002 tour. "Boom Boom Mancini," "Accidentally Like a Martyr," "Mutineer," and "Lawyers, Guns and Money" were a regular part of Dylan's live set list while touring. (A live Dylan version of "Mutineer" is included in the *Enjoy Every Sandwich* [2004] Zevon tribute record.) In a 2009 interview with longtime critic Bill Flanagan that appeared in the *Huffington Post*, Dylan, presumably not standing on Steve Earle's coffee table, though likely wearing cowboy boots, named Zevon as one of his favorite songwriters, citing how he "straddled the line between heartfelt and primeval," and that "there might be three separate songs within a Zevon song but they're all effortlessly connected" (n.p.)

The Wind, benefitting from Zevon's "terminal exposure," sold 48,000 copies its first week in late August 2003, debuting at number 16 on the *Billboard* Top 200 chart, marking Zevon's first Top 20 appearance since *Bad Luck Streak in Dancing School* in 1980. The album was certified gold (100,000 copies sold) in December, and also received five Grammy nominations, eventually winning in two categories. The nominations were for Song of the Year ("Keep Me in Your Heart"), Best Male Pop Vocal ("Keep Me in Your Heart"), Best Rock Song ("Disorder in the House"), Best Contemporary Folk Album, and Best Rock Performance by a Group or Duo ("Disorder in the House" with Springsteen). According to Calderón, as the end neared, Zevon did not read many of *The Wind*'s reviews "because they all talked about him dying. I remember him telling me, 'Just tell me the good news'" (Fricke 2003, 49).

The Wind cast critics in an unusual position. Considering the album's inescapable context of finality, the renowned supporting cast, and their outstanding contributions to the record, any critical disapproval could be delicate, and potentially viewed as insensitive and nitpicking. At the opposite end of the evaluation spectrum, tour-de-force proclamations might be read as opportunistic overstatement fraught with sentimentality. Reviews of *The Wind* were uniformly favorable and fair, with a reverent tone and admiration for Zevon's courage. "Under normal circumstances" was a frequently used phrase. Those who found the album marked with Zevon's characteristic unevenness were empathetic and conceding. Critics commonly focused on *The Wind*'s unsettling poignancy. While some found the album an oddly invasive experience with personal expressions almost too intimate to bear, most agreed the farewell work was undeniably unique and unforgettable.

PROCESSION TO PASSAGE: A RECONFIGURED ROCK REQUIEM

Warren spent his whole life expecting death, so he was ready for it.
Maybe more than most of us who are trying to live clean and decent
lives. I'd say he kicked death right in the balls.
                                        —humorist Dave Barry (C. Zevon)

Zevon's desperado Deteriorata was a distinctive and dignified requiem, a captivating small-scale spectacle of compassion, curiosity, and chronicle. The rich rite of passage embodied qualities of the human condition and meanings that transcended the rock-and-roll sphere. With death an anticlimactic inevitability, preface and process proved more compelling than pinnacle or postscript. In addition to Zevon having the opportunity to say goodbye, the death-watch circumstances afforded journalists, fans, and cultural observers a unique opportunity to contemplate and prepare preemptive eulogistic career retrospectives. The grim nature of the narrative was enriched by the looming shadow of irony cast by Zevon's dark songwriting preoccupations, wry humor, and excessive lifestyle for much of his life.

The portrayal, permission, and participation in Zevon's dying day reflected the "reality show" realm of media and celebrity culture where an endless cycle of compulsive coverage matches a boundless consumer attraction and appetite. The value shift from private to public was deeply entrenched, with even the most intimate details of lives and lifestyles such as sex and death a vital part of the all-access pass and audience expectations.

As a narrative ritual form, Zevon's Deteriorata reconfigured the conventional rock-and-roll mortal methodology and martyrdom from plane crashes, gunshot wounds, murder, suicide, and accidental overdoses to a dieography that was a more honorable sacrament. Mingling ceremonial elements of tour, recording session, and living funeral, the Deteriora-ta's devices and arrangement reflected a more reverent staging and tone than the sensationalism that tends to characterize the media satu-ration and audience fascination in the immediate wake of a sudden or expected death of a public figure. In Zevon's case, the shock came with the public disclosure of his terminal diagnosis rather than the death itself. The death-watch circumstances afforded journalists and fans the opportunity to ponder and prepare eulogistic career retrospectives and appreciations in what was ironically a familiar role for the songwriter who had been spokesperson for the doomed.

The Zevon Deteriorata set a precedent. An analogous arc of notable parallels and waning documentation unfolded in the wake of country music legend Glenn Campbell's Alzheimer's diagnosis in 2011. *Ghost on the Canvas* (2011) was Campbell's version of *The Wind*, in his words, "the last studio album I ever plan to make." The record was followed by *See You There* (2013), which featured Campbell's most popular songs with new vocals recorded during the *Ghost* sessions and mixed with different instrumentation. Similar to the VH1 documentary on Zevon's final recording sessions for *The Wind*, *Glenn Campbell: I'll Be Me* (2014) is an intimate, unflinching career chronicle centered on Campbell's struggles with Alzheimer's and framed by his farewell tour. The song, "I'm Not Gonna Miss You," recorded in 2013, is Campbell's "Keep Me in Your Heart," his final studio recording that won a Gram-my and was nominated for an Academy Award for Best Original Song. Due to the progression of Campbell's disease, he was admitted to a care facility in Nashville months before the film's New York premiere in October 2014. The documentary's television debut aired on CNN on June 28, 2015.

While Zevon's non-superstar status as an artist may have not been the only motivating factor for the exposure inherent within his Deteri-orata, it also contributed to the process of the ritual being more man-ageable. Arguably, a similar preface and procession for Beatle Harrison, who was in Zevon's relatively young age range when battling brain cancer before his death at age 58, or the elder legend Cash during his prolonged illness, may have proved overwhelming due to the magni-tude of their careers.

It may have taken death's career-enhancing cliché and a little help from his musical friends and family, particularly an amp-melting

Springsteen guitar solo, but Zevon crossed over from the peripheries. From the announcement of his terminal condition in September 2002, through the posthumous Grammy tribute in February 2004 and the continued flurry of afterlife activity, Zevon received more press coverage than he had his entire career. Perhaps that was part of the plan, both personally and professionally. Grudgingly pondering posterity and the "vast indifference of heaven" following his diagnosis, Zevon quipped that his hope was to be remembered better than the "bad watercolor" of Humphrey Bogart on the DVD case of *The Maltese Falcon* (Pareles 2003, 25).

Zevon's son Jordan, reflecting on his father's final year, said that beyond his undeniable strength and courage, Zevon displayed intuitive marketing savvy, and "was not going to go out John Prine–style with the record that sells ten thousand copies:"

> He'd been in the business for his entire life, and he hit it right on the head. I mean, there are gold records, the things keep selling, people talking about him. It really proves that even though he made music that wasn't geared toward instant commercial success or trying to conform to something . . . and though he may have had times when he was frustrated by the sales or poor attendance at concerts, when it all came down to it, he knew what he was doing more than anybody at any of these labels did. (C. Zevon, 399)

"KNOCKIN' ON HEAVEN'S DOOR"

At 56, Zevon was, as he cowrote with T-Bone Burnett on "Bed of Coals," "too old to die young, too young to die now." But Zevon was lucky and he knew it. He lived the familiar, full-force, fatally flawed rock-and-roll fable much longer than his perished predecessors. Zevon was mystified by and perversely proud that he was not "deader than a Door." "I chose a certain path and lived like Jim Morrison, but lived 30 more years, who knows why?" he told Letterman. Morrison appeared to be the benchmark, his name and fate frequently invoked during Zevon's interviews. Zevon was routinely reminded of his emblematic, excitable "Wild Age" tales and corresponding "cowboy days" of "running straight in their graves" lifestyle. Looking back in 2003, he observed his route from recklessness to redemption with the realization that "I lucked out big time because I got to be the most fucked-up rock star on the block, at least my block, and then I got to be a sober dad for 18 years. I've had two very full lives" (Gunderson, 12D). One reckless, and one of recovery and redemption after a stay at Rehab Mountain. His career retrospective windblown, from "Hasten Down the Wind" to *The Wind*.

Familiar lines of questioning persisted during the Deteriorata as journalists prodded Zevon about his continual deciphering of death in songwriting. As far back as 1981, Zevon explained in an interview in *Songwriter*, "I consider that what we're essentially dealing with is an existence that we don't understand. That's why a lot of my work is about death" (Alfonso, 24). More than 20 years later, in 2002, as the mystery unraveled within the context of his own dieography, Zevon's view was slightly more comprehensible:

> I've often infuriated sincere interviewers who asked why I write all these 'death songs.' I'd tell them "I don't know." I guess I have the answer now. Maybe we as writers carry some kind of physical knowledge of our fates, and work through them. To me the message of my songs, of all songs, is "enjoy life." . . . It's the only message I ever thought art had any business having. (Gunderson, 12D)

CODA: DIE WITH YOUR BOOTS ON

> *It was the role he was preparing to play all his life. [Cancer] gave him the chance to be like one of his tough-guy heroes. He got to be John Wayne, at last.*
>
> —Jordan Zevon (Jones, 2014)

Zevon got to go out on his own terms in an extraordinary exit, dying like the antihero in F. Scott Fitzgerald's *Tender is the Night*, exiting in the shadows he so often wrote and sang about, the shadows that lurked and those he chased, the shadows he cast and those that cast him. And the waning shadows cast by the glare of media coverage. Rather than dying in what he called in his *Rolling Stone* interview with Paul Nelson "a coward's death" as a drunk, or by a drug overdose or gunshot wound— all three well within Zevon's realm of reckless roulette at one time— Zevon died with dignity. He had played the doomed protagonist, the hard-boiled poet saboteur, for so long; this was his apotheosis. The noir hero, and the noir hero redeemed, blazoned. In 2003, more than 30 years after Zevon defiantly wrote "I'll Sleep When I'm Dead," his life-long piano-pounding pledge converged in chorus with Zevon's more current decrees, "Life'll Kill Ya" and "My Ride's Here," into prophecies fulfilled. On September 7, Warren Zevon died in his sleep at his home in Los Angeles. The desperado died with his boots on.

POSTHUMOUS SCRIPT

"Eat My Dust"

Serious writers, serious lovers of language, will be discovering [Zev-on's songs] for a long time to come.

—Jackson Browne (Fricke 2003)

"THE OTHER SIDE OF GOOD BYE"

Warren Zevon's ashes were scattered in the Pacific Ocean near Los Angeles during a private ceremony of family and friends. True to death's ripple effect on an artist's mythic ascension and marketability, Zevon articles proliferated. The groundwork for commemorative momentum that was established during the course of his Deteriorata from 2000 through 2003 sustained in the immediate aftermath of his death, and over the course of the next four years, in ceremony, awards, music, song, visuals, art and artifact, performance, and literature.

On February 8, 2004, at the 46th Grammy Awards, Zevon won two Grammys for *The Wind* in somewhat contrasting categories—Best Contemporary Folk Album and Best Rock Performance by a Group or Duo ("Disorder in the House" with Springsteen). Placing *The Wind* in the Contemporary Folk category may have been a sympathetic stretch, a genre designation that may have been further contradicted by removing "Disorder in the House" to place it in the Rock Duo category. Whether it was industry exploitation, or a current or career parting gift—a Lifetime Achievement for the dying—was a mortal moot point. The recognition may not have been about Zevon's "best for last," but rather affirmation that Zevon's best work *will* last. "This album has one soul but it has many hearts," reiterated Jordan Zevon when accepting the awards on his father's behalf. The morning of the Grammy Awards broadcast, Jordan appeared on the cable network A&E's (Arts and Entertainment) *Breakfast with the Arts*, where he discussed his father's life, music, and final recording.

The Grammy ceremony further celebrated Zevon with a lovely live choral tribute, with Ariel and Jordan Zevon, Jorge Calderón, Billy Bob Thornton, Jackson Browne, Emmylou Harris, Timothy B. Schmidt, and Dwight Yoakam singing "Keep Me in Your Heart." The beautifully reflective song, augmented by its mortality milieu, was instantaneously enshrined into the canon of pop music eulogies, advancing to the forefront of a hymnal that includes Sarah McLachlan's "Arms of an Angel" and "I Will Remember You," Jane Siberry's elegant "Calling All Angels," fellow Los Angeles songwriters James Taylor's "That Lonesome Road" and Karla Bonoff's traditional "The Water is Wide," Jackson Browne's "For a Dancer," and Elton John's "Candle in the Wind," reconfigured from its 1973 Marilyn Monroe version into a Princess Diana tribute single following her death in 1997.

"Keep Me in Your Heart" approached "Werewolves of London" as the Zevon song most frequently incorporated into television and film soundtracks. The song's sentiment, tone, and context proved ideal for closing montages and for framing emotional moments, among them: the drama series, *Boston Legal*, a woman researches alternative treatments for terminal lung cancer for her love interest (played by Michael J. Fox) asleep beside her; a father's funeral on the crime procedural *NCIS*; a 50th birthday commemoration in the Jim Belushi sitcom *According to Jim*; the farewell scene of the series finale of the curmudgeonly hospital drama, *House*, titled "Everybody Dies"; and in a memorial video on *Joan of Arcadia*, a "what if God was one of us?," hallowed halls of high school series, which also featured Zevon's "Back in the High Life" in another episode.

In a scene in the Judd Apatow film *Funny People* (2009), Ira (Seth Rogan) previews a playlist for his friend, George Simmons (Adam Sandler), hoping to cheer him following his leukemia diagnosis. After leading with samples of Bob Marley's "Three Little Birds" ("Don't worry about a thing") and the *Dirty Dancing* (1987) theme, "(I've Had) The Time of My Life," Ira's rotation gets to "Keep Me in Your Heart." As the song plays, the shots linger, cutting back and forth to Ira and George intently listening. Zevon's sentiment strikes too deep a chord of vulnerability in George, who stands up, utters a profanity and leaves. "Numb as a Statue" from *The Wind* is also featured in the film.

The song's lineage is further advanced by singer Madeleine Peyroux, who adopted the title for her *Best of* (2014) collection, which includes her interpretations of both "Keep Me in Your Heart" and "Desperados Under the Eaves." Peyroux was among the many artists who recorded individual Zevon songs in the years following his death, in a variety of styles and genres, carrying the Zevon cover tradition established by Linda Ronstadt in the 1970s into the new millennium, from the fringe to international hits like Kid Rock's sample of "Werewolves" inventively inserted alongside Lynyrd Skynyrd. Folkie Phil Cody, who opened for Zevon during the mid-1990s, paid homage to his stage partner with a rare single-artist tribute on the ten-song cover collection, *Phil Cody Sings Zevon* (2014).

The same month as the 2004 Grammys, the VH1 *(Inside)Out: Warren Zevon* DVD became available in the marketplace, followed by a steady stream of Zevon record releases over the next three years. There was a varied trio of tribute albums, beginning with *Dad Get Me Out of This* (2003)—the name derived from a "Lawyers, Guns and Money" verse—a captivating string quartet collection that renders ten Zevon songs symphonic; and two multi-artist compilations, *Hurry Home Early* (2005), an alternative independent-label record titled after the opening line to "Boom Boom Mancini," preceded by an accessible pop/rock set, *Enjoy Every Sandwich* (2004), featuring Springsteen, Browne, Henley, Dylan, Bonnie Raitt, Jill Sobule, Steve Earle, and Adam Sandler among its contributors, with Jordan Zevon premiering his father's unrecorded "Studebaker." Loyalist David Letterman helped showcase the album on the *Late Show*, as Jordan performed "Lawyers, Guns and Money" with Jakob Dylan's band Wallflowers shortly before the tribute's release; months later, Sandler did "Werewolves of London" on the show, marking the song with celebrity karaoke novelty.

The Zevon family affair was further manifest in daughter Ariel's touching liner notes for *Reconsider Me* (2006), a compilation of 13 of her father's romantic ballads, with the majority drawn from his last three albums. As a nifty promotional tie-in on Valentine's Day, VH1 Classic premiered a music video from the compilation, "She's Too Good For Me," which aired every hour on the hour throughout the day.

Before he died, Zevon commissioned his former wife and lifelong friend, Crystal, to conduct and compile exhaustive interviews with friends, family, lovers, cavorters, and cohorts. The result was an unflinching oral history, *I'll Sleep When I'm Dead: The Dirty Life and Times of Warren Zevon*, published in May 2007. The brutally honest, frequently fascinating, and unflattering and unsettling "sex, alcohol, and rock and roll" saga of antihero excess, redemption, and tortured genius matches, if not eclipses, the numerous incisive accounts of the Los Angeles music scene mythology, among them *Riot on Sunset Strip: Rock 'N' Roll's Last Stand in '60s Hollywood* (2007) by Domenic Priore, Michael Walker's *Laurel Canyon: The Inside Story of Rock and Roll's Legendary Neighborhood* (2006), and Barney Hoskyns's *Waiting for the Sun* (1996) and *Hotel California* (2006). In the view of Jackson Browne, the intimate patchwork portrait of Zevon "reads like a rock and roll Rashomon." The 452-page chronicle, with a foreword by Carl Hiaasen, immediately followed by a breathtaking account of Zevon's final moments from his close friend and confidante, Ryan Rayston, eventually reached the *New York Times* best-seller list, perpetuating Zevon's legacy of tortured brilliance. The book's publication in 2007, coinciding with the reissues of Zevon's Asylum catalog of albums that same year, marked a postmortem peak for Zevon activity.

AFTERLIFE ENDEAVORS: "SO MUCH TO DO"

Subsequent acknowledgments of Zevon, though steady to present, were more scattered than the concentration of activity in the four years following his death. As Zevon's dust settled, his songs sustained. "Poor Poor Pitiful Me" is one of ten tracks featured on the music CD of the two-disc DVD/CD, *Troubadours: The Rise of the Singer-Songwriter* (2011), a documentary package on the legendary West Hollywood club. The meager number of songs in the set is disappointing considering the impact of the Santa Monica Boulevard venue during the era.

Zevon's songs routinely surfaced in television and film soundtracks, from the aforementioned widespread use of "Keep Me in Your Heart" to "Lawyers, Guns and Money" as the theme song for the short-lived Jerry Bruckheimer series *Justice* (Fox 2006) to "Detox Mansion" in a scene as a character comes back to consciousness during the second season of HBO's *True Detective* (2015). In the Showtime cable series *Californication* (2007–2014), Zevon's presence is deeply embedded beyond his original songs and cover versions that permeated the series soundtrack during its seven-season run. Zevon is the musical touchstone and rock-and-roll alter ego for David Duchovny's lead character, Hank Moody. Hank, a novelist whose alliterative code of (mis)conduct includes women, "whisky, weed and Warren Zevon," is caught between the hedonism of Los Angeles and his quest to reclaim lost love. Duchovny, who "got into Zevon" around the time the series began (Baltin, n.p.), thought that lyrically, and in terms of consciousness and attitude, Zevon was really close to what he wanted Hank to be, and that Zevon reflected his character's love-hate relationship with California.

Hank seems to channel Zevon, regularly referencing the antihero and freely quoting from his songs. One scene inventively features "Z-e-v-o-n" as the answer to a crossword puzzle clue Hank is working on: "Five-letter word for 'Excitable Boy.'" In what is perhaps the series' consummate "Hank Zevon" scene, "Keep Me in Your Heart" is playing as source music as a point-of-view camera tracks toward a faint constant clicking sound through the house, arriving at Hank behind his typewriter. He types, "THE END," triumphantly snatches the sheet of paper from the carriage and places it on his manuscript stack, then pours a drink and lights a joint, as the camera pans a candleholder with a skull. The subject of Hank's novel, an ex-rock-and-roller, appears in the doorway, curiously observing his ritual. A satisfied Hank pronounces, "Every time I finish a book—whiskey, weed and Warren Zevon," then slyly slips in a Zevonian phrase, "dirty life and times," in his next sentence.

The standard afterlife archival activity also included a profusion of remastered, reissued editions of the early Zevon catalog. The stream of releases began in 2003 during Zevon's waning months with *First Sessions*, featuring lyme and cybelle recordings, followed by reissues of his two Virgin albums. Rhino released Zevon's modestly upgraded Asylum catalog in 2007 and 2008, with the long-out-of-print live set, *Stand in the Fire*, the most heralded and welcome return. The requisite rare and unreleased songs in the editions were limited, as Zevon was notorious for recording virtually everything he wrote with very little material left-

over for archiving. New West's two-CD set, *Preludes* (2007), was indic-
ative of the sparse vault, as the edition contained one disc of music, and
a companion disc labeled "Primate Discourse," which was primarily
devoted to a Zevon interview circa 2000 with Jody Denberg, interspersed with three songs from *Life'll Kill Ya.*

Zevon's live performance legacy was buoyed by increased accessibility of his concert recordings. In 2009, with the approval of Zevon's
family, Archive.org released a definitive collection from Zevon's live
soundboards between 1976 and 2003—a total of 89 shows and over
1,137 songs—for downloading and streaming. Crystal Zevon noted that
"Warren's fans have this unbelievable collection of stuff" that Jordan "at
one point gave them permission to swap music." Jordan green-lighted
the concert archive project out of respect for his father, saying that his
"Dad had a liberal attitude towards taping," reasoning that "fans are
going to trade anyway. And there's no reason they shouldn't be able to"
(Clarke, n.p.).

Among the most widely circulated "unofficial concert recordings"
were from shows during *The Envoy* tour in 1982—*Headless in Boston*
(All Access, 2013), a live broadcast from the Metro; *Live at the Capitol
Theatre* in Passaic, New Jersey; and an FM broadcast, *Simple Man,
Simple Dream* (Laser Media, 2016), its title a J. D. Souther song covered by Zevon. The shows, a few days apart, feature similar 14–19 song
set lists highlighted by a medley that segues from "Poor Poor Pitiful
Me" into Springsteen's "Cadillac Ranch." In another memorably amusing and irreverent moment during the Passaic performance, Zevon tells
the audience: "They say that everything that dies will come back—and
if that is true, I hope I come back as Suzanne Somers," before he
launches into "I'll Sleep When I'm Dead." The Jersey concert, although
generally regarded by Zevon devotees as slightly inferior to his 1980
Philadelphia show with Willie Nile for the *King Biscuit Flower Hour*,
was notable as it was originally broadcast on FM radio in October 1982,
and more significantly in the era, cablecast on MTV with VJ Mark
Goodman as the emcee.

The posthumous appreciation for Zevon transcended music. As
Browne accurately anticipated, the admiration for Zevon within the
literary sphere was prominent. Members of the Rock Bottom Remainders also paid homage to their lit rock band member. Carl Hiaasen
dedicated his outrageous novel *Skinny Dip* (2004) to the memory of

Zevon, as did Stephen King in *Doctor Sleep* (2014), the Danny-Tor-rance-grows-up sequel to *The Shining*. In King's tribute, the prolific horror writer reminisced about Zevon's sage advice on how King should approach the Rock Bottom Remainder rendition of "Werewolves of London": "Key of G, howl like you mean it. And most important of all, play like Keith (Richards)." King concludes the dedication, "This howl is for you, wherever you are."

My Ride's Here collaborator Paul Muldoon wrote a streaming three-part elegy in memory of Zevon called "Sillyhow Stride," the final poem published in his collection *Horse Latitudes* (2006). Irish literary scholar Tara Christie Kinsey analyzes Muldoon's poem, and his and Zevon's relationship and writings, in an extensive critical essay, "Rave on John Donne: Paul Muldoon and Warren Zevon," published in *The Yellow Nib* (2013).

The "serious" literary types to whom Browne alluded also reached the scholarly realm. Among critical inquiries, Michael Flood's essay, "Lord Byron's Luggage: Warren Zevon and the Redefinition of Litera-ture Rock," credits Zevon as the precursor of "literature rock," tracing strands of influence to bands such as the Decemberists, Modest Mouse, and Belle and Sebastian. One of the most ambitious Zevon-related pro-jects is Kelly Lynn Thomas's MFA creative writing thesis, *Miss Gun to a Knife Fight: Stories* (2013), an engaging collection of 12 short stories that are feminist interpretations of Zevon's songs, exploring multiple contexts of violence, sexuality, and masculinity.

Zevon's spirit also attracted riffraff writing. Rae Murphy's self-pub-lished pseudo-memoir, *Reconsider Me: My Life and Times with Warren Zevon* (2010), is the counter to the *My Dirty Life and Times* oral histo-ry. Murphy, who is not interviewed nor mentioned in Crystal Zevon's compilation, appears torn between fiction and nonfiction in her chroni-cle of an alleged relationship with Zevon. The book's "big reveal" is Murphy's brazen claim that Zevon is the father of her daughter. The tone is similar, though more credible, in *You Turn Me On I'm a Radio: My Wild Rock 'N' Roll Life* (2012), a self-published memoir by Phila-delphia radio personality and rock groupie Anita Gevinson, who lived with Zevon for a year and was briefly engaged to him. It's rather telling that of the many Zevon trysts and relationships named and interviewed in Crystal Zevon's oral history, Gevinson is the only one never identified by name in the book; she is referred to as "the disc jockey."

The most intriguing Zevon tribute may be artist/author/American Studies scholar Greg Metcalf's "Zevon *Nkisi*," a Congolese ritual sculpture of "power figures." The detailed one-foot-tall monument is hand carved out of aged wood, with stain, found objects, mirror, and rusted nails (*mbau*), part of Metcalf's meticulous "cultural heroes" series. A rich and resourceful ricochet off of Andy Warhol's silkscreen celebrity *Myth Series*, Metcalf's carved collection includes Zevon heroes Hemingway, Fitzgerald, and Hunter S. Thompson; artists Magritte, Pollock, Matisse, Frida Kahlo, Egon Schiele, Joseph Cornell, Victorian illustrator Edward Gorey, Max Ernst, and Käthe Kollwitz; writers Shakespeare, Poe, Kerouac, Kafka, Samuel Beckett, Samuel Clemens/Mark Twain, Gertrude Stein, Bram Stoker, H. P. Lovecraft; Theodore Geisel (Dr. Seuss), and Maurice Sendak; Sigmund Freud, Albert Einstein, folksinger Steve Goodman, escape artist Harry Houdini, John D. Rockefeller, mythology scholar Joseph Campbell, media theorist Marshall McLuhan, Alfred Hitchcock, Walt Disney, and Elvis Presley, among others.

The status of numerous other Zevon-related projects lingered between works in progress and wishful thinking. Among those rumored to be close to completion are Kevin Smith's film *Hit Somebody!* and Zevon aide-de-camp George Gruel's documentary, *Reconsider Me*, a companion piece to the long-time road manager's impressive collection of rare photographs compiled scrapbook-style in *Lawyers Guns & Photos* (2013)—the cover a gun barrel, point-blank close up of Zevon taking aim. Notions of a Broadway musical based on Zevon's life surfaced around 2009 without ever gaining much traction.

The petitioning for Zevon's induction into the Rock and Roll Hall of Fame, which gained its initial momentum following his terminal diagnosis, has remained more sporadic than steady, ebbing and flowing with waning discussion on Internet fan pages, from *The Warren Zevon Other Page* to the cleverly titled fan forum *Just an Excitable Board*, with "Keep Calm and Zev On" allegiance and hopeful updates of Zevon's high ranking on random "Artists Who Should be in the Hall of Fame" lists. The movement leveled off somewhat in the aftermath of the ten-year anniversary of Zevon's death in 2013. While very few of his fans, critics, or musical peers question Zevon's merit as a songwriter worthy of the Hall of Fame, there is uniform skepticism and frequent resignation in regard to a selection process that is at once subjective, seemingly arbitrary, and often puzzling.

"DON'T LET US GET STUPID, ALRIGHT?"

> One thing that impressed me about Warren was how damned smart he was. I haven't found that to be necessarily the case in the music world. . . . I'm used to dealing with highly bright people, and let's just say Warren was unusually smart for anybody.
> —Jonathan Kellerman, psychologist, medical school professor, author

During the four-plus-decade span of his career, Warren Zevon lived many roles, literally and figuratively: songwriter, satirist, cartoonist, storyteller, classically trained pianist, rocker, romantic, intellect, literate prick, alcoholic, obsessive compulsive, firearm fanatic, and entertainer, among them. And, he was frequently his lyrics incarnate: a desperado and outlaw; an excitable boy and a howling werewolf, the gent who ran amok; the wild age, the restless kind, listening to some song inside; a piano fighter, thin-ice walker; accidental martyr and innocent bystander; a mercenary, a thorn trying to find a side; a renegade, rebel all his days; Model Citizen and Mr. Bad Example; intruder in the dirt; mutineer, born to rock the boat; genius.

Scattered whispers of "genius," albeit a typically tortured one, were routinely affixed to Zevon's name and his body of work in the Songwriter's Neighborhood. Such canonization is impulsively seductive, if not clichéd, posthumously. Zevon himself may have slightly nudged the notion with the self-mythologizing title of his song and the "Best of" collection in 2002. Carl Hiaasen was among his many admirers who considered Zevon a genius "in the truest sense . . . troubled, but an immense, unbelievably prodigious talent." Musically or otherwise, that lofty designation is always delicate, even when directed at mythical figures such as Brian Wilson, who is among rock's commonly anointed virtuosos for his surf and orchestral productions with the Beach Boys, notably *Pet Sounds* (1966) followed by his "teenage symphony to God" in *Smile* (1967).

Whether or not Zevon is worthy of wearing the thorny crown of genius, his intelligence, greatness, and originality are indisputable. His

signature comic noir is authentic, his berserk brilliance unique, no matter the context or writing realm. Zevon got sick, but he never got stupid.
After all, he swore to self-accountability in "I'll Sleep When I'm Dead":
"If I start acting stupid, I'll shoot myself." Zevon may have been the
most reckless person in the room for much of his career, and he was
usually, if not always, the smartest person in *any* room, not just those
occupied by songwriters. Even when he wrote what he called "a stupid
song"—"Werewolves of London"—he was shrewd enough to write it
"for smart people."

Legendary music industry figure Jon Landau, who witnessed Zevon's Asylum arrival, adds Zevon's perseverance to another "sign of
greatness" beyond his writing, intellect, humor, and melodic and complex music arrangements. Landau found it "interesting and unusual"
how productive Zevon remained, and how he got better creatively and
continued to grow despite all of his issues. Zevon was "really the exception" among the talented late-1970s songwriters circle in Los Angeles,
many unable to sustain over a 25–30 year period the way Zevon did.
Drawing from his experiences producing and managing Bruce Springsteen, Landau recognized similar qualities in Zevon:

> For most genuinely great artists, it's a lifetime endeavor. They're at it
> forever . . . Bruce is still there today trying to write the best song he
> ever wrote. Maybe he will, maybe he won't, but that's what he's
> interested in doing. He's as interested in it today as he was the day I
> met him. Warren was like that, too, but with him what was unusual
> was his level of perseverance mixed with the level of adversity he
> created for himself. It is a fascinating combination. (C. Zevon, 112)

Zevon did persevere. He withstood his own demons and torments of
the "cowboy days" and the "wild age," teetering on the edge of a vodka
vista, persisting through several record-label exiles and significant shifts
within the music industry and marketplace. Through eras marked by,
among other things, disco, MTV, music format evolution from vinyl to
compact disc to digital downloading, boy bands, and the *American Idol-
atry* of television's reality karaoke contests featuring poseur participants
and panelists, Zevon never strayed from his smartly sinister and sensitive steps that marked his singular songwriting path.

As a "mad magical poet," Zevon displayed the courage, and the
crazy, to rush in head first where other songwriters feared to tread,

confronting subjects that most dread, and never look back. And he did it consistently, not on a whim or as a novelty or diversion. Years of sobriety did not appear to significantly diminish nor enhance his songwriting and music. No matter his condition, whether wrecked or redeemed, Zevon wrote with profound sensitivity. Calamity was always at the core of Zevon's compositions, with mayhem among his main motifs, desperation and amok frequent attributes, humor and vulnerability counterpoints. As those closest to him testified, Zevon was consistent and without compromise, remaining true to his smart self and dark preoccupations, without selling out or reinventing himself (beyond rehabilitation) to fit in anywhere at any time. It was appropriate that compadre Jorge Calderón's observation that Zevon "traveled down his own road" punctuates the *I'll Sleep When I'm Dead* compendium of quotes and conversations. Jackson Browne, another of the indelible marks on Zevon's chronology from start to finish to Great Beyond, routinely offered ardent affirmation of Zevon's greatness, stating, "He [Zevon] was an independent thinker. I never saw him dumb down or simplify what he had to say so more people would recognize him" (C. Zevon, 430).

RESTLESS SLEEPER: A GHOST IS BORN

> *I thought of him [Zevon] as one of the aliens. I think he captured the spirit of that time. His tormented soul was like a deeper expression of what was going on than anybody else was even thinking about, let alone writing about.*
>
> —drummer Eddie Ponder (C. Zevon)

More than any personal or artistic qualities, Zevon's way with words exceeds his notorious wayward ways as *the* distinguishing mark that anchors at the core of his influence and lasting mythology. His hard-boiled and humorous *noir*ratives, characters, and settings; the clever couplets, rhymes, and turns of phrase; the rich and vivid language at once literary, cinematic, romantic, idiosyncratic, and dotted with cultural references make up a songbook that will remain distinctive as one of popular music's best reads from any era and artist. Repeated Zevon readings and listenings relinquish limitless revelations of a unique artistic vision.

Zevon's underappreciated and abundant body of works is smart and sophisticated, scornful and sensitive, evocative, exquisite, and enduring. His refreshing lyrical conceits and music will continue to loiter and lurk in his spirited legacy, a ghostly presence and restless sleeper whispering "eat my dust" beneath a lovely line or merry melody. They will hover, haunt in verse, phrase, and melody, and inevitably howl "Aahh-woooo," wreaking occasional havoc; soliciting smirks and sentimentality, moments of abandoned amusement and confessional grace, of parting and yeaning; all spectral souvenirs of songwriting brilliance.

When those ethereal vestiges visit, they do so with delight, wonder, intrigue, and grace. Some of the most recent relics, more than 12 years post-Zevon, are among the most evocative and captivating. In December 2013, an animated Zevon shows up, in an unlikely locale—a video for the Killers' "Christmas in L.A.," one of the band's annual charity Christmas singles. The melodic, melancholy tune is cowritten and performed by the L.A. roots-rock group Dawes, who are frequently compared to and paired with Jackson Browne. The video features actor Owen Wilson seeking advice from Harry Dean Stanton, before morphing into his animated likeness that meanders through Los Angeles on Christmas morning. Zevon's cartoon cameo is subtle. When Wilson stops into an empty church along the way, Zevon is sitting in the background, "the slumming angel," leaning in a pew as the despairing lyrics cleverly reference one of his notable L.A. songs: "Another Christmas in L.A., hold me tighter 'Carmelita,' I don't know long I can stay." The song exhibits a nuanced *Warren Zevon* undercurrent, ending with a somber extrapolation of "White Christmas" before fading out on Wilson, still alone in his apartment. And maybe a moment of winter whimsical wondering what a Warren Zevon Christmas song or holiday collection would have sounded like.

Zevon's ghostly grin emanates from an another curious afterlife endeavor that may be one of his best punch lines—his best known song, "Werewolves of London," used in an ad campaign for Three Olives Vodka. Latvian Chanteuse Masha (Shirin) delivers one of the most disparate interpretations of a Zevon original, particularly among the chorus of female vocalists who have covered Zevon. Masha's slinky, subdued rendition—half spoken, half sung; part Marianne Faithful, part Lana Del Rey, and some Lorde—helps create a sultry, sophisticated, noir atmosphere for the "Werewolves of London" music video that never was in 1978. The adaptation is literal, with a stylish lothario/lycanthrope on the loose in London.

The most current Zevon specters come full circle to David Letterman, nearly 13 years after Zevon's memorable final appearance in October 2002. As the host's 33-year run in late-night television approached the May 20, 2015, finale, part of Letterman's and bandleader Paul Shaffer's exit strategy was to treat the *Late Show* musical segments as a personal playlist. Letterman was a music medium summoning Zevon's participation in his ongoing farewell celebration. On the Friday, April 24 show, at Letterman's request, Jason Isbell and Amanda Shires, backed by Willie Nelson's harmonica player Mickey Raphael, encored their gorgeous version of Zevon's "Mutineer," which they had recorded on their *Sea Songs* EP. The homage conjured Zevon's memorable *Late Show* performance of "Mutineer" on October 30, 2002, with the line, "Grab your coat, let's get out of here," now translating to Letterman's sendoff. As Letterman stepped in afterward to thank the trio, it was evident that he was moved by the performance.

One week later, on May 2, in a *Late Show* web exclusive, Zevon again was the focus, as Dawes performed "Desperados Under the Eaves" as a favor to Letterman. During Letterman's lengthy intro, he summarized Zevon's significant history with the show. Letterman explained that when Zevon returned for his final appearance on the show, "Desperados Under the Eaves" was the one song he "really, really wanted to hear but was uncomfortable pressing Warren to do nine or ten songs for me." Letterman gushed with gratitude, saying how meaningful it was to him and Paul that Dawes said, "Hell, we can do that (song)." He concluded the intro stating, "this is for Dawes, for myself and for Warren Zevon." Dawes, who frequently performs Zevon songs, often jointly with Browne, was comfortable with the Zevon classic, delivering an impressive and faithful rendition along with some keyboarding from Shaffer. In his outro following the song, Letterman again returned to the "beyond emotional" Zevon appearance in 2002, which obviously made an indelible mark and was close to the surface. He vividly recounted going upstairs to the dressing room, where Zevon placed his guitar in his case and presented it to Letterman, saying simply, "Here, take care of this for me."

In June, a few weeks into his departure from television, Letterman reaffirmed the lasting impact of the Zevon farewell show in his interview with Ron Pearson for *Indianapolis Monthly*. Letterman revealed that over the course of his career, the two interviews that created the most anxiety for him as a host (for different reasons) were Warren Zevon and Bill Clinton. Singling out Zevon among more than three decades' worth of guests and juxtaposing him with a president was an extraordinary distinction for the singer-songwriter.

"KEEP ON RIDING, RIDING, RIDING"

> *He [Zevon] would reawaken my interest in music, in songs, in litera-*
> *ture. I mean, he was that kind of guy who would really wake you up.*
> —Jorge Calderón (C. Zevon)

Since the mid-1970s, around the time of his Asylum debut, through his death in 2003 and to the present, Zevon and his songs woke up a lot of people, in many ways and on many levels. David Letterman was clearly one of the awakened. Zevon's songwriting continually struck a chord of profound admiration among fans, critics, and especially his contemporaries within and outside music. As one of America's most prolific authors, Stephen King spoke universally for the Every Writer when he said, "When I listen to some of the stuff Warren wrote . . . I think, if I could write something like that I'd be a happy guy" (C. Zevon, 428). As if reading lines from the same script, Browne echoed, "[Warren] was always the writer who said the things I wish I said, the things I wish I could say." Springsteen also recited the familiar verse: "He continued to write terrific songs. I would rarely see Warren when he hadn't written something that I wished in another lifetime I'd written. It's very telling—right down to the last record, that beautiful stuff Warren came up with" (C. Zevon, 156).

Such fervent appreciation, celebration, and acclamation directed toward Zevon has been profuse and poetic, with admirers in line from Browne, Calderón, Springsteen, Raitt, and Dylan to Paul Nelson, Landau, Letterman, Thornton, Hiaasen, King, Muldoon, Thompson, among many others. Within the voluminous reverence, writer and intellectual Gore Vidal's commanding and comprehensive précis of Zevon's brilliance and uniqueness persists: To this day, there is simply nobody else who writes like Warren Zevon.

A DYLAN COFFEE TABLE AFTERTHOUGHT

Warren Zevon is a poet. He has written more classics than any other musician of our time, with the possible exception of Dylan.
—Dr. Hunter S. Thompson (Jones, 2014, 46)

Warren Zevon is still ahead of his time. He is one of the Late Greats. It is not an overstatement to suggest that Zevon will always be one of the most intelligent and interesting songwriters in any era, past, present, or future. He is an original. A virtuoso. A mad magical poet. Mr. Lyrics. One of the aliens. A slumming angel with a romantic presence. A prick, but a literate one. The guy who made someone like Randy Newman even seem normal. Who hung out with Igor Stravinsky. Who was the only person Linda Ronstadt knew with a subscription to *Jane's Defence Weekly*. Who laid his head on the railroad tracks waiting for the Double E. Who hastened down the wind. Who went down to dinner in his Sunday best and rubbed the pot roast all over his chest. Who was bound and gagged and dragged behind a clown mobile. Who listened to the air conditioner hum. Who rhymed "gender" with "Waring blender." Who needed some sentimental hygiene. Who hurled himself against the wall at the Louvre Museum. Who was always one joke away. Who was obsessed with the color gray. Who traveled down his own road. And yes, the guy who "saw a werewolf with a Chinese menu in his hand." That kind of guy who would really wake you up.

The desperado of Los Angeles. Keep on riding, riding, riding . . .

FURTHER READING

Alfonso, Barry. "Warren Zevon: Rock's Stout-Hearted Man." *Songwriter* magazine, April 1981, 23–25, 48–49.

Avery, Kevin. *Everything Is an Afterthought: The Life and Writings of Paul Nelson.* Seattle: Fantagraphics Books, 2011. Excellent collection and commentary on the life and works of one of rock criticism's preeminent figures. Includes the unedited version of the renowned Zevon interview/profile that was the basis for a *Rolling Stone* cover story in March 1981.

Baltin, Steve. "Q&A: David Duchovny on the Rocking New Season of *Californication.*" *Rolling Stone*, 3 January 2013. www.rollingstone.com.

Boucher, Geoff. "Facing Mortality with Mischief Rather Than Tears." *Los Angeles Times*, 13 September 2002, F1.

Bowman, David. "My Lunch with Warren Zevon." Salon, 17 March 2003. www.salon.com.

Brown, G. "Rock Talk: Zevon Presents Role Model for Living in Face of Death." *Denver Post*, 23 March 2003, F8.

Browne, David. "The Knights of Soft Rock." *Rolling Stone*, 11 April 2013, 52–59, 70. Long overdue profile of premiere L.A. session players, the "Mellow Mafia."

Catlin, Roger. "Warren Zevon's Twists on Rock 'N' Roll." *Hartford Courant*, 27 December 1991. http://articles.courant.com/1991-12-27/features/0000207754_1_ugly-one-morning-excitable-boy-warren-zevon.

Christgau, Robert. "Warren Zevon: *My Ride's Here.*" *Rolling Stone*, 6 June 2002.

———. "Warren Zevon: *Excitable Boy.*" Consumer Guide Reviews, n.d. www.robertchristgau.com.

"Christmas in L.A." Music video. Brandon Flowers, Mark Stoermer (the Killers), Taylor Goldsmith (Dawes). Directed by Kelly Loosli, 2013. Cool animated Zevon in background in a church pew as the Christmas song references "Carmelita."

Clarke, John. "Warren Zevon Live Shows Hit the Web, Possible Film in the Works." Rolling Stone online, 3 June 2009. www.rollingstone.com.

Connelly, Christopher. "Why Joe Jackson Said No to Rock Video." *Rolling Stone*, 30 August 1984, 32.

———. "Warners Drops Van Morrison, Thirty Others." *Rolling Stone*, 5 July 1985, 41.

Cromelin, Bruce. "'Excitable Boy' Now 'Mr. Bad Example': Warren Zevon's Latest Album Recalls Twisted Wit, Rocking Sound of His Defining Works." *Los Angeles Times*, 6 February 1992. http://articles.latimes.com/1992-02-06/entertainment/ca-2050_1_warren-zevon.

Crowe, Cameron. "Neil Young: The Last American Hero." *Rolling Stone*, 8 February 1979, 44, 62.

Dansby, Andrew. "Warren Zevon Dies." *Rolling Stone*, 8 September 2003. http://www.rollingstone.com/music/news/warren-zevon-dies-20030908.

Deas, Kyle. "Warren Zevon: *Warren Zevon.*" PopMatters, 8 January 2009, http://www.popmatters.com/review/66981-warren-zevon-warren-zevon/.

DeCurtis, Anthony, and James Henke, eds., with Holly George Warren. *The Rolling Stone Album Guide*. New York: Random House, 1992.

Dees, Jim. "Intruder in the Dust: The Savage Wit of an American Original." *Oxford Eagle*, September 2003; email correspondence.

Deming, Mark. "Warren Zevon Album Reviews." http://www.allmusic.com/album/warren-zevon-mw0000312155.

Denberg, Jody. "Primate Discourse" (interview with Warren Zevon), Bonus disc on *Preludes: Rare and Unreleased Recordings*, New West, 2007. KSRG-radio (Austin, Texas) program director's interview with Zevon, circa *Life'll Kill Ya*. Zevon is articulate, forthright, and engaging during the conversation that covers a lot of ground—mortality, noir, songwriting, influences, classical music, fans, acting, Los Angeles, Elvis.

Devenish, Colin. "Zevon's Fight." *Rolling Stone*. 17 October 2002,13.

Dretzka, Gary. "Warren Zevon: Mutineer." *Chicago Tribune*, 24 August 1995.

Eliot, Marc. *To the Limit: The Untold Story of the Eagles*. New York: Little, Brown, 1998; paperback edition, Boston: DaCapo Press, 2005.

Erlewine, Michael, Vladimir Bogdanov, and Chris Woodstra, eds. *All Music Guide to Rock*. San Francisco: Miller Freeman Books, 1995.

Fawcett, Anthony, with photos by Henry Diltz. *California Rock, California Sound*. Los Angeles: Reed Books, 1978. The earliest chronicle of the L.A. music scene and the "Southern California sound," features an excellent introduction essay on region and genre convergence, "The Emergence of Folk Rock," followed by profiles of some of the essential singer songwriters. Diltz, the renowned photographer of the L.A. music scene, captures the youthful artists in a variety of settings, in candid and colorful images that may be more revealing portraits than Fawcett's essays.

Fishman, D. B. "Warren Zevon: In Memoriam." PopVerse, 7 September 2013. http://popverse.com/2013/09/07/warren-zevon-in-memoriam/. Ten-year commemoration of Zevon's death.

Flanagan, Bill. "Bob Dylan Exclusive Interview." *Huffington Post*, 16 May 2009. http://www.huffingtonpost.com/2009/04/15/bob-dylan-exclusive-inter_n_187216.html. During the lengthy interview, Dylan lists Zevon as one of his favorite songwriters.

Flood, Michael. "Lord Byron's Luggage: Warren Zevon and the Redefinition of Literature Rock." Paper presented at the Popular Culture/American Culture Association Annual Conference, New Orleans, LA, April 2015.

Freeman, Hadley. "Warren Zevon: The Man Behind the Demons." *Guardian*, 1 August 2013. http://www.theguardian.com/music/2013/aug/01/warren-zevon-werewolves-of-london-demons. Another piece honoring ten-year anniversary of Zevon's death.

Fretts, Bruce. "He Puts His Licks on *Route 66*: Rocker-turned-scorer Warren Zevon." *Entertainment Weekly*, 4 June 1993, 44.

Fricke, David. Liner Notes. Warren Zevon, *Stand in the Fire* (reissue). Rhino, 2007.

———. "Tribute: Warren Zevon." *Rolling Stone*, 16 October 2003, 49.

———. "Browne Remembers Zevon." *Rolling Stone* online, 19 September 2003. http://www.rollingstone.com/music/news/browne-remembers-zevon-20030919. Typically well-informed questions from outstanding music journalist leading to usual astute responses from Browne.

Gevinson, Anita. *You Turn Me On, I'm A Radio: My Wild Rock 'N' Roll Life*. Philadelphia: Anita Gevinson, 2012. Self-published memoir by Philadelphia radio personality and rock groupie who was briefly engaged to Zevon.

Gilmore, Mikal. "Warren Zevon Takes Control." *Rolling Stone*, 16 September 1982, 39, 49–50.

Goldberg, Danny. Liner Notes. *Warren Zevon: Preludes: Rare and Unreleased Recordings*. New West, 2007.

Gruel, George. *Lawyers Guns & Photos: Photographs and Tales of My Adventures With Warren Zevon*. Big Gorilla Books, 2013. A treasure trove of photos curated by Zevon's longtime road manager and aide-de-camp, niftily presented in scrapbook style with commentary, quotes, lyrics, captions, maps, artifacts, and anecdotes. A must for Zevon devotees.

Gunderson, Edna. "Sad Fate for an Excitable Boy." *USA Today*, 13 September 2002, 12D.

Hiaasen, Carl. *Basket Case*. New York: Knopf, 2002. Title based on the fictional character Jimmy Stoma's hit song, and cowritten with Zevon on *My Ride's Here*. Lyrics quoted throughout the book and printed entirely at the end, credited to Zevon and Stoma.

———. *Native Tongue*. New York: Knopf, 1991. Lead character copes by listening to Zevon songs full blast.

"Hollywood Desperado." *Time*, 2 August 1976: 62–63.

Hoskyns, Barney. *Hotel California: The True-Life Adventures of Crosby, Stills, Nash, Young, Mitchell, Taylor, Browne, Ronstadt, Geffen, the Eagles and Their Many Friends*. Hoboken, NJ: Wiley, 2006. Focuses on L.A. music scene and setting during revolutionary and prolific era from late 1960s through late 1970s.

———. *Waiting for the Sun: A Rock 'N' Roll History of Los Angeles*. New York: Backbeat Books, 2009. Most recent edition of 1996 original, and 2003 reprint. Comprehensive and absorbing music chronicle of the Los Angeles setting and West Coast music mythology from jazz to rock by noted Brit music historian and founder of Rocksbackpages.com.

Jones, Allan. "I'll Sleep When I'm Dead: Warren Zevon 1947–2003." *Uncut*, November 2003, 34–38.

———. "Life'll Kill Ya." *Uncut*, June 2014, 44–50.

Jurek, Thom. "*Wanted Dead or Alive*" (Record review). *www.allmusic.com*.

King, Stephen. *Doctor Sleep*. New York: Scribner, 2013. Sequel to *The Shining* with an adult Danny Torrance includes a nice dedication to Zevon. Redrum.

Kinsey, Tara Christie. "'Rave On, John Donne': Paul Muldoon and Warren Zevon." *Yellow Nib* 8 (2013): 33–51. Princeton point of view on Muldoon and Zevon, their writings and relationship.

Kubernik, Harvey. *Canyon of Dreams: The Magic and the Music of Laurel Canyon*. New York: Sterling, 2009. Coffee-table volume with interesting narrative and excellent photos, with a foreword by the Doors' Ray Manzarek and afterword by record producer Lou Adler.

Lim, Gerrie. "Warren Zevon: The Mutineer and His Bounty." *Big O*, Spring 1993, 1.

Macdonald, Ross (Kenneth Millar). *The Zebra-Striped Hearse*, 1962. Zevon identified with the kidnapped kid in this Lew Archer mystery written by his literary hero Macdonald.

Marsh, Dave. "Rock 'N' Roll 1980: Hold On Hold Out." *Rolling Stone*, 25 December–8 January 1981:1–2.

———. "Warren Zevon on the Loose in Los Angeles." *Rolling Stone*, 9 March 1978.

Maslin, Janet. "Salty Margaritas." *Newsweek*, 2 August 1976, 72–73.

Mehr, Bob. Liner Notes, *Warren Zevon* (reissue). Asylum/Rhino Records, 2008.

Metcalf, Greg. Zevon *Nkisi*. http://gregmetcalfritualart.blogspot.com/. Although the figures are obviously best viewed up close and in person for their remarkable detail, this is a fine alternative exhibition and catalog for the "collect the whole set" compulsives, with insightful creative context and commentary for each of the Nkisi ritual sculptures in the extensive "cultural heroes" series.

Milward, John. "Rehabilitation Enriches Warren Zevon's Music." *Philadelphia Inquirer*, 26 September 1987. http://articles.philly.com/1987-09-26/news/26209943_1_sentimental-hygiene-warren-zevon-rolling-stone.

Muldoon, Paul. "Sillyhow Stride," in *Horse Latitudes*. London: Faber and Faber, 2006. Irish poet's meandering three-part elegy to Zevon.

Murphy, Rae. *Reconsider Me: My Life and Times with Warren Zevon*. Create Space Independent Publishing Platform, 2010. Really?

Nelson, Paul. "Warren Zevon Comes Out of the Woods." *The Village Voice*, 21 June 1976, 21.

———. "Warren Zevon: How He Saved Himself from a Coward's Death." *Rolling Stone*, 19 March 1981, 28–34, 70. Rock journalism masterpiece from legendary critic is the definitive Zevon profile within vortex of his alcoholism.

———. "Warren Zevon: *Wanted Dead or Alive*" (Record review). *Rolling Stone*, 24 January 1980, 63.

Newton, Steve. "Warren Zevon Says the Odds Have Pretty Big Feet." *Georgia Straight*, 6 February 1992.

Nolan, Tom. *Ross Macdonald: A Biography*. New York: Scribner, 1999.

Pareles, Jon. "In His Time of Dying: Warren Zevon's Last Waltz." *New York Times Magazine*, 26 January 2003, 22–25.

———. "Work Hard, Play Hard." *Rolling Stone*, 3 January 1985, 137.

Pearson, Ron. "Exclusive Post-Retirement Interview with David Letterman." *Indianapolis Monthly*, June 12, 2015. http://www.indianapolismonthly.com/arts-culture/exclusive-post-retirement-interview-david-letterman/.

Priore, Dominic. *Riot on the Sunset Strip: Rock 'N' Roll's Last Stand in '60s Hollywood*. London: Jawbone Press, 2007.

"Random Notes" (Column). *Rolling Stone*, 12 July 1979, 34.

Reid, Graham. "Warren Zevon Interviewed (1992): Tales from the Dark Side." *New Zealand Herald*, September 1992. Posted on Reid's site, Elsewhere: http://www.elsewhere.co.nz/absoluteelsewhere/1897/warren-zevon-interviewed-1992-tales-from-the-dark-side/.

Reilly, Sue. "The Next Big Quake Has Already Rocked L.A.; It's The Excitable Boy Warren Zevon." *People*, 22 May 1978, 97–99. Fairly fluff piece that nonetheless manages to affirm Zevon mythology by leading with vodka. Great photo of Zevon behind his Smith Corona.

Rockwell, John. "Living in the USA." In Greil Marcus, ed., *Stranded: Rock and Roll for a Desert Island*. New York: Knopf, 1979, 188–218.

Roeser, Steve. "Left Jabs and Roundhouse Rights." *Goldmine*, vol. 21, no. 17, Issue 393, 18 August 1995, 16–24, 28–38, 80. One of the most revealing, in-depth, career-spanning interviews in the Zevon print archive.

Ronstadt, Linda. *Simple Dreams: A Musical Memoir*. New York: Simon & Schuster, 2013.

Strauss, Neil. "The Man Who Disappeared," *Rolling Stone*, 28 December 2006/11 January 2007, 52–64. Riveting profile of legendary music critic Paul Nelson and his sad and lonely fadeaway.

Sutcliffe, Phil. "Filter Albums: A-to-Zevon." *Mojo*, April 2007, 124.

Tannenbaum, Rob. "Reconsider Me." *Buzz*, September 1987, 23–26.

Thomas, Kelly Lynn. *Miss Gun to a Knife Fight: Stories*. MFA creative writing thesis, Chatham University, PA, 2014. A collection of short stories composed of feminist interpretations of Zevon songs. Thomas is founder and editor-in-chief of the Zevon title–inspired Wild Age Press, an edgy independent literary publisher.

Thompson, Hunter S. *The Curse of the Lono*. New York: Bantam Books, 1983. Another Zevon writing hero whose Gonzo memoir set in Hawaii cites Zevon's "The Hula Hula Boys."

Torn, Luke. "How to Buy . . . Warren Zevon on Record Part 1 & Part 2." *Uncut*, June 2014, 47–48.

VH1.com. "*(Inside)Out*: Interviews: Warren Zevon: Dirty Life and Times." August 2003. http://archive.is/gJd6Q.

VH1 (Inside)Out: Warren Zevon: Keep Me in Your Heart. Documentary DVD produced/directed by Nick Read. MTV Networks/Artemis Records, 2004. Captivating, emotional two-hour chronicle of all-star cast of music contemporaries gathered for requiem recording session of Zevon's final album, *The Wind*. The production fuses elements of reality shows, New Orleans Jazz funeral, Irish wake, and *The Last Waltz*. DVD features two music videos and expanded interviews with Zevon.

Walker, Michael. *Laurel Canyon: The Inside Story of Rock and Roll's Legendary Neighborhood*. New York: Faber and Faber, 2006. Outstanding L.A. canyon chronicle.

Ward, Steven. "Whatever Happened to Rock Critic Paul Nelson?" RockCritics.com, 6 March 2000. www.RockCritics.com.

Wild, David. Liner Notes. Warren Zevon . *The Envoy* (reissue). Asylum/Rhino, 2007.

Wilner, Paul. "Poor, Poor, Pitiful Zevon." Obit-Mag.com, July 2007. www.Obit-Mag.com.

Zevon, Crystal. *I'll Sleep When I'm Dead: The Dirty Life and Time of Warren Zevon.* New York: Ecco Books, 2007. Before he died, Zevon asked his ex-wife Crystal to tell his story. She complied, with 400-plus pages assembled from interviews and conversations with more than 80 Zevon cohorts. The intimate and honest oral history is a captivating antihero portrait of genius and excess.

"Zevon Hastens Down the Wind." *Ice*, July 2003: 4, 26.

Zevon, Warren. Liner Notes, *I'll Sleep When I'm Dead (An Anthology).* Elektra/Rhino Records, 1996. Zevon's concise personal riffs on each of the anthology's 44 songs provide unique context.

———. Liner Notes, *Stranger Than Fiction.* Don't Quit Your Day Job Records, 1998. Zevon's witty essay for the vanity band of bards the Wrockers' charity compilation reveals his inner critic that deftly blends smart with smart ass. Further evidence that Zevon could write in any context. A fun read.

http://zevonatacism.tripod.com/presskitbio.htm. Archived in *The Warren Zevon Other Page*, the only currently active Zevon Internet fan page. Established in 1998, the site features bio, articles, links, definitions, and a useful overview of the Zevon online community. The *Other Page* includes a chronology of the cluster of Zevon websites, message boards, and resources from the official Warrenzevon.com (1999–2003) and fan forum cleverly titled "Just an Excitable Board" to unofficial sites from 1994 to present.

FURTHER LISTENING

Wanted Dead or Alive (1969), Imperial Records. Zevon's forgivable first album, in his words, was "like a terrible John Hammond album, with drums"; to others, "a shambolic mess . . . that wears it excesses everywhere." Psychedelic, folk, rock, country, and blues converge in a sound initially produced by Kim Fowley before creative differences. The songs provide glimpses of what lay ahead: the title tune and "Bullet for Ramona" establish the desperado songwriting motif and outlaw tone; "Iko Iko" foreshadows curious cover selections; "Tule's Blues," the first of a series of songs about Marilyn "Tule" Livingston, Jordan's mother, provides a glimpse of the Romantic, and heartache. Notably obscure, "She Quit Me" was regendered for the soundtrack of the Academy Award–winning film, *Midnight Cowboy* (1969). The album has not yet, nor will likely be, revisited as "buried treasure," even following its reissue in 1996, with no bonus tracks for enhancement or diversion; it is largely relegated to first footnote status as a distant anterior debut or "independent release" in the Zevon discography. As Paul Nelson recapped, "Hey, he just wasn't ready then. Simple as that."

Warren Zevon (May 18, 1976), Asylum Records. A masterpiece. Striking on so many levels—first and foremost, the songwriting—and the noir tone, arrangements, demystifying and delightfully dark view of Hollywood and vicinity, the cast of L.A. luminaries and Mellow Mafia members contributing, Jackson Browne's producing, and David Geffen's touchstone record label. Beyond the four songs from the album that Linda Ronstadt covered, "Desperados Under the Eaves" is an era epic—"listening to the air conditioner hum, it went mmm, mmm . . ." Though overshadowed by the Eagles' *Hotel California*—same year, same label—the lurking, literate *Warren Zevon* is transcendent, an essential within the substantial 1970s California singer-songwriter sound and sphere. The Rhino reissue in 2008—a two-disc edition with 15 "previously unreleased" tracks of demos and alternative versions, and a booklet with an insightful essay by Bob Mehr—is the most comprehensive reissue package of any Zevon album.

Excitable Boy (January 18, 1978), Asylum Records. Draw blood. As his most popular album (number 8), with his biggest hit and signature song, "Werewolves of London" (number 21), *Excitable Boy* became the Zevon brand, for better or worse. A slyly smart album in between the hairy-handed howling and headless mercenary ghosts. The incongruence in a song such as "Excitable Boy" is berserk brilliance, abandoned amusement, and menacing merriment at its finest; with emotional equilibrium and sensitivity from "Tenderness on the Block" and "Accidentally Like a Martyr"; speckled with history and geography in "Veracruz"; and punctuated with the amplified rocklamation: "Send lawyers, guns and money, the shit has hit the fan." Of note among the 2007 reissue's four extra tracks is the self-mocking confessional "I Need a Truck" ("to haul my pain/To haul my Percodan and gin"); and a David Fricke liner note essay.

Bad Luck Streak in Dancing School (February 15, 1980), Asylum Records. The third Asylum album—the one with "brucellosis"—reveals a glimmer of redemption in the aftermath of the 1970s Lost Weekend. There are numerous curiosities—two gunshots that bridge classical strings and an edgy guitar in the title track opening, an Eagles desperado satire, Western allusions in cowrites with Springsteen and T-Bone Burnett, a baseball bio ditty, a jungle mercenary sequel. The album showcases Zevon's classical ambitions with excerpts of his unfinished symphony as song interludes. Contrasts are stark: the graceful vulnerability in "Empty Handed Heart" with a lovely Ronstadt descant counters one of Zevon's most stunningly strange and scathing songs, "Play It All Night Long," that features incest and a mocking Lynyrd Skynyrd chorus. Despite an outlook and tone that are self-revelatory and repentant throughout, Zevon still clings to the "Wild Age." The sly cover of Ernie K. Doe's "A Certain Girl" reached number 57, while the album itself, despite its unevenness, charted at number 20. The album is dedicated to detective fiction writer Ken Millar (Ross Macdonald). Turn those speakers up full blast.

Stand in the Fire (December 26, 1980), Asylum Records. "Karate on speed period." Zevon's second album released during the year; dedicated to director Martin Scorsese. Gleaned from five nights of rousing live performances at the Roxy in West Hollywood, the compact ten-song set draws from Zevon's first three albums, with predictable emphasis on songs such as "Poor Poor Pitiful Me" and "Lawyers, Guns and Money" that were suitable for hard-rocking, no-holds-barred live renditions with his backing band, Boulder. The album avoids "greatest hits live" exclusivity with the inclusion of new material, notably a Bo Diddley medley. The energetic performances merited double-album treatment rather than a scant ten songs. A welcome reissue with four bonus tracks in 2007 following a prolonged exile in Out of Printville.

The Envoy (July 16, 1982), Asylum Records. "Excitable boy grows up." In his first album in the MTV and music video era, Zevon steps back from the edge, with the exception of a punishing postcard from the Louvre Museum where he's going to hurl himself against the wall. His relatively restrained view unsettled some critics into "talent on the wane" suspicions. Among the less chaotic, well-crafted nine songs are a Thomas McGuane cowrite, a sparse Elvis dirge, three sweetly optimistic tunes, a homage to Middle East diplomat Philip Habib, a drug dealer death, and a humorous Hawaiian cuckold. The 2007 reissue extras include a soundtrack-worthy instrumental "Word of Mouth"; a synth- driven "The Risk"; and a plodding, raucous "Wild Thing," with liner notes by David Wild.

A Quiet Normal Life: The Best of Warren Zevon (October 24, 1986), Asylum Records. The thinnest of Zevon's three "Best of" collections is a predictable playlist that closes his Asylum catalog. Ten of its 14 songs are from his debut and *Excitable Boy*, with three from *The Envoy* and "Play It All Night Long," the lone selection from *Bad Luck Streak in Dancing School.*

Sentimental Hygiene (August 29, 1987), Virgin Records. Considered an impressive "comeback" after a five-year record label hiatus. Guests include Dylan, Neil Young, Jennifer Warnes, and R.E.M. Rhythmic riffs on the 1980s, fame, celebrity rehab at "Detox Mansion," music biz disdain, karma, a boxing tragedy, and working-class heroes in "The Factory." The romantic, redemptive "Reconsider Me" sustains as the album's Bartók centerpiece.

Transverse City (October 1989), Virgin Records. Synthesizers and cyberpunk, *Metropolis* and *Modern Times*, noir prophet William Gibson and Thomas Pynchon's *Gravity's Rainbow.* Zevon's misanthropic vision of a futuristic dystopia digs deep into the heart of the last days of the Reagan era and perestroika. Complex, dense, occasionally overwrought arrangements that incorporate Stravinsky influences combine with rich vocabulary to conjure an image-laden noir landscape. "Nobody's in Love This Year" may summarize the prevailing pessimism. The tuneful homage to the virtues of seclusion, "Splendid Isolation," lingers as a melodic memento and link to the overlooked, conveniently dismissed record (and as a wistful wish that Zevon would have played more harmonica on his songs). The conceptual album is Zevon's most ambitious and least accessible work. An undeniable acquired taste, *Transverse City* is well worth revisiting, if for nothing else, Zevon's apocalyptic gaze and, as always, his writing. The lone bonus track on the 2003 reissue, an acoustic Dylanesque demo version of "Networking," provides a glimpse of the simpler album that might have been.

hindu love gods (1990), Giant Records. Small-scale "super group" collaboration with Zevon fronting R.E.M. members Bill Berry, Peter Buck, and Mike Mills from an all-night jam in the studio during the *Sentimental Hygiene* sessions. Primarily a blues record, with good-natured, occasionally clumsy renditions of Chicago, New Orleans, and Mississippi Delta blues standards. Also a worthwhile Western riding rendition of Woody Guthrie's "Vigilante Man," and a vigorous version of the artist-formerly-and-currently-known-as-Prince's hit "Raspberry Beret," which reached number 28 and remains on the Zevon "best of" playlists.

Mr. Bad Example (October 15, 1991), Giant Records. Darkness at the end of the cul de sac. A vitriolic veer into some of his nastiest narratives and creepy comic character sketches, such as the whirling-word polka, "Mr. Bad Example," "Renegade," and "Model Citizen," which solicit cringes of irresistible amusement. Balancing the hovering pessimism are the country-tinged charmer, "Heartache Spoken Here," one of the buried treasures in the Zevon songbook; and the smooth single and closing cut, "Searching for a Heart," a song that "out-Eagled the Eagles" and was used in two soundtracks.

Learning to Flinch (April 13, 1993), Giant Records. Zevon *Unplugged*. Carefully curated, 17-song, 75-minute set—culled from 100 songs during the 1992 world tour—is a riveting, unadorned acoustic complement to the electric Roxy shows from 1980 on the live *Stand in the Fire*. Zevon is strictly solo, playing piano and steely 12- and 6-string guitars, with no instrumental or vocal backing, and no audience repartee. The recontextualization is frequently fascinating. Prolonged preludes, bridges, and finales of the versions provide some of the purest showcases on record of Zevon's musical virtuosity and dexterity on guitar and piano, and his inventiveness as an arranger. The set features a new bluesy tune, "Worrier King," and previews "Piano Fighter" and "The Indifference of Heaven," which would be recorded on his next album. The record was also released in a deluxe edition in a gray velvet case with "Old Velvet Nose" embossed on silver plate, and an attractive booklet with lyrics and images of road relics and souvenirs.

Mutineer (May 23, 1995), Giant Records. One of Zevon's most anonymous records, with the worst sales of his career. Dedicated to Hunter S. Thompson, and self-produced in Zevon's home studio with sparse instrumentation. Humor, heartache, and intelligence persist in the lyrics, though the melody is minimal, arrangements frequently disjointed, and the tone bleak. Two collaborations with novelist Carl Hiaasen, and a Judee Sill cover. The title song lingers, performed by Dylan during his 2002 tour, and recorded as a duet by Jason Isbell and Amanda Shires.

I'll Sleep When I'm Dead: An Anthology (1996), Elektra/Rhino Records. Box set quality. Comprehensive 44-song collection, with Asylum songs on disc one and Virgin and Giant sharing disc two. Zevon's concise, droll comments on each song in the package's booklet, along with quotes from others about him, are as big a bonus as the exclusive tracks from Zevon's television and film soundtrack/score credits in *Route 66*, *TekWar*, and the film *Love at Large* with Mark Isham. Another rarity is "Frozen Notes," which, according to Zevon, was "written during the Mesozoic era" and recorded for *Excitable Boy*, though it did not make the original sequence.

Life'll Kill Ya (January 25, 2000), Artemis Records. A gem. Zevon's sturdiest, sharpest, most cohesive set of (12) songs from start to finish since his Asylum debut in 1976. The mortality motif is enhanced by the eerie prescience of the title tune, the doomed diagnosis of "My Shit's Fucked Up," the lovely benediction "Don't Let Us Get Sick," a meditative "Ourselves to Know," another reflection on Elvis's life and death, "Porcelain Monkey," and a cover of Steve Winwood's "Back in the High Life." The array of peculiar opening lines, which mention among other things an "invalid haircut" and being "dragged behind the clown mobile," are some of Zevon's most distinctive language and phrasing. An extraordinary record that deserved a better fate and wider listenership.

Genius: The Best of Warren Zevon (October 2002), Elektra/Rhino Records. At 22 songs, the mid-size of Zevon's three "Best of" compilations, and the only one to span four record labels. Carefully curated, despite the curious omission of "Desperados Under the Eaves." The booklet's various portraits of the Zevon logo "Old Velvet Nose" with props and costumes, such as a raspberry beret and a Chinese menu, playfully reflect song lyrics and themes.

My Ride's Here (May 7, 2002), Artemis Records. A pastiche of popular culture references—highlighted by "Albert Einstein making out like Charlie Sheen"—and literary collaborations, including Hiaasen again on "Basket Case," the title of his novel published months before the album's release; Mitch Albom, Hunter S. Thompson, and Irish poet Paul Muldoon on two songs, including the understated title tune, a Western fever dream involving Jesus, John Wayne, Charlton Heston, Shelley, Keats, and Lord Byron. Also includes the novelty tune "Hit Somebody! (The Hockey Song)" with David Letterman shouting the chorus, and a quirky Serge Gainsbourg cover *en francais*. Of note are the classical proficiencies on the sophisticated string arrangement in the self-alluding "Genius."

The Wind (August 26, 2003), Artemis Records. Captivating context, prophecy fulfilled, emotion, and an all-access pass to recording sessions via VH1's *(Inside)Out: Warren Zevon* documentary, may slightly elevate the album's status to another level without exaggerating its musical merit. The all-star cast's contributions musically and vocally stand out. The fond farewell and career climax, "Keep Me in Your Heart," is one of the era's most stirring and beautiful songs, one that continues to gracefully surface throughout the cultural soundscape.

SUPPLEMENTAL LISTENING

The Offender Meets the Pretender: Warren Zevon with Jackson Browne (December 8, 1976). Unofficial recording. Along with shows from the renowned Main Point coffeehouse venue in Philadelphia, this is perhaps the most notable Zevon bootleg, recorded at the VPRO Studio in Hilversum, Holland. The set, which includes interviews, is often packaged with an abbreviated set by Zevon with David Lindley one day later at the RAI Congress Building in Amsterdam.

hindu love gods, "Gonna Have a Good Time Tonight"/"Narrator," 7-inch single (1986), I.R.S. Records. Single not included on the hindu love gods album in 1990. The A-side is a cover of "Good Times" by the Easybeats, an Australian band best known for their 1966 hit, "Friday on My Mind." The B-side composition by Bill Berry was a quirky surf-riff homage to the famous French undersea explorer Jacques Cousteau. The single, a hip collectible packaged in a picture sleeve, was released as a 45 rpm on R.E.M.'s I.R.S. label.

Deadicated (April 23, 1991), Arista Records. Zevon and David Lindley collaborate on "Casey Jones" on a various artists' tribute to the Grateful Dead that marks Zevon's only guest spot on another album in his entire career, either as a musician or singer.

The Wrockers, *Stranger Than Fiction* (1998), Don't Quit Your Day Job Records. Two-disc, 32-song charity collection by reconfigured merry band of bards Rock Bottom Remainders, comprised of Hiaasen, Albom, Dave Barry, Stephen King, and many others, included Zevon as one of the house band's special guests, along with Jimmy LaFave, Jerry Jeff Walker, and Doobie Brother Jeff "Skunk" Baxter. Zevon backs Barry with guitar on "Tupperware Blues," plays keyboards on King's nod to his novella *The Body* with "Stand by Me," and offers his deepest Ike Turner vocal on "Proud Mary," performed with Tananarive Due. He also writes some nifty liner notes for the compilation.

The First Sessions (2003), Varése Sarabande Records. Compilation of early recordings and demos, primarily lyme and cybelle songs, notably their 1966 single "Follow Me"; "Outside Chance" and "Like the Seasons," which were recorded by their White Whale label mates the Turtles; and Dylan, Beatles, and Jimmy Reed covers. Good accompanying historical essay. Buried treasure for any Zevon completist.

Dad Get Me Out of This: The String Quartet Tribute to Warren Zevon (November 25, 2003), Vitamin Records. Classical interpretations of ten Zevon songs and homage to his unfinished symphony that bring his arrangement proficiencies and sense of melody to the forefront. Those familiar with Zevon's music will appreciate the record cover's x-ray image of a smoking skull wearing headsets, and likely be captivated by the musical recontextualization and incongruence, particularly songs such as "Werewolves of London," "Excitable Boy," "I'll Sleep When I'm Dead," and "Lawyers, Guns and Money," as opposed to the more classical-compatible "Keep Me in Your Heart." Those unfamiliar with Zevon will find the music and arrangements a pleasurable listen.

Enjoy Every Sandwich: The Songs of Warren Zevon (October 19, 2004), Artemis Records. The most mainstream and cohesive Zevon tribute, featuring many artists who participated in *The Wind* sessions—Browne, Springsteen, Calderón, David Lindley, Ry Cooder, Don Henley. The impressive chorus also features Dylan, Bonnie Raitt, Jill Sobule, Pete Yorn, Steve Earle, Reckless Kelly, the Pixies, Billy Bob Thornton, the Wallflowers, Jennifer Warnes, and Adam Sandler, who, of course, covers "Werewolves of London." Jordan Zevon's performance of his father's previously unrecorded "Studebaker" is a family heirloom highlight delivered with a 1970s L.A. sound.

Hurry Home Early: The Songs of Warren Zevon (July 8, 2005), Wampus Multimedia. Good cross-section of the Zevon catalog in a 13-song tribute by indie artists, among them Jordan Zevon, who sings another of his father's unreleased songs, "Warm Rain," with Simone Stevens.

Reconsider Me: The Love Songs (January 31, 2006), New West Records. Affirmation of Zevon as the Hopeless Romantic, and his songs of parting and longing being as integral to his songwriting signature as his menacing and macabre compositions. The collective sensitivity is striking, and at the same time, some of the emotional resonance may be altered slightly when recontextualized from their original sequence, juxtaposed with or bridging darker and violent narratives. "Empty Handed Heart" would have been a more apt inclusion than the Winwood cover, "Back in the High Life." Daughter Ariel's intimate passages written in the liner notes provide a tender context; Mike Marone, program director for The Loft on Sirius XM Satellite Radio also contributed a thoughtful essay.

Preludes: Rare and Unreleased Recordings (May 1, 2007), New West Records. Two-disc set; disc one features stripped-down versions of songs, and several unreleased rarities, including "Studebaker." Disc two, "Primate Discourse," is Jody Denberg's conversation with Zevon in 2000 on a variety of topics. Disc two also features a solo acoustic version of "Don't Let Us Get Sick" and two other cuts off *Life'll Kill Ya*. This edition includes an attractive booklet containing essays by Jordan Zevon and Artemis CEO Danny Goldberg, photographs, and, in shrewd marketing synergy, ruminations on Zevon excerpted from the *I'll Sleep When I'm Dead* oral history, published the same month.

Californication: Music from the Showtime Series (2007–2014), ABKCO. Zevon's presence is prevalent in the Showtime cable series and in its lead character, Hank Moody, a writer, womanizer, alcoholic, and Zevon-quoting acolyte. Zevon songs, both originals and covers, were automatic on the series soundtrack during its seven seasons.

David Lindley, *Big Twang* (2007), self-release. The longtime Zevon music collaborator, friend, and admirer has covered more Zevon songs, live and recorded, than any single artist, Linda Ronstadt included. Among his renditions are "Werewolves of London" in 1988, and "Play It All Night Long" on the official bootleg *Live in Tokyo: Playing Real Good*, with Hani Naser. On this album, Lindley provides his signature exotic string-instrument interpretations of three Zevon songs from *Mutineer*—"Monkey Wash Donkey Rinse," "Seminole Bingo," and "(Beneath) the (Vast) Indifference of Heaven."

Warren Zevon: Original Album Series (2010), Rhino Records. The Zevon Asylum bundle: *Warren Zevon, Excitable Boy, Bad Luck Streak in Dancing School, Stand in the Fire, The Envoy*. The "Original Album Series" features back catalogs of artists with the Warner Group. The attractive CD five-packs are presented as mini-LP replicas in cardboard sleeves, a can't-resist, cost-efficient, and comprehensive alternative to Best of, Greatest Hits, or Anthology releases.

Troubadours: The Rise of the Singer Songwriter (2011), Rhino Records. Two-disc set that includes a documentary on the legendary West Hollywood club and accompanying ten-song CD. In addition to Zevon's "Poor Poor Pitiful Me," the collection features songs by James Taylor, Linda Ronstadt, Elton John, Little Feat, Tom Waits, Bonnie Raitt, Randy Newman, Kris Kristofferson, and Carole King.

Warren Zevon: Headless in Boston (September 29, 1982) (2013), All Access Records. One of the widely circulated Zevon concert recordings. Live 1982 broadcast from the Metro in Boston by WBCN-FM, with a virtually identical set list as the well-known concert at the Capitol Theatre in Passaic, New Jersey. One of the highlights is a medley that segues from "Poor Poor Pitiful Me" into Springsteen's "Cadillac Ranch."

Phil Cody, *Cody Sings Zevon* (2014), Back and Belly Recordings. Twelve-song salute from the folkie who opened for Zevon in the mid-1990s, with vocals that drift between Cat Stevens (Yusuf Islam), John Hiatt, and Burl Ives.

Warren Zevon: Simple Man, Simple Dream (2016), Laser Media. Another "unofficial" recording from an FM broadcast during *The Envoy Tour* in 1982. Five songs shorter than a similar set in the *Headless in Boston* bootleg, the title is borrowed from a J. D. Souther song that Zevon routinely covered on piano.

INDEX

ABOUT THE AUTHOR

George Plasketes is professor of media studies and popular culture in the School of Communication & Journalism at Auburn University in Alabama. Among the courses he teaches are Popular Culture, Soundtracks, and Fame, Celebrity & Media Culture. A native of Chicago, Plasketes studied in Oxford (Mississippi, that is), receiving two degrees, and earned a doctorate at Bowling Green State University in Ohio. He is the author/editor of three books for Ashgate's Popular and Folk Music series—on B-sides, cover songs, and debut albums—and two books on Elvis Presley images and fanaticism in American culture. He has published essays, articles, and book chapters on a variety of music, media, and popular culture subjects, including *Saturday Night Live* creator Lorne Michaels, baseball pitcher Bill "Spaceman" Lee, *Cop Rock*, TaB diet cola, and the music of the television series *Northern Exposure*.